THE
RUSSIA CONUNDRUM

THE
RUSSIA CONUNDRUM

MIKHAIL KHODORKOVSKY
WITH MARTIN SIXSMITH

HOW THE WEST FELL FOR PUTIN'S
POWER GAMBIT – AND HOW TO FIX IT

ST. MARTIN'S PRESS
NEW YORK

First published in the United States by St. Martin's Press, an imprint of St. Martin's Publishing Group

THE RUSSIA CONUNDRUM. Copyright © 2022 by Mikhail Khodorkovsky. All rights reserved. Printed in the United States of America. For information, address St. Martin's Publishing Group, 120 Broadway, New York, NY 10271.

www.stmartins.com

The Library of Congress Cataloging-in-Publication Data is available upon request.

ISBN 978-1-250-28559-1 (hardcover)
ISBN 978-1-250-28560-7 (ebook)

Our books may be purchased in bulk for promotional, educational, or business use. Please contact your local bookseller or the Macmillan Corporate and Premium Sales Department at 1-800-221-7945, extension 5442, or by email at MacmillanSpecialMarkets@macmillan.com.

Originally published in Great Britain by WH Allen, a Penguin Random House company

First U.S. Edition: 2022

10 9 8 7 6 5 4 3 2 1

CONTENTS

PREFACE

As I was writing this book, the world changed. Vladimir Putin's invasion of Ukraine on 24 February 2022 unleashed potentially the most brutal conflict on European soil since the end of the Second World War. Seven decades of commitment to the cause of peace were replaced by a return to the era of great power intimidation. A paranoid dictator launched an unprovoked war against a peaceful neighbour, ordering missile attacks on civilians that killed women and children, toying with Armageddon by shelling nuclear power stations, exposing his own young conscripts to untold horrors, watching thousands of them return in body bags.

Putin lied to the Russian people. He claimed his aim was to de-Nazify a country that was in reality a law-abiding democracy, led by a Jewish president. He called it a special military operation and attacked those who spoke the truth about his wanton act of aggression. He banned independent newspapers and broadcasters, personally dictating the distorted version of events that would appear in Russian state media. Readers and viewers were told the same lies hour after hour, day after day, and most of them believed them. Russians did not see the images of cities in ruins, terrified child refugees, burned out Russian tanks and defiant Ukrainians defending their homeland. They did not hear about the captured Russian soldiers, the international outrage and the speculation about the state of Vladimir Putin's mental health. All they heard was that Putin's 'operation' was going to plan.

So scared was the Kremlin by the power of the truth that it passed a law imposing 15-year jail terms on anyone deemed to be spreading 'false information' (for which, read 'true information') about the military campaign. The result was an escalating barrage of absurdities, in which the Ukrainians were blamed for everything – including bombing their own nuclear power plants, deliberately placing their civilians in the path of Russian bullets, using Chinese students as human shields (a nod to Beijing that it should offer more support) and shooting at refugees to stop them fleeing. The only thing the Russian media were unable to supply were the heartening TV pictures of Moscow's troops being greeted as liberators by a grateful population.

Even in Putin's deluded world of cynical realpolitik, the invasion had little logic. Whatever the outcome of the initial offensive, it was evident that he would be left with intractable problems.

He might eventually declare Ukraine defeated, but he would be manifestly unable to subdue an angry, resentful population, tens of thousands of whom had been equipped with automatic weapons. Even the Russian-speaking minority in the east of the country, in whose defence the invasion was supposedly launched, were left dismayed by the extent of the violence. The prospect of a protracted insurgency, with occupying troops being shot at and partisans roaming the countryside, was hardly an attractive one.

Despite his sneering dismissal of Western sanctions, Putin knew they were a danger. Russia's economy had long been on the slide and exclusion from the global banking system promised to leave it in limbo. Russians were hit by exchange controls, soaring inflation and cash shortages; the withdrawal of electronic payment systems resulted in queues to get into the Metro; and the younger generation was left disgruntled by the curtailment of messaging services and computer gaming, all of which promised to fuel social discontent.

Anti-war demonstrations in Moscow and St Petersburg in the weeks after the invasion were quickly repressed, but even Putin cannot arrest everyone. The prospect of domestic opposition coalescing around the Ukraine issue was a worry for him, made worse by the emergence on social media of images of killed and injured Russian soldiers and prisoners of war.

The world was taken aback by the February invasion. Putin had previously massed troops on the Ukrainian border in the spring of 2021, but withdrew them after ratcheting up tensions. When troop deployments resumed in December 2021, the global community assumed that this time, too, Putin was bluffing. There was speculation about his aims, some sympathy for his complaints about NATO expansion into Eastern Europe and discussions of concessions that the West might make. All the sympathy – and all the suggestions among Western liberals that Putin should be given the benefit of the doubt – evaporated when Russian tanks rolled over the border.

The world's shock and horror left me a little bemused. Unlike those who have persisted in appeasing Putin, turning a blind eye to his provocations in the hope that he might be mollified into 'being nice to us', I don't harbour any illusions about him, although I admit that the methods and the scale of his invasion were a surprise to me. My long and painful personal experience of dealing with Vladimir Putin showed me that he can never be trusted, that he is capable of the most terrible crimes, and that his smiling promises of cooperation and understanding have always been less than worthless.

Today, I am more convinced than ever that he is a dictator who must be stopped, regardless of the risks and regardless of the costs that we will have to bear; our sufferings pale by comparison with the shelling and bombing of innocent civilians. For if we do not stop Putin in Ukraine, he will inevitably lead us into global war. Comparisons to Hitler may seem exaggerated to some, but we should be very wary of appeasing Putin in the manner that gave Hitler free rein in the 1930s. We must not repeat that mistake – it will be too costly for all of us.

My purpose in writing this book is to explain the damage that two decades of Putin have inflicted on Russia and on East–West relations, and to suggest constructive ways forward now that the international community is aware of the truth.

21 March 2022

INTRODUCTION

I'm a fairly calm fellow; I don't usually get wound up about things. But I was, let's say, concerned when I tuned in to the Moscow Echo radio station and heard that the Kremlin had put a price on my head.

'It has been stated,' said the radio, 'that a bounty of five hundred thousand dollars will be paid for the capture of the former head of the Yukos Oil Company, Mikhail Borisovich Khodorkovsky, who is currently hiding in London. The reward will be payable to any Russian citizen who brings the former oligarch back to Russia.'

The announcement didn't quite say 'Dead or alive', but it came close.

This was in March 2021, after I had completed my ten years as a political prisoner in Vladimir Putin's jails and seven years after I had been exiled to the West. My understanding has always been that serving a prison sentence – even those imposed for non-existent crimes – means the end of the matter, but that is evidently not the Kremlin's view. Sergei Skripal had served his term and been released, but it didn't stop Putin sending GRU killers to try to poison him, so why would I be any different? The radio announced that the bounty on my head had been promulgated by a member of Vladimir Putin's inner circle, so it was clear that it came from the top.

1

In functioning democracies – among which I number most Western nations – people are protected from abuse at the hands of their rulers. The people vote politicians in and they can vote them out. There are safeguards that prevent the accumulation of excessive power by potentially unsuitable individuals and stop them exploiting that power for personal ends.

But this is obviously not the case in authoritarian states like Putin's Russia. It pretends it is a democracy, but in reality it is a personal dictatorship. And that makes it vitally important for Russians and the world to learn as much as possible about the character of the individuals who run the Kremlin. My own history has forced me to pay more than passing attention to this, and what I have learned is not reassuring. The extent of institutional criminality in Vladimir Putin's Kremlin is staggering. The oligarchs of the 1990s, myself among them, were reproached for accumulating wealth, but they did so through the cut-and-thrust of business. Now, the oligarchs are inside the Kremlin and their wealth is derived from the brazen abuse of power.

It has reached the point where Putin and his cronies will fight any fight, commit any crime, destroy any opponent in order to preserve their wealth and keep the nation in their pernicious grip. Their bunker mentality and fear of what might come afterwards make them cling to power. The methods they are using to do this increasingly put the Russian people and the world in danger.

Things have to change, for Russia's sake and for all humankind. Real change in Russia is possible only through the will of the Russian people; but the West can play its proper and constructive role in facilitating Russia's transition from Putin's mafia state to a more open, democratic country, as part of the community of nations. This is my attempt to examine the West's efforts to curb the Kremlin's repression at home and aggression abroad; to explain the reality of power in

Putin's Russia and how the West has frequently misunderstood it; and to show how the mistaken perceptions of leading figures – politicians, journalists and commentators – have shaped Western public opinion and led to misguided policies in East–West relations. It's a story that looks back at how Russians have long admired the West, and how they took Western values and Western prosperity as an ideal to which they could aspire – a source of inspiration that has, in recent times, become tarnished. It's a story that looks ahead, to ask if and how Russia can change. Can reforms end Russia's status as a pariah state acting outside the democratic norms of the international community? What is the end goal for Russia's future? What model of power would best serve the interests of the Russian people and the world as a whole? Can Russia become a part of the global solution, instead of part of the problem – and can the West help bring that transformation about? These questions must be addressed seriously and with urgency. Russia is one of the most important – and powerful – countries in the world. The world must not ignore her.

• • •

You might think that being locked up as a political prisoner in Vladimir Putin's prisons and labour camps is unlucky, but I might disagree. I have read enough Shakespeare to understand the fate of his tragic heroes who attain worldly success, ascending to the heights of power and fortune, only to be struck down by reverses that strip them of all their gains. But as they plunge into ruin and despair, Shakespeare sometimes endows them with something they never had: the ability to see things clearly in themselves and in the world.

Before my arrest in October 2003, I had been close to the highest levels of power in Russia. In the early 1990s, I was an adviser to the first Russian prime minister, then a deputy minister myself, before returning to the business I had founded in the late 1980s and becoming one of the country's leading industrialists. I was extremely wealthy, admired, envied and hated all at the same time.

My familiarity with the highest levels of power in Russia – and my subsequent experience of the punitive repression that such power routinely inflicts – followed by years living in a Western society that so many Russians admire and fear, has given me insight. Seeing and witnessing so much in both societies has convinced me that East and West have misunderstood each other so badly and so completely that, together, they are leading the globe into grave danger.

I was close enough to Vladimir Putin to discover how he thinks and to intuit the psychology of the man, to understand what his goals are for Russia and for himself. Few have had the opportunity to read Putin's mind; even fewer have had the chance to say to his face everything they think about the corruption that exists right at the very top. I did exactly that in February 2003, in an angry, televised exchange between us that lifted the lid on the dark side of his regime and unleashed a chain of dramatic events for both of us.

Speaking truth to power – and doing so publicly – led to my arrest and incarceration. My experience of the capricious, personalised model of authority that Putin exercises taught me that there is a crucial difference between the Russian state and the men who now run the Kremlin. Putin is not Russia and Russia is not Putin. My prison years deepened my appreciation of Russia's importance, her beauty and her future. They helped me to understand that Russia can be saved from an endless succession of dictatorships, that she can become a normal country, taking her rightful place in the community of nations, instead of a pariah state constantly embroiled in confrontation and acrimony.

When, finally, I was released from prison in December 2013, the authorities kicked me out of Russia, promising a life sentence should I ever return. Since then, while living in London I have gained an understanding of how Russia is seen from the West. It has helped me

Earlier times: Vladimir Putin and I in discussion in the Kremlin, 2002

Putin and I debating the future of Russia in February 2003

Kierkegaard wisely pointed out that life can only be understood backwards, even though we are condemned to live it forwards. As well as looking to the future, I will look back at how today's crisis developed over the past three decades, to consider why things in Russia have gone so wrong. It is 37 years since the then Soviet president Mikhail Gorbachev advocated the establishment of a Common European Home uniting East and West in a cooperative endeavour, and nearly 30 years since Boris Yeltsin proposed that Russia should join NATO. Why was that moment of mutual respect and conciliation squandered? What condemned Russia to return to anti-Western autocracy? Why were the hopes of the Russian people, with their long-standing admiration for Western democracy and desire to share in its benefits, left dashed and disappointed?

Russia succumbed to the weight of its thousand-year history, to the seductive paradigm of an autocratic leader who sometimes makes the trains run on time but always takes away freedom, prosperity and dignity. Until the beginning of the 2000s we were building a demo-cratic state, with all its initial-stage shortcomings, similar to what happened in eighteenth- and early nineteenth-century America. From 2001 on – and especially after the Yukos affair, the battle over prop-erty rights and political values, in which the very public clash between Vladimir Putin and myself brought into focus the choice between the two contrasting futures available to the nation – the analogy is closer to early fascist Spain and Latin America: 'To my friends, everything; to my enemies, the law.' The fork in the road and the unfortunate path that Russia followed are obvious. Under Putin, Russia is in thrall to a brand of authoritarian state capitalism based around one leader. Society and the state apparatus are controlled through corruption, blackmail, intimidation and the arbitrary enforcement of the law, while the substance of independent civic institutions has been system-atically undermined. This is no way to build a modern country.

realise that the West can help Russia to solve her problems – not just for Russia's sake, but for the West's own sake, and for the world.

I would define the West as those countries in Europe and the Americas where human rights are protected, where democratic values ensure that people have a choice in who governs them and where – despite the well-publicised challenges of recent years – civic institutions, checks and balances enshrine the right of the people to oversee and control those they have elected.

I live in a city and country where powerful Russians, exiled from their homeland, have been targeted and murdered by the agents of the Kremlin. The United Kingdom is a democracy, but Putin's powers know no borders. I know that the same fate could befall me at any moment – the polonium slipped into my tea, the Novichok on my doorhandle – but I have learned to live with it. What I have not learned to live with is the thought that my country is in the hands of men who strive only to increase their own wealth and power. Living in the West, I have seen how politicians here have mistaken and misinterpreted Putin's Russia, trying to accommodate him and the threat he poses; how they fell into the traps that Putin set for them.

Like many people in the public eye, I often feel that my identity has been taken from me and moulded into a shape that I do not recognise. Politics has become an acutely personalised business. When someone is involved in a public conflict, their image is appropriated and conflated with the values and prejudices of those who use it for their own ends. I was involved in one of the fiercest political controversies of modern Russia, and for me that made the process all the more extreme. For my supporters, I was a passionate champion of democracy, battling to save the nation's soul; for my detractors, I was a greedy oligarch who stole the people's inheritance. Neither version is the whole truth, but both have become ingrained in the polarised way I am now viewed.

Riot police clash with demonstrators during a protest against Alexei Navalny's jailing in January 2021

But the West, which continues to inflict unnecessary damage on itself, is also to blame. The Kremlin has benefited enormously from democracy's crisis globally, and from the realisation that Western liberal democracies have turned out to be more vulnerable to political corruption than many thought they were. When Vladimir Putin is criticised for political corruption and intolerance, he now simply points to the West. You may think there are imperfections here at home, he says to the Russian people, but just look how much worse things are in the countries of so-called Western democracy. It is an old tactic: I remember very well how, when Soviet leaders were attacked for their human rights abuses, they would retort that Black people in America or Catholics in Northern Ireland were being treated much worse. Such arguments have become an existential crutch for the Putin regime.

At times, it seems that both sides recognise the need for fundamental change, but neither seems capable of securing it. What should matter to all of us are the shared origins of our common European-Atlantic civilisation. Russians should not be strangers in the Western world. We are Europeans; we have helped to build and grow this civilisation, and I believe we will be an important part of it once again.

The 2020s have the potential to be a turning point for Russia. The invasion of Ukraine has thrown the future of the Putin regime into uncertainty and given ammunition to Russia's democratic opposition. Putin's decision to jail Alexei Navalny in 2021 made the popular lawyer and anti-corruption activist into a political prisoner, in the same way that I was in the 2000s. Navalny's 'crime' was the same as mine: to have pointed out the corruption and self-enrichment of the president. He took the same decision that I did: to continue the fight, even if it means going to prison. It gave both of us status in the struggle for freedom and democracy. Modern technology now makes that struggle very public. Navalny's exposé of Putin's theft of public funds to build his extravagant palace on the Black Sea was viewed over 100 million times on the internet. Social media helped coordinate demonstrations against Navalny's imprisonment all over Russia, not just in Moscow and St Petersburg; and hundreds of thousands of those who took part said they were motivated to protest against the Kremlin for the first time in their lives. They are mainly young people and their protest is not just about Navalny, but about the injustices that run through Putin's Russia.

Discontent with the Putin regime has reached new heights. We are at a historic moment of opportunity that offers the chance of a better future. If it were to be spurned, the issues that divide East and West will become entrenched beyond redress. The security not only of Russia but also of the Atlantic alliance will suffer and global peace be put at risk. Men and women of goodwill on both sides must come together now to ensure this is not allowed to happen. What follows is my attempt to reveal how this can be done.

PART ONE
A GREAT EXPERIMENT

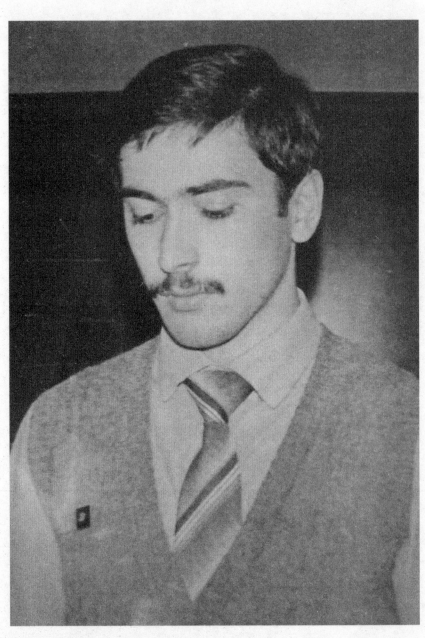

Early years: an image from school

CHAPTER 1
HOPES AND ASPIRATIONS

I grew up on Cosmonaut Street in north-east Moscow, where gangs of youths and petty criminals ruled the roost. There were street fights and at times it could be scary. I decided early on that I didn't want to live my life in fear; I didn't want the unending stress of living with outside forces that can bully you. For the hooligans, the answer was simple: I trained in martial arts, beefed up my muscles and refused to give in to their threats. But there were other forces in Soviet society that were also aimed at making people cower, and they were harder to confront.

As a child in the 1960s and 1970s, like most Soviet people I believed in the Party. Communism was our universe; it was here to stay and we never even thought there could be other ways of doing things. That's pretty much how children are: parents, friends, teachers – what they say is a fact; most of the time you accept it without questioning. Sure, we had a little snigger when our leader Leonid

Brezhnev used to come on TV mumbling and stumbling or awarding himself yet another medal. That was funny. But maybe it was like that everywhere? I didn't see a connection between our system and empty shelves in the shops. I didn't even know that shops could be full.

When I look back, I wonder if I was too naive, too blinkered to see clearly. I understood that lots of things were wrong, and I certainly knew there were plenty of contemptible people running the country, but I didn't draw a general conclusion from those individual facts. Perhaps I didn't do a lot of thinking.

I could have protested. There were dissidents at the time, and human rights advocates who pointed out the injustices of our society, but they didn't make much of an impression on us. The state controlled all the sources of information and there was no internet back then. In those years, a person needed to come to the decision to protest from his or her own independent thinking, from his or her own sources of information. If you didn't have that spontaneous personal conviction, it was hard to comprehend what the dissidents were saying. Most people – including me – had got used to the world we grew up in and we tended to accept the reality to which we were accustomed.

I was a good student. I was getting good marks and encouragement from the system, so I suppose that made me think twice about opposing it. I specialised in chemistry and I earned a place at the Moscow Mendeleev Chemical Technology Institute, which was a good place to study. I graduated with honours in 1986, a crucial time in Russian history. Mikhail Gorbachev had been in charge of the Soviet Communist Party for just over a year and he was beginning to shake up things that hadn't been shaken for a long, long time.

My first jobs from the age of 15, while I was still a student, were as a street cleaner, then as a carpenter and finally on the overnight shift in a Moscow bakery. But I also took on another post. In 1986, I became the deputy secretary for organisational affairs of the Committee of the All-Union Leninist Young Communist League – the Komsomol – at the Chemical Technology Institute. Why? Well, first of all because it allowed me to enrol at the All-Union Correspondence Law Faculty. But, to be truthful, it was also an important credential for people like me who were looking to move up in the world. The Komsomol youth movement was an integral part of Soviet society; it gave a seal of approval to the young men and women who joined it, and it brought them into contact with important people who wielded influence in different areas.

My duties were mainly organising Komsomol meetings and collecting subscriptions, but it meant I was in the best place to maximise my future job prospects, something that remained the case when Gorbachev's perestroika reforms kicked in. Gorbachev figured out that the Soviet centralised command economy, with the state taking all the economic decisions and telling people what to do and how to work, had sucked the energy and enthusiasm out of the country. People had no incentive to work hard; there was no initiative or innovation, because those things were not encouraged or rewarded. We used to say, not altogether jokingly, 'We pretend to work and the state pretends to pay us.' Gorbachev decided it was no good and the only way to get things moving was to allow a little bit – really just a *little* bit – of private enterprise.

At first, it was only work such as driving a taxi, cutting people's hair, baking bread or running a café. You could own a private business and were allowed to make a profit, but for appearances' sake, the companies were officially called cooperatives and they had to be run as a communal enterprise, without shareholders and with a strictly limited number of people involved. Gorbachev's halfway-house approach was like trying to be 'just a little bit pregnant', but once the profit motive was accepted, I knew he would have to go all the way. So I decided to get in on the ground floor. A few friends and I used our

Komsomol connections to open a café, where we served some very basic food and drink. It wasn't much, but it gave us an insight into what it was like to work hard and make money. And if perestroika took off, we knew we'd be able to grow and grow.

. . .

I met my first wife while we were students and we were married by the time I was 20. But I had another, secret love: like many of my contemporaries, I loved Western pop music – Boney M, ABBA and, most of all, the fabulous Annie Lennox!

Western music was frowned on in Soviet Russia. The old men in the Kremlin said it was a CIA plot to weaken the moral fibre of our youth and infect us with capitalist values. Well, it certainly worked! Like all young people, being told that something was forbidden made us doubly determined to get it. We set up a (short-lived) disco in our school; my classmates pestered Western tourists for LPs or had them mailed by circuitous routes, then we copied them using whatever means we could concoct. The appearance of recordable cassettes in the 1980s sent the black market into overdrive. A young fellow named Artyom Troitsky, who organised covert discos at Moscow Uni, was said to be able to get you pretty much anything you wanted.

When Gorbachev decided to ease the stagnation of the Brezhnev era, he allowed some British and American pop to be played on the radio. The Soviet state label Melodiya put out a couple of Paul McCartney albums and Billy Joel played a gig in Moscow in 1987. But it was Annie Lennox I was waiting for … and in 1989, she came.

Along with Peter Gabriel, Chrissie Hynde and the Thompson Twins, Annie was in the USSR to launch a double album titled *Breakthrough*, with music by 25 different artists, including Sting, Bryan Ferry, Sade, Dire Straits and the Grateful Dead. Soviet fans mobbed the state record stores and the discs were sold out within hours. But

An image of me in my youth

Annie Lennox in Red Square, Moscow 1989

what was most remarkable to us was that the singers and musicians had given their services for free and that all the profits were going to the environmental pressure group, Greenpeace. This made a big, big impression. Along with hundreds of thousands of other Russians, I suddenly understood that the world outside was very different from the one we were living in. The West now appeared to me as a world of freedom and energy and colour. I loved the music, the outspokenness, the lack of fear and the independence of mind. I loved how these stars were devoting their time and energy to global issues like the environment, matters that affected and united all humankind. It was the polar opposite of how we were living – in a country that repressed music, freedom and thought. It aroused my first serious doubts about the communist system and autocratic rule; it made me admire the West and want to be part of a free, prosperous, equitable society.

• • •

It was Mikhail Gorbachev's acceptance of economic free enterprise that allowed me to improve my own fortunes. A group of us, mostly students in our mid to late twenties with backgrounds in physics, chemistry, economics and geology, had a shared desire to prove ourselves, to make a success of our lives, to take on the world. It all began with a little computer cooperative we opened in 1987. That was what set us on a lifetime adventure, beset with both triumph and tragedy.

When Gorbachev announced in 1987 that universities could form research and development centres, and could use their expertise to offer services and earn an income, we jumped at the chance. We founded the impressively named Centre for Inter-Industry Scientific and Technical Progress, known by the acronym Menatep, selling computers and providing programmers to service the IT systems of state enterprises and government ministries. It was the age of the computer revolution, IT experts were in short supply and the country needed us to keep all the new technology running. We provided a quality service, charged high fees and made big profits.

What's more, demand for personal computers was about to go through the roof. These weren't being made in the USSR, so we arranged for people to bring them back from abroad when they went on official business trips. We bought the computers from them, reprogrammed them with Russian keyboards and Russian software, and sold them on for a profit. By late 1988, we'd accumulated some substantial cash reserves that were sitting unused, just in time for Gorbachev's announcement that, after 72 years of banning private capital, the Kremlin was going to allow private banks to be formed. It was a massive change and we weren't going to miss the chance.

Looking back, I don't think the men who were introducing all those reforms understood that they were sealing the fate of Soviet communism. They were permitting an element of free enterprise because they needed to kick start the moribund economy. Capitalist aspiration, the urge to work hard and get rich, is, in my view, an instinct in the human brain. The communists had repressed it for seven decades, and now they let people see that it was possible again. Russians, I thought, weren't going to be satisfied until the whole nation had returned to free-market capitalism. People wanted to work hard and improve the quality of their lives, which they hadn't been able to do under Soviet rule. They wanted the freedom to start their own businesses, feed their families and achieve a level of prosperity that had eluded them for so long.

• • •

By the end of the 1980s, our little computer cooperative had 150 employees and around 5,000 people contributing to its research and development. These were brilliant, sparky youngsters, mainly students and recent graduates, who were coming to me every day with ideas for new projects. We were desperate to develop the ground-breaking innovations they came up with, but we didn't have the funds. In a free, democratic society, we would have tapped up investors, explained the potential of our new projects and everyone would have benefited. But in those days, the only source of money was the official state banks. Loans were available only to state industries as part of the State Loan Plan.

Someone must have been watching over me, because out of nowhere an angel appeared: the remarkable Mrs Krushinskaya, manager of the state bank branch where we had our account. For some reason, she took it upon herself to help us. She took me aside and said, 'Look, I've heard you're after a loan. And maybe you've heard that the government has just authorised the creation of independent banks. Well, if you were to go out and create a bank like that, I might be able to give you a loan as an official banking institution ...' She gave me the number of a contact at head office and suggested I try my luck. I met the man in question, Viktor Bukato, who told me, much to my surprise, that he would provide the recommendation needed to get our charter written. 'What would you like your bank to be called?' he asked me. It really was as easy as that.

Within a month, we had set up the **KIB NTP Bank** (later called the Menatep Bank), one of the first private Russian banks since 1917, with an authorised capital of 100,000 roubles and an approved credit line. It was the start of a new world. Finally, we could expand into new areas, develop new IT solutions and kick start the projects we'd been sitting on for a year or more. We bought a company car and moved into bigger premises. I started wearing a suit and a tie, and all at once we started to look like a grownup business.

The loan money and the excitement of owning our own bank went slightly to our heads. We branched out into some wacky projects, including the import of Napoleon brandy, but we weren't much good at anything other than our core speciality. Computers and IT

An interview during the peak of my business years

remained our mainstay, especially when we discovered a way for our clients to buy and sell them in hard currency, i.e. using stable foreign currencies rather than roubles. At that time, the rouble was non-convertible – you couldn't use it for purchases outside of Russia – so there was a premium attached to being able to trade in dollars and other foreign denominations. We were eventually earning so much hard currency that I was summoned to see the state bank chairman, Viktor Gerashchenko, who wanted to know how we did it. I explained it all to him and he looked through the regulations, hoping to catch us out, but in the end he had to admit we hadn't broken any rules.

We were pretty good at exploiting any opportunities that the rules allowed. Because there had never been any private enterprise in the Soviet Union, people just accepted that it wasn't a possibility: the guiding principle of Soviet law was, 'everything which is not authorised is forbidden'. But Gorbachev's new spirit of enterprise flipped that to, 'everything which is not forbidden is allowed'. We took him at his word.

We moved into so many fields of IT supply and cornered so many markets that several government departments, including the Soviet Committee for Science and Technology, took an interest in us as an example of the success of the new economic policies. It was while we were working for them that the Moscow mafia took an interest in us.

Organised criminal gangs had always existed, but they became much more powerful in the perestroika era. It was a time when businesses were turned over by the mafia as a matter of course. In our case, contact came from the Izmailovo crime syndicate, who invited me for a 'friendly chat' and offered us 'protection' from their own henchmen. As you can imagine, I was on my best behaviour. I conversed politely and respectfully, and agreed that we would be in touch.

When I got back, I wrote to the local KGB department (back then, it was the KGB that took the lead in the fight against organised crime), where we had good contacts – they were responsible for the Mendeleev Chemical Technology Institute, where I had been a student, our office was on their territory and, what's more, we had plenty of defence industry clients, so they paid attention to us. That was the last we heard from the Izmailovo mob. Years later, I learned that the boss of the Organised Crime Unit of the regional KGB had a quiet word with the mafia and told them that our contracts with official government departments meant we were off limits. That's how things worked in those days. There were endless reports of premises being blown up and entrepreneurs having their throats cut, but I never had a problem. Perhaps I should have been more worried. On a few occasions, I was warned there was a contract out on me so I hired a couple of bodyguards, but I never paid for 'protection'. I told my staff that I didn't want any security briefings so that I could try to remain oblivious. I didn't want to live in fear.

. . .

My son Pavel was born while my first wife and I were still students. We were very young, times were hard and the marriage didn't last. The fact is that I met someone else. It happened while I was doing my stint as Komsomol deputy secretary at the Mendeleev Chemical Technology Institute. I was 23, Inna was just 17 and she was pretty wary of this cocky fellow with big ambitions; but I knew from the very first moment that I loved her and wanted to be with her for the rest of my life. I moved out of my family apartment and slept in my car until Inna took pity on me. We are now in our fourth decade of married life together, with a grownup daughter and twin boys. In my business life, I always felt I was in control, but I learned that love is a lot less predictable.

At first, Inna and I lived in rented flats with two small rooms and second-hand furniture, plus chairs and a table that I borrowed from the office. The business climate was cutthroat. It is no exaggeration to say that I had enemies and could have been killed, and Inna was also at

My wife, Inna Khodorkovskaya

risk. But she stayed with me, stayed cheerful, supportive and endlessly beautiful; I can't thank her enough for all she has done for me.

Progress became easier as the years went by. It was a lawless decade in Russia, but we worked hard and Menatep Bank gained a reputation for honesty and reliability. People came to understand that their cash was safe with us. It helped us not only to acquire many private investors, but also to build relations with ministries, departments and state organisations, which opened accounts with us. Within a couple of years, we had a large number of branches and a substantial turnover. We were the first Russian bank to list its shares.

Things were changing fast in the USSR and anyone with the nous and agility to keep up could make a lot of money. There was no stock exchange back then and no developed system of private banks, so if a company managed to earn hard currency it could only exchange it through the state bank at a very uncompetitive rate. Our idea was to find companies in that position and offer them a better exchange rate to convert their hard currency to 'soft' roubles. At the same time, we knew that many state enterprises had massive reserves of soft roubles that they were desperate to turn into foreign currency in order to purchase vital technology from abroad. We travelled up and down the country looking for such firms, offering to help them out and charging healthy margins for doing so. This in turn allowed us to enter the field of foreign currency trading, which had been forbidden under the old Soviet Constitution, punishable by long prison sentences or even death, but was not specifically banned under the new legislation of the Gorbachev era. We were a bunch of youngsters – most of us were still under 30 – but we had grown Menatep into one of the biggest commercial banks in Russia, and the future offered even greater possibilities. Gorbachev's liberalisation was beginning to allow us to see how things were done in the West and we wanted the same freedoms for ourselves.

CHAPTER 2
AN OPEN SOCIETY

Russians who have struggled for freedom and democracy have traditionally looked to the West for inspiration. The values of Western liberal democracy, and the prosperity associated with it, inspired generations with the knowledge that the repressive autocracy imposed on their homeland was not inevitable, and that there was a better way of doing things. In the years of Bolshevik rule, the Kremlin recognised the danger of such aspirations and strove to prevent the Russian people from learning about the advantages of life in the West. The communist state exercised a monopoly on the sources of mass information, bringing the media under its control, preventing access to foreign news outlets and banning travel abroad. The Kremlin's censors decreed what could be written in the press and dictated how the media should describe life outside of the Soviet Union. Much was made of the defects of capitalist society – the inequality, the poverty, colonial exploitation, crime and racial discrimination – and only very limited reporting was permitted of its achievements. Many Soviet citizens – me included – grew up believing what the Kremlin told them. It took independence of mind and assiduous curiosity to discover that the reality was different from the official portrayal. We did catch glimpses of the good things in the West, however, amplifying them through word-of-mouth and samizdat publications that were consumed with great eagerness, largely because they contrasted so sharply with the unpleasantness of day-to-day life in the USSR.

Matters changed in the late 1980s, when Mikhail Gorbachev permitted a cautious easing of the secrecy practised by his predecessors. There were several reasons for Gorbachev's policy of glasnost (openness), including his need to circumvent the old-style orthodox communists in the Kremlin who were opposed to his liberalising reforms. Because the hardliners controlled many of the official levers of power, Gorbachev took the bold decision to appeal directly to the Soviet people, over the heads of the apparat, the hidebound politicians and officials who ran the system. In order to encourage a groundswell of support for his perestroika policies, he actively encouraged people to think for themselves – something that had long been frowned upon – by allowing them access to much greater information than in the past, including greater truth about life in the West.

When UK Prime Minister Margaret Thatcher came on an official visit to the USSR in March 1987, Gorbachev took it as an opportunity to expand his glasnost initiative. Not since Richard Nixon in 1959 had a Western politician been permitted to speak openly on Soviet television, and on that occasion things had ended badly, when Nikita Khrushchev was widely seen to have come off worse in an ill-tempered exchange with the then US vice-president. Gorbachev knew it was a gamble to accept Mrs Thatcher's demand that any interview with her should be broadcast unedited, but he did so.

Margaret Thatcher greets the crowds in Moscow during her official visit in 1987

Many Russians who saw her realised for the first time that the West was different from what they had been told.

Three of the Soviet Union's top journalists were assigned to grill the *zheleznaya leidi* – the iron lady – whom the Kremlin had long portrayed as an enemy of the USSR, a capitalist ogre who had described Moscow as 'bent on world dominance' and Soviet communism as 'synonymous with getting one's way by violence'. Boris Kalyagin, political editor of Soviet Television and Radio, Tomas Kolesnichenko, international editor of *Pravda*, and Vladimir Simonov, a political commentator from the Novosti Press Agency, agreed that the interview would last 45 minutes and that all of Mrs Thatcher's answers would be broadcast in full. Speaking many years later, Kalyagin said the three of them were confident they could run rings round any capitalist.

It didn't work out that way. The journalists pressed Mrs Thatcher on why Britain insisted on maintaining nuclear weapons and, at first, the iron lady was studiously polite. When the interviewers tried to cast doubt on her answers, however, she showed her steely character, saying things that the Soviet people had never heard before.

'Well, you have more nuclear weapons in the Soviet Union than any other country in the world,' declared an unflustered Prime Minister. 'You have more intercontinental ballistic missiles and warheads than the West. You started intermediate weapons; we did not have any. You have more short-range ones than we have. You have more than anyone else and ...' The hapless interviewers tried to cut her off, but Mrs Thatcher was having none of it. 'One moment!' she commanded. 'Please may I say this to you ... All weapons of war are dangerous. Would it not be marvellous if we did not have to have them? But we can only get to that stage when we have more trust and confidence in one another. That means much more open societies. And let me put this to you: since the First World War, which finished in 1918, there has been no case where one democracy has attacked another. That is why we believe in democracy. So, you want to get rid of the weapons of war. It would be marvellous if we could, but we have to get more trust and confidence.'

Mrs Thatcher had steered the debate to the relative merits of Western democracy versus Soviet communism. Millions of television viewers pricked up their ears.

'We have an open society,' the prime minister continued. 'This goes to the depth of our fundamental freedoms: freedom of speech, freedom of worship, freedom from fear, and freedom from want; a much more open society means that you [in the USSR] could discuss all of the things in the same way as we do ... You really have two ways in which you can work: you either have a completely centralised control system in which you are told what to produce, how much it will cost, how much you are paid – and that does not really work to best advantage, as you have discovered, because it does not pay people if they do better. Or you go to what is called an incentive society when the harder you work, the more reward you get; and one has to recognise, you know, that people work not only for their country but they work to better their families. They work for a higher standard of living and so if they see the point of working harder, they will. And, you know, no matter what the theory, and there are lots of political theories – I wish there were fewer – no matter what the theory, there is no person alive and no computer which can plan a country as large as the Soviet Union, take into account all its various different conditions in all its various republics, all the various ambitions and needs and wants, the requirements of the people. You have got to disperse responsibility to the people who are much nearer to the life in those republics, towns, rural areas and then you have got to give them responsibility – and for that they must have incentives.'

The *Pravda* man, Tomas Kolesnichenko, tried to argue with Mrs Thatcher. The principles of a socialist society, he suggested, were the right ones and they brought real advantages. 'Well, you have tossed out a quite provocative comment there!' she replied. 'So, what exactly do you think are the advantages of a socialist society?' 'Its planned economy,' ventured Kolesnichenko. 'In economy that is an advantage; and all the years of planning, not just a centralised plan, but also local …' Mrs T pounced – her list of advantages was considerably longer: 'Life in Britain, you know, the standard of living is high. It is higher than it has ever been. We are working very hard. In our housing we have perhaps a different system from you. Out of every hundred families, sixty-four families … own their own home, they own it! It is my ambition to get that up to seventy-five families out of every hundred. We have an excellent health service, very, very good indeed* and we are building more and more hospitals … Unfortunately, we do have unemployment and I do not run away from it. When you get technological change, you are almost bound to get some unemployment. It is now falling. But let me make this clear: the people who are unemployed, they live like other people, in houses. They are rented and their rent is paid for them, because they have not the income to pay. And every week they get a weekly benefit, a considerable weekly benefit. It is more if they have children and the weekly benefit for some of them will be as much as some of the wages which some people get in industry. They will get that weekly sum for as long as they are unemployed and after six months when they have been unemployed, we will take each one of them in. We will try to get them a job or will try to get them fresh training or we will put them on what is called a community programme. So, we are tackling our problems and we are hoping that we shall gradually get unemployment down so that those people too may have the higher standard of living which our other people enjoy.'

---

* Nowadays this claim may be debatable, but the National Health Service remains undoubtedly better than anything in Russia outside of Moscow.

For Mikhail Gorbachev, who watched the interview in the Kremlin, there were several important wins. Mrs Thatcher had pointed out the stifling effects of the old-style Soviet command system that he was struggling to transform; she had laid out the benefits that accrue from incentivised work, just as he was about to introduce limited competition in some areas of the economy; and she had praised his liberal reforms, calling on the Soviet people to support his open-society initiatives: if the USSR were to become more open and more democratic, she said, its people would begin to enjoy the 'Western' benefits of freedom and prosperity.

'You [in the USSR] are introducing a much more open society; you can discuss things much more openly than you ever have done before. That is part of our beliefs … I have a much better idea now of Mr Gorbachev's hopes and this tremendous challenge for the Soviet people under your restructuring [perestroika] and the new open society. We wish you well in this great endeavour and we hope it will be very successful.'

Mrs Thatcher ended the interview by painting a picture of the future that many Russians wanted for themselves; a future in which they would be permitted not only to travel to the West, but to share in the advantages that seemed to flow from liberal free-market democracy.

'We want you to travel more frequently to us because we think it is more and more important to build up friendship between peoples and to build up trust and confidence between the people of the Soviet Union and the people of Western Europe and in particular the United Kingdom. I have loved my visit here. I have very much enjoyed the warm welcome you have given me. I will not forget it and I hope to see quite a lot of you in the United Kingdom so you may know more of our way of life and how we do things and more of our people will come to see you. Thank you for your good wishes, thank you for your kindness. Let us hope that there is a better future ahead for all of us.'

It was a powerful message and it was greeted with approbation by the majority of those watching. Unused to challenging debate, the three Soviet interviewers felt they had been trounced by a masterly opponent. One of them, Vladimir Simonov, reflected that he and his colleagues had been 'as ineffective as village chess players taking on Garry Kasparov'. Boris Kalyagin agreed. 'She was excellent; very quick; and she always found the right words to answer us. We didn't make any cuts, any changes; so for the first time, everything she said, everything was on air. People could listen to it and make their own conclusions. I think it was the beginning of glasnost in international affairs. Mrs Thatcher was the winner of the discussion.'

An estimated 100 million people tuned in, and the broadcast sparked a lively debate. Many viewers complained about the interviewers' 'aggressive' and 'impolite' conduct. Women especially leapt to Mrs Thatcher's defence. 'You lost the battle – three men against a single woman,' Kalyagin recalled people saying. The admiration for Mrs Thatcher as a representative of Western values was evident. In despatches assessing the impact of the prime minister's appearance, the British ambassador, Bryan Cartledge, wrote about the 'Maggiemania' that had gripped the country, with Russians reportedly referring to her as *Nasha Masha* – 'our Maggie' – and hanging on her words as if they were the promise of a new life. 'Spectaculars like MT's visit, and especially the live TV interview, dramatically demonstrated his [Gorbachev's] commitment to glasnost,' Cartledge suggested. 'One might add perhaps the importance to Gorbachev of giving the Soviet public a sense of progress in the direction he sought to go.'

Barely 18 months earlier, Britain and the USSR had been at loggerheads, engaged in a bitter round of diplomatic expulsions following the defection of Oleg Gordievsky, the London KGB chief. And Mrs Thatcher was not slow to confront Gorbachev. On the eve of her visit, a demonstration in Moscow by Jewish families denied

Margaret Thatcher hugs a little girl during her
Moscow visit in 1987

Margaret Thatcher waves and smiles at the crowds during the same trip

permission to emigrate to Israel had been broken up by police. At a meeting in the Kremlin, she brought up the incident and spoke on behalf of persecuted dissidents such as Anatoly Shcharansky, Josef Begun and Andrei Sakharov. Her refusal to go soft on the Kremlin's human rights record enhanced her moral authority and her reputation; she was seen as close to Ronald Reagan and speaking on behalf of 'the West.'

Mrs Thatcher made a visit to a church service at the Russian Orthodox monastery at Zagorsk, outside Moscow, and attended a performance of *Swan Lake* at the Bolshoi with Gorbachev and his wife Raisa. But most memorably, she went walkabout, mingling with the Russian people, listening to their views and answering their questions. There was no attempt to curb her interaction with the crowds who turned out to greet her on the streets of Krylatskoe, a recently built but already down-at-heel suburb in western Moscow, and their excitement was plain to see.

The enthusiasm for the West was real, and it was at least in part explained by the next stop on Mrs Thatcher's itinerary. In the long-standing tradition of Potemkin villages* – fake facades to impress outsiders – the prime minister was taken on a tour of a supermarket that had been specially stocked with supplies of bread and cheese, tinned fruit and fresh veg. Looking back, it is amusing to imagine what

---

* Potemkin villages are as old as the times of Catherine the Great. When Catherine came to inspect the newly conquered Crimea in 1787, the province's governor (and Catherine's former lover) Grigory Potemkin was desperate to impress her. There is a historical story – perhaps true and perhaps not – that in order to disguise the reality of poverty and destitution, he built fake villages consisting solely of wooden facades that could be erected along her route, hastily dismantled and then reassembled further on as if they were additional examples of the region's prosperity. In the same way that Gorbachev created his own Potemkin village for Thatcher, Putin is doing the same, on a grand scale, to show off to the Russian people and the West – an idea I will address later, in chapter 15.

Mrs Thatcher thought to herself when she saw this array of very basic foodstuff – which for us back then represented unimaginable luxury. Those reporters who stayed behind after the motorcade had departed saw the efforts of local shoppers trying and failing to empty the shelves before the goods were all packed away.

Five decades earlier, the great Russian poet Anna Akhmatova had recorded in her epic verse drama, *Poem Without a Hero*, how a brief encounter with a charming British diplomat had opened her eyes to another, undreamed of universe beyond the grim reality of Soviet life. Akhmatova called him a 'guest from the future', because she regarded him as the intimated herald of a future that Russia, too, might one day enjoy.

> *The future ripens in the past ...*
> *All the mirrors on the wall*
> *show a man not yet appeared*
> *who could not enter this white hall.*
> *He is no better and no worse,*
> *but he is free of Lethe's curse:*
> *his warm hand makes a human pledge.*
> *This guest from the future, can it be*
> *that he will really come to me ...?*

In 1987, Mrs Thatcher with her self-confident optimism and unwavering belief in Western values, her stylish hats, glamorous sable-collared coats and beige suede boots, also seemed like a 'guest from the future', a portent of what Russia's future could be if the right choices were made and history were to look kindly on the nation's efforts.

CHAPTER 3
A TURNING POINT

Gorbachev's reforms created opportunities for those capable of seizing them. But decades of the Soviet state had destroyed people's capacity for initiative and few took up the challenge of private enterprise. People were so used to the state taking all the decisions for them – providing them with a minimal wage for minimal work, basic accommodation, heating and food – that they had lost the ability to think and act for themselves. For those of us willing to risk it, perestroika offered the possibility of great rewards. Menatep Bank thrived; by the standards of the time, my partners and I were well off.

But there was a problem. The hardline communists were angry at Gorbachev's flirtation with capitalism and were threatening to overthrow him. In August 1991, they staged a putsch. Tanks were on the streets, Gorbachev was detained in his holiday home in Crimea and the coup leaders were promising to take Russia back to the old days by reversing his political and economic reforms. If they succeeded, our businesses would have been crushed and there could have been personal consequences for us and our families. People were scared that all the rights and freedoms that had come to us since perestroika began would be lost forever. That's why I joined Boris Yeltsin on the barricades around the Russian parliament, even though not every-thing about the Yeltsin administration – including the nepotism and incipient corruption – was to my liking. The coup plotters ordered tanks and troops to take over the streets of Moscow and sent the elite Alfa KGB unit to storm the Russian parliament building to destroy us. The people of Moscow linked arms and swore to stand in the way of the tanks. Some of them were shot or crushed to death, but we were defending freedom and democracy. We were defending ourselves and everything we had achieved. That is why we took the decision not to surrender. It was one of the most emotional moments of my life.

When I stood on the barricades in those dramatic August days, I was 28 and a successful businessman. Since earlier that year, I had been an adviser to the prime minister of the Soviet Union, Ivan Silayev. I had a personal stake in the economy and in the reformist policies of Gorbachev and his team. I went to defend the Russian White House because Silayev was there and because it was my duty to stand up for the liberal policies we had been promoting, policies that the coup plotters were seeking to destroy. Perhaps I didn't fully realise the signif-icance of what was happening, but I went with passions running high. The August events confirmed my commitment to democracy and the market economy.

August 1991 changed everything for Russia, and for me. The heroism of the Russian people and the collapse of the coup secured the way for a free-market democracy. In a few turbulent months between August and December 1991, the USSR was dissolved and Boris Yeltsin, president of a newly independent Russia, inherited power. Mikhail Gorbachev had started the move towards a market

People stand on a barricade in front of the Russian White House in Moscow,
21 August 1991

economy, but his measures were limited and tentative. He wanted to strengthen the communist system by encouraging a minimal amount of economic enterprise; the last thing he wanted was to bring communism crashing down. But that was exactly what happened.

The unexpected turn of history thrust Boris Yeltsin into a role that I don't think he had fully anticipated. In opposition, he had espoused radical economic reforms, including an end to the old centralised Soviet command system, but now he had to implement them. In the exhilaration of his victory over the hardline communists, Yeltsin committed himself to the programme of 'economic shock therapy' propounded to him by Western economists. These were the so-called 'Chicago Boys', young technocrats led by Harvard University's Jeffrey Sachs, who came flooding into Russia at the behest of the US leadership, aiming to transform Russia from a stagnant communist central command system into a rejuvenated market economy where private enterprise would breathe new vigour into the state. Their ideas were enthusiastically backed by economic liberals in Yeltsin's Reform Cabinet, most notably Prime Minister Yegor Gaidar and the privatisation guru Anatoly Chubais. The Chicago Boys convinced Yeltsin that he had no time to lose, that delay would increase the scale of the task, and that the transformation had to be completed before the communists could regroup and turn back the clock. Only by creating a new business elite and a middle class with a stake in the system, they argued, could they be sure the communists would never regain power; leaving the economy full of nationalised industries would make it easy for communism to return. The Chicago Boys had previously had some success in post-Jaruzelski Poland, and even more so in Augusto Pinochet's Chile – but these were countries with a living memory of capitalist traditions, while Russia, a country that had no such history, was totally unprepared for the radical changes they were proposing.

The reformers accepted that the speed of the change would cause short-term pain, but believed the long-term gain would make it worthwhile. Yeltsin's first step in late 1992, masterminded by the Chicago Boys and implemented by Gaidar and Chubais, was a voucher scheme that aimed to transfer ownership of Russia's state industries to the Russian people. Every citizen was sent a voucher worth 10,000 roubles (approximately $60), each one representing a very small stake in the country's economy. It was an attempt to create a shareholding middle class, but it was destined to fail.

As an adviser to Yeltsin's Reform Cabinet, I followed the process from the inside. I was never particularly close to Yeltsin himself, but in 1992 I was appointed chairman of the Investment Promotion Fund, with the rank of deputy minister of fuel and energy. I saw at firsthand the mistakes that were being made and I raised the alarm about the pitfalls that awaited us. Many of the problems were down to the Chicago Boys. Much has been written about their role, but I saw with my own eyes how systematically they took apart the country's national economy and dismantled structures that had taken decades to build up, breaking things that should never have been broken. I don't know exactly what authority these American consultants had been given – or who gave it to them – but our Russian politicians deferred to them and, when disputes arose, it was the Americans who got their way.

The thing that made me most angry – and one of the reasons I decided to quit – was the way in which the Russian oil industry was unnecessarily torn apart. Despite all advice, the decision was taken to privatise the main branches of activity – mining, processing, marketing and distribution – separately from each other, with the inevitable result that production collapsed. In an industry where the product is mined in inhospitable conditions hundreds or thousands miles from ports and even from populated areas, with little capacity for prolonged storage, it is obvious that any disruption to the established supply chain

Boris Yeltsin meets with leading industrialists and bankers, including myself, in the Kremlin, 1997

will lead to problems of shortages, the loss of wells frozen because of inactivity and the destruction of expensive equipment in processing facilities. I argued against the decisions that were taken, but my views were ignored. Ironically, just a few years later, it would fall to me to undo the damage that was done to the oil industry by the misguided policies of the Chicago Boys and their Russian counterparts.

I saw so much going wrong that, in 1993, I stood down from my role in the Reform Cabinet. I told the cabinet that if entrepreneurs like me were not listened to, then we would inevitably take advantage of their mistakes. I decided to go fulltime into business.

The voucher scheme failed because it distorted the realities of the Russian economy. The sums involved were illogical. The population of Russia was 150 million, so 150 million vouchers were issued, meaning that the greater part of Russian industry was being valued at a mere $9 billion. Anyone who did the maths could see this was wrong, and anyone with a business brain could see it presented an opportunity. But most Russians had no experience or understanding of the concept of private ownership and were more than happy to sell their bits of paper for a few roubles. Group Menatep bought up large numbers of vouchers, which were being traded on street corners, and acquired shareholdings in many different industries, including textile mills, chemicals, metallurgy, glass, food processing, wood pulp and paper, fertilisers and oil. It was a risky process because no one was sure what condition these industries were in – the Soviet way was never to open the books; official profit and loss figures were unreliable, and we often discovered huge debts that had not figured in the accounts – but we took the gamble. Many of the firms we bought turned out to be hard to resurrect, several produced no returns and one even went bankrupt; but all enterprise involves an element of risk. When things worked out for us, we were accused of buying businesses on the cheap, but the fact is that we played by the rules that were in force at the time.

I took a hands-on role in running the companies we acquired, some of which we grew into multimillion-dollar businesses; but it soon became clear to me that our portfolio of interests was too big. Menatep needed to slim down; we needed to concentrate on one thing and, in 1996, I chose oil. The decision was partly influenced by the experience I had gained at the Ministry of Fuel and Energy and by my own background in chemical engineering, as well as my business partners' qualifications in oil engineering. Russia has vast natural supplies, but her state-owned oil companies had been appallingly inefficient, operating at a loss for many decades. The industry was in sharp decline. I could see the wasted potential and I knew how things could be turned round; but Russian law specified that strategic industries should not be sold to private owners. While Yeltsin had managed to privatise many branches of industry, the remaining communist faction in the Russian parliament had fought to block the sale of land, iron and steel, oil and gas.

Times changed, however, when a combination of the inevitable crisis in the old state industries (especially defence), the splintering of the Soviet economic space, the Chicago Boys' shock therapy and Boris Yeltsin's clumsy management of the economy resulted in a massively inflated budget deficit that came close to bankrupting the country. Wages and pensions were left unpaid and people lost their jobs. To make things worse, presidential elections were due the following year and the Communist Party, under its new leader Gennady Zyuganov, was leading in the polls. Yeltsin needed cash to keep the economy going and get a grip on the main industries that were spiralling out of control if he were to have any chance of being re-elected. He asked Russia's leading businessmen, including myself, to come to his aid and we agreed to do so. It was certainly in our interests to prevent a Communist Party victory, as it was already promising to renationalise our businesses and restore the state-run economy of old. In return for our help, the government agreed to revise the law on state industry and put up for sale the assets we were keen to purchase. The whole deal was quite remarkable: we were a bunch of young men who had started out less than a decade earlier doing petty business deals in defiance of a disapproving Soviet state, and now the state was coming to us for help.

Russian businesses advanced Yeltsin around $1.8 billion and, most importantly, helped to end the chaos and stabilise the situation in the big industries, which resumed the payment of taxes to the state and wages to their millions of employees. It allowed the government to head off the massive wave of strikes in both the cities and the regions, and to pay pensions and wages. Yeltsin's poll numbers rebounded and, in July 1996, he was elected to a second presidential term. In a state-run auction, my partners and I bought the oil company, Yukos. It was a turning point for me that would define the rest of my life.

CHAPTER 4
GAMBLING BIG

Yukos was a major oil producer, but it had been run by uninterested state bureaucrats for so long that it was unprofitable, inefficient and deeply in debt. In 1996, we paid $309 million for a controlling 78 per cent of the holding company, despite knowing that it controlled only a minority of the shares in its oil production and other assets, and had debts exceeding $3.5 billion. We did so because we understood the potential that Yukos offered – and because we were sure we could bring the leadership, enterprise and commitment that would turn it around.

It worked. Under our leadership, Yukos would ultimately grow into the biggest oil producer in Russia, responsible for 20 per cent of the nation's output, and one of the largest in the world. By 2003, its value on the Moscow stock exchange would rise to a market capitalisation of over $30 billion. But it wasn't easy. Back in 1996, the Russian oil sector was in chaos. The major companies were in meltdown, not paying wages to their workers, not paying taxes and threatened with bankruptcy. Yukos owed $2 billion in taxes to the state; wage arrears and debts to contractors were spiralling; output had fallen from 45 million to 35 million tons per year, with the result that the infrastructure for production, processing and transportation had collapsed. The Kremlin was unhappy, the workers were unhappy and tensions were growing. When Boris Yeltsin agreed to privatise the oil industry, he knew that that was the only way to save it, and he laid down strict conditions. 'We have to immediately ensure the receipt of taxes from the largest industrial enterprises,' the Kremlin negotiators told us. 'That is why we are ready to sell those enterprises to you. But, to begin with, you must go and persuade the directors of those enterprises to hand over power to you. You have to do that yourselves. And you have to start paying workers' wages and state taxes immediately.'

I remember very clearly what Yukos was like back then. Salaries were six months in arrears and employees were either grumbling to themselves or complaining out loud. The level of theft of company property and corruption by workers and managers was staggering. Yukos was running a massive operating loss, and the company was only functioning in nine regions of Russia. When I left Yukos seven years later, however, average salaries had reached $1,000 per month; there were no delays in pay; production had doubled; and tax payments reached $3.5–4 billion per year at an oil price of just over $20 a barrel. Privatisation had allowed us to establish proper management, which simply did not exist in the era of the 'red directors' – the old Soviet bureaucrats who continued to run the big national industries.

We had to do it the hard way. As I mentioned before, Soviet era employment practices were based on the old mantra of 'we pretend to work and they pretend to pay us', with the result that Yukos was saddled with hundreds of middle managers who turned up, clocked

on and did nothing. To knock the company into shape, we had to move most of them on. Many people were fired. We introduced severe penalties for drunkenness on the job, which was running at catastrophic levels. And we cracked down on corruption, showing no mercy to those workers and contractors who were seen to be cheating the company or stealing its property. After seven years, Yukos was active in a total of 50 Russian regions, with an annual production of 80 million tons and a distinct upward trend. It became the second largest taxpayer in the whole country, after Gazprom, accounting for almost 5 per cent of all federal budget revenues – and all of this was achieved in a country that had just emerged from 70 years of communism, where we had to struggle to find managers and workers able to adapt to the new ways of private enterprise.

Turning round Yukos's fortunes meant struggling against the backwardness and mental entropy of the Russian business world. In addition, we had to contend with sharp practice from Western business as well. There was underhand dealing, a systematic failure to respect agreements and an unscrupulous Wild West capitalism at play, which helped to undermine the esteem in which we Russians had held the West, denting our admiration for the 'shining light' of free-market democracy.

In particular, I saw how large Western companies used their negotiating experience to exploit the business illiteracy of Russian officials, trying to bargain with the government to snap up oilfields for 2–4 per cent of their real value. And I encountered examples of economic blackmail, so-called 'greenmailing', by Western investors. This was done by buying a minority stake in a company and then accumulating enough shares to be able to veto its management's plans for restructuring and modernising the business. The greenmailers would offer to lift the veto in return for the management's agreement to buy out their shares at a price well above market value. In our case,

Western investors did this to us when we were trying to integrate some of Yukos's subsidiary companies. We eventually managed to fend off the greenmail attempt, but the underhand methods they used against us shook my faith in the West as a model to be followed.

Then, in the second half of 1998, things went from bad to worse. Following the sudden plunge in world oil prices, the rouble was sharply devalued and the energy-dependent Russian economy went into a nosedive. The stock market lost billions of dollars. Many firms that had previously appeared impregnable went to the wall and it seemed Yukos might become one of them. The price of oil on world markets plunged to $8.50 per barrel, while the cost of production remained at $12 per barrel. It meant we were producing oil and then paying out money for doing so. With bankruptcy looming, I took drastic action. I had to cut the staff by 30 per cent: tens of thousands of people in just one year. It is not something I found easy, or am proud of, but there was no alternative. Those who remained, nearly 100,000 employees, agreed to take a 30 per cent reduction in their salaries (which was softened to less than half of that because of the devaluation of the rouble).

I went to Yukos's main oil production facility in the town of Nefteyugansk and invited representatives of all the company's workers to a meeting in the local theatre. I spoke with them to explain why I was asking them to vote to take a pay cut. Their agreement in a formal vote was legally necessary and the initial reaction was hostile, but by the end of the meeting I had convinced them that it was better to agree a temporary drop in wages to save the company for better days ahead. I promised I would make up for their lost wages within a year, and I am proud that I managed to do so. But even more important for me was the fact that I had gained the trust of the workers.

The economic crisis of 1998 was a wakeup call, though not everyone heeded it. Many Russians complained and blamed the West, but I

My partners and I were lucky. We teamed up with consultants from the oilfield services specialists, Schlumberger, and other advisers from Western countries, who were marvellous to work with. They not only advised us on how to transform and restructure our company, they helped us to restructure our whole way of thinking. The Schlumberger team showed us the best things about Western business ethics and why integrity matters. They worked according to proper codes of conduct, honest people who commanded respect both as professionals and as decent folk with real values. Even today, I remember them with the greatest admiration. This convinced us that the conmen who had previously rushed into Russia were perhaps not the true face of Western capitalism after all.

My respect for Western values was boosted and restored but, for the majority of Russians, things seemed very different. Many had been badly hit by the economic collapse of 1998 and a substantial number of people came to blame the West. Russian government officials who had to cut public spending and imposed economic austerity measures were quick to cite the demands of the International Monetary Fund as the reason for their tough decisions. The result was a growing, generalised antipathy towards 'Western interference'. When Russian banks failed and people's savings were lost, the public seized on the explanation that this too was the result of conditions imposed on Russia by the IMF. They believed that the West was implementing a deliberate policy of destroying Russian banks in order to clear the way for Western financial institutions to come and take their place. Things had gone badly wrong and the West – especially its financial institutions – was a convenient scapegoat. A wave of national resentment grew, attaching itself to the 'traitors' in the Russian government who had 'sold Russia out' to foreign interests. The Yeltsin administration's commitment to Western-style market democracy was blamed for all the nation's ills, and the conditions were created for the coming to decided it was time to concentrate on taking practical steps. Together with my business partners, we resolved to transform Yukos into a completely open and transparent operation, adopting Western reporting standards and respecting world-class environmental, employment and ethical practices. Without this, it was evident that we could not thrive in an international business sector where competition was fierce. We invited the best specialists from around the world to help us reorganise our production processes, and we secured the buy-in of the company's employees. It paid off: production increased, costs fell, we were welcomed into the global market and our profits grew.

Yukos became one of the first Russian companies to adopt Western standards of corporate governance and respect for shareholder rights, including the preparation of financial accounts that complied with US Generally Accepted Accounting Principles (GAAP). An independent board of directors was appointed, with a mix of Russian and Western representatives, such as the international investment specialist Bernard Lozé, the prominent French banker Jacques-Antoine Kosciusko, the Washington lawyer Sarah Carey Reilly and others. We revealed who owned what in the company, with details of all our shareholdings, and we adopted a new company motto, 'Honesty, Openness, Responsibility'. The result was that Yukos American Depository Receipts (ADRs) were accepted for trading in the US market, and US investors – including state pension funds – bought nearly 15 per cent of our shares. By conforming to Western norms, we boosted our standing and our profits at the same time. Yukos became a poster-child company, a symbol of how the Russian economy and its shady business culture could transform itself. *BusinessWeek* wrote that US investors were rewarding our new approach. Yukos's share price rose 250 per cent. 'If Khodorkovsky can keep this up,' *BusinessWeek* concluded, 'the Russian energy industry with Yukos as its standard bearer may finally get some respect.'

on and did nothing. To knock the company into shape, we had to move most of them on. Many people were fired. We introduced severe penalties for drunkenness on the job, which was running at catastrophic levels. And we cracked down on corruption, showing no mercy to those workers and contractors who were seen to be cheating the company or stealing its property. After seven years, Yukos was active in a total of 50 Russian regions, with an annual production of 80 million tons and a distinct upward trend. It became the second largest taxpayer in the whole country, after Gazprom, accounting for almost 5 per cent of all federal budget revenues – and all of this was achieved in a country that had just emerged from 70 years of communism, where we had to struggle to find managers and workers able to adapt to the new ways of private enterprise.

Turning round Yukos's fortunes meant struggling against the backwardness and mental entropy of the Russian business world. In addition, we had to contend with sharp practice from Western business as well. There was underhand dealing, a systematic failure to respect agreements and an unscrupulous Wild West capitalism at play, which helped to undermine the esteem in which we Russians had held the West, denting our admiration for the 'shining light' of free-market democracy.

In particular, I saw how large Western companies used their negotiating experience to exploit the business illiteracy of Russian officials, trying to bargain with the government to snap up oilfields for 2–4 per cent of their real value. And I encountered examples of economic blackmail, so-called 'greenmailing', by Western investors. This was done by buying a minority stake in a company and then accumulating enough shares to be able to veto its management's plans for restructuring and modernising the business. The greenmailers would offer to lift the veto in return for the management's agreement to buy out their shares at a price well above market value. In our case,

Western investors did this to us when we were trying to integrate some of Yukos's subsidiary companies. We eventually managed to fend off the greenmail attempt, but the underhand methods they used against us shook my faith in the West as a model to be followed.

Then, in the second half of 1998, things went from bad to worse. Following the sudden plunge in world oil prices, the rouble was sharply devalued and the energy-dependent Russian economy went into a nosedive. The stock market lost billions of dollars. Many firms that had previously appeared impregnable went to the wall and it seemed Yukos might become one of them. The price of oil on world markets plunged to $8.50 per barrel, while the cost of production remained at $12 per barrel. It meant we were producing oil and then paying out money for doing so. With bankruptcy looming, I took drastic action. I had to cut the staff by 30 per cent: tens of thousands of people in just one year. It is not something I found easy, or am proud of, but there was no alternative. Those who remained, nearly 100,000 employees, agreed to take a 30 per cent reduction in their salaries (which was softened to less than half of that because of the devaluation of the rouble).

I went to Yukos's main oil production facility in the town of Nefteyugansk and invited representatives of all the company's workers to a meeting in the local theatre. I spoke with them to explain why I was asking them to vote to take a pay cut. Their agreement in a formal vote was legally necessary and the initial reaction was hostile, but by the end of the meeting I had convinced them that it was better to agree a temporary drop in wages to save the company for better days ahead. I promised I would make up for their lost wages within a year, and I am proud that I managed to do so. But even more important for me was the fact that I had gained the trust of the workers.

The economic crisis of 1998 was a wakeup call, though not everyone heeded it. Many Russians complained and blamed the West, but I power of a new breed of politicians – people with a background in the security services, who would restore order with the iron grip of centralised autocracy.

It seems to me that Russia in the late 1990s was suffering from a sort of Weimar syndrome. In the 1930s, the population of the Weimar Republic had become convinced that Germany's poverty and humiliation were caused by the harsh terms of the Treaty of Versailles, imposed on them by the victorious First World War allies. In a similar mood of national discontent, Russians now began to blame Western Europe and the United States.

The Russian people had seen living standards fall and many were plunged into poverty. After decades of artificially maintained price controls, backed by billions of roubles of state subsidies (which even then did not manage to keep the shelves filled), Yeltsin and the Chicago Boys had freed prices for all but the most essential goods. Inflation had rocketed; people's savings were being spent on just a few days' worth of food. Hordes of beggars appeared on the streets; people were forced to sell their family possessions to stay afloat. The collapse of the USSR and the Soviet system of central planning had left factories without suppliers and without government orders. Unable to adapt to market conditions, they could no longer pay wages to their workers or taxes to the state. In an attempt to balance the national budget, Yeltsin slashed state spending and raised taxes. When entitlement to free healthcare was sharply reduced, few could afford the paid services that replaced it. Illnesses and infant mortality increased, along with alcoholism and suicide; male life expectancy fell to 57 years. The result was that the nation felt cheated and belittled. And at the same time, Western Europe and North America seemed to be thriving. Many Russians resented the apparent decline of their country from a global superpower to an impoverished third world country. And they knew who to blame. Powerful voices in society accused malevolent foreign powers of trampling on Russia's national interests and called for the restoration of national pride by the rejection of all cooperation with the West.

By a stroke of ill fortune, the Yugoslav crisis – following reports of Serbian ethnic cleansing of Kosovar Albanians – broke out just at the moment when revanchist demands in Russia were at their height. In 1999, the Kremlin was still actively engaging with the international community, pursuing internationalist policies and in return receiving Western financial support. With Boris Yeltsin incapacitated by a series of heart attacks, the country was effectively being led by the prime minister, Yevgeny Primakov. On 24 March that year, Primakov was due to fly to Washington to ask the International Monetary Fund for an additional $4.2 billion, and he took me with him as a member of the Russian business delegation. As we took off from Moscow, Primakov explained that he was not optimistic that the loan would be granted: the West had already pumped large sums into Russia, with little indication that it was making any difference to the crisis in our economy. In addition, there was growing popular anger in Russia that Yeltsin was perceived as going cap-in-hand to the Western 'enemy' who had brought us to our knees. A further flashpoint had emerged: NATO countries announced their intention to intervene in the Yugoslav conflict by bombing Serbian military forces accused of the ethnic cleansing of Muslim Albanians in Kosovo, further inflaming Russian opinion.

We were already in the air when Vice President Al Gore called Primakov to tell him that the bombing campaign was about to begin. Primakov had to decide what to do. Most Russians regard the Serbs as our historical allies, fellow Slavs who fought with us against Muslim forces threatening from the east. After hurried discussions, Primakov ordered the crew to turn the plane around in mid-flight over the Atlantic and return to Moscow, scrapping a long-scheduled round of high-level economic and security talks with the Clinton administration. It was a dramatic protest against Western military action against Serbia, but also a symbolic U-turn in Russia's whole relationship with the West. Even though I was on that plane, I am not sure that I fully understood at that moment the fateful consequences of what was happening. There was, however, a very real sense of a historic drama being played out before our eyes. At Shannon airport in Ireland, where we landed for refuelling on the way back home, I bought a box of Irish whisky and we all shared it to drown our anxiety about the future. We didn't know it, but in a little over six months Yeltsin would be gone, and Russia would be under the rule of a very different type of leader.

CHAPTER 5
THE HUMBLING

An enduring memory of my childhood was being allowed to stay up late on New Year's Eve. From my earliest years, I knew that at a few minutes before midnight – in the moments before national television broadcast the Kremlin chimes, signalling the advent of a new year – the country's leader would address us, the Russian people. The tradition had begun in 1941, in the darkest days of the war, when the titular head of state Mikhail Kalinin took to the radio to rally Soviet spirits in the face of Hitler's inhuman onslaught against us. In my early memories, it was Leonid Brezhnev who would slur his way through a summary of what had been achieved and what was expected in the year ahead. In 1985, we watched with especial excitement as the new broom in the Kremlin, Mikhail Gorbachev, outlined his vision for change. Then in 1987 and 1988, there was the extraordinary spectacle of Gorbachev and Ronald Reagan swapping roles, so that Reagan spoke to us and Gorbachev addressed the American people on New Year's Eve, which brought us tangible proof that the Cold War was thawing.

But it was 1999 that produced the biggest surprise. The millions of viewers switching on their TV sets at midnight, expecting to see the familiar red-nosed, puffy-cheeked face of Boris Yeltsin, champagne glass in hand, were in for a shock. In his place, a small, unfamiliar man in an ill-fitting suit was sitting in front of a decorated Christmas tree, trying to look presidential. Breaking with years of tradition, Yeltsin had already made his New Year speech, and instead of the usual, well-worn expressions of national congratulation, he had startled us. 'I want to apologise,' Yeltsin said, 'for failing to make all our dreams come true, for failing to foresee that what at first seemed easy would turn out to be agonisingly hard. I apologise for betraying the hopes of all of us who believed we would be able to jump in a single leap from the grey, retrograde, totalitarian past to the shining, rich and civilised future.' Yeltsin announced that he was resigning, in order to hand over the presidency to a new man, 'a strong person who deserves to become President', who would ensure that Russia never again regressed to its discredited, authoritarian past. For those who did not know who this 'strong person' was – possibly the majority of those watching – a helpful caption appeared, naming him as 'Acting President of the Russian Federation, Vladimir Vladimirovich Putin.'

To most of us, the first words of the new president seemed reassuring, a categorical reaffirmation that he would continue the open, West-friendly policies of his predecessor so that Russia would remain on the path of liberal, free-market democracy. 'I assure you there will be no vacuum of power,' Putin pledged. 'The Russian state will stand firm in the defence of freedom of speech, freedom of conscience, freedom of the media, private ownership rights and all the fundamental elements of a civilised society. Russia has opted irrevocably for democracy and reform and we will continue to pursue those goals …

New Year is a holiday when dreams come true, and that is certainly the case this year. I believe the hopes and dreams that all of us cherish will undoubtedly come true.'

Putin's promises were comforting; most of us went to bed relieved. But we might not have done so if we had known what had occurred earlier, behind doors. When Yeltsin told Putin on 14 December that he was about to become the leader of a superpower, the 'strong man' replied that he 'wasn't ready' (at least, that is what both Yeltsin and Putin wrote in their account of the meeting). But it wasn't long before the 'strong man' allowed himself to be persuaded. A meteoric rise from obscurity had whisked him from an undistinguished career in the lower echelons of the Soviet Union's intelligence service, the KGB, via civil service posts in St Petersburg and then the Kremlin, to a surprise one-year stint as boss of the KGB's successor organisation, the Federal Security Service (FSB), before three months as interim prime minister and, finally, the commanding heights of power.

Having received the news of his elevation, Putin knew exactly who he must report to; a day or so later, he went straight to his old stamping ground – the Lubyanka, the headquarters of the FSB and formerly that of the KGB. At a gala evening in honour of Lenin's punitive organ of repression, the Cheka secret police,* Putin raised a glass to his former FSB colleagues. 'Comrades,' he had just declared in a speech of welcome, 'I wish to inform you that the group of FSB colleagues despatched by you to work undercover in the national government has succeeded in the first phase of its mission!'

At the time, it may have seemed a harmless joke – if somewhat tasteless, given the brutality and suffering dished out in the basements of the Lubyanka over the years – but in retrospect, the story has

---

* The first incarnation of the Bolshevik secret police after the 1917 revolution was called the Cheka.

acquired distinctly sinister overtones. Putin's braggadocio at the secret policemen's ball needs to be seen in the context of the time. By 1999, the Soviet Union had been dead for nearly a decade and its brutal enforcers, the once dreaded KGB, were no more. The collapse of the USSR had left all Russians dazed and confused, but for members of the security services the upheaval had been even more painful. The event that signified the downfall of the USSR and the end of seven decades of communist rule was the shambolic attempted coup of August 1991 to halt Gorbachev's liberalising reforms and return Russia to socialist orthodoxy. When the hardline communists' putsch was defeated, the plotters were vilified and sent to jail. Prominent among them were the leaders of the KGB, including its then chairman Vladimir Kryuchkov. For the secret police, the consequences were immediate and ultimately catastrophic. The KGB, already held in dubious regard by many Soviet citizens, was now identified in the minds of millions as the malevolent force behind an attempt to seize control of their country's future and deprive its people of the freedom and prosperity that Gorbachev's reformers were promising.

On 22 August 1991, as it became clear that the coup had failed, thousands of people gathered in front of the Lubyanka. Demonstrations, long banned in the USSR, had been tolerated under Gorbachev, so it wasn't surprising to see people on the streets. But the events of the hours that followed were so iconoclastic, in their most literal sense, that I will never forget them.

In the centre of Lubyanka Square, the lowering statue of Felix Dzerzhinsky, the founder of the Cheka, was a very visible symbol of KGB repression. The crowd daubed its pedestal with slogans – 'murderer', 'tsar-killer', 'antichrist' – while chanting 'Freedom!' and 'Down with the KGB!' Someone managed to wrap a rope around Dzerzhinsky's neck, like a hangman's noose, and attempt – unsuccessfully – to topple him with the help of a bus. Dusk began to fall. From

Protesters celebrate after toppling the statue of Felix Dzerzhinsky on Lubyanka Square, 23 August 1991

A view of the Lubyanka, and the statue of Felix Dzerzhinsky before it was toppled

somewhere – at the time, no one knew from where – three mobile cranes rumbled into the square, led by a group of construction workers who ushered them through the crowd. One of the men was hoisted high in the basket of a cherry-picker, until he came face to face with 'Iron Felix'. The rope was replaced with a metal hawser attached to the jib of a crane. Shortly before midnight, the 15-tonne statue rose uncertainly into the air, swaying like a hanged man. Fireworks exploded. The crowd cheered. People kicked and spat on the toppled statue. In the Lubyanka itself, not a single light burned in any of the windows. The once-untouchable KGB had been humbled, its fearsome reputation for omnipotence destroyed. It felt like a seminal moment.

In the climate of freedom that came with the collapse of the USSR, the new Russian leadership strove to ensure that the country could never return to the police state of the past. A reformist chairman, Vadim Bakatin, was appointed to dismantle the KGB monolith, declaring, 'The traditions of Chekism must be eradicated.' Bakatin introduced measures to curtail the security services' extrajudicial control over society: the KGB would be broken up and replaced by independent agencies, competing with one another as equals; they would be transparent, subject to the rule of law and respect for human rights; and their focus would henceforth be the fight against crime, not the policing of political opinion.

The next decade was a hard time to be a secret policeman. The KGB's successor organisation, the FSB, was a pale shadow of its predecessor, having been restructured and seemingly neutered, operating with greatly reduced budgets and only half its previous staff. It meant that 200,000 former KGB employees, people accustomed to wielding unchecked power over their fellow citizens, were made unemployed. Thousands of them found work in private security, as bodyguards, analysts and enforcers, assisting politicians, businessmen or – in many cases – shady figures from the increasingly prominent world of organised crime. The nexus of KGB and mafia would become a phenomenon of national concern. Even those agents who were retained by the FSB found their wages uncertain and frequently unpaid. As a result, they, too, were vulnerable to recruitment by private business and criminal gangs, using their inside knowledge and authority to make money on the side, learning to serve the state and their own private interests at the same time.

There was a further category of KGB employees – those men and women whose ideological outlook had been formed by the organisation, and who were devoted to bringing it back from the dead. Even as the jubilant crowd was celebrating the end of terror in August 1991, a small group of officers had slipped out of the Lubyanka, staying in the shadows as they discreetly unscrewed the iron plaque commemorating Yuri Andropov, saving it from the crowd's wrath. Andropov had been a revered KGB chairman, serving for over 15 years at the height of the organisation's power in the 1960s and 1970s, before succeeding Leonid Brezhnev as general secretary of the Soviet Communist Party in 1982. His early death had truncated his reign as Soviet leader, but Andropov's reputation in KGB circles remained high. As the 1990s turned to political disappointment and economic collapse, his name would be invoked by secret policemen hankering for their glory days – if only Andropov had lived, they told each other, he would have saved communism, averted the chaos of gangster capitalism and instituted something akin to the Chinese state model. Their nostalgia for the past was redoubled by the trouble they had finding a role in the Russia of the present; they did what they needed to do to survive while biding their time, dreaming of regaining their place at the top table. Most significantly, as we were to learn to our cost, it was to this category of disenchanted apparatchiks that Vladimir Putin belonged.

Many Russians do not share the view that today's FSB are villains, trampling on people's rights at home and murdering innocent victims in the UK. Even in the 1990s, our nation's time of greatest openness, there was a feeling that disbanding the KGB had deprived Russia of a powerful force for law and order, in whose absence the country might spiral out of control.* Without the levers of oversight and coercion provided by a strong security apparatus, Boris Yeltsin's government had few means of combating an unprecedented surge in organised crime that swept the nation. Alternative arrangements needed to be found. Of necessity – or perhaps through choice – the FSB looked for accommodation with the criminal world. In most of Russia's major cities, the FSB took on the role of mediator between gangsters, businessmen and city bureaucrats, often with the assistance of former KGB men working in all three camps. The aim was to broker a compromise, an informal truce under which the criminals would moderate their behaviour, allowing the authorities to maintain a semblance of order on the streets, while turning a blind eye to their criminal activities.

In St Petersburg, the arrangement became institutionalised. The mayor, Anatoly Sobchak, instructed Putin, who was then the first deputy chairman of the St Petersburg city government, to work with the city's underworld. Putin's role was to co-opt organised crime

---

* People in the West have a fairly uniform view that the Cheka, the OGPU, NKVD, KGB and FSB are a bad thing – run by sinister thugs, dedicated to repressing the Russian people and sowing evil abroad. But that is not how many Russians view them. For every Russian who reviled the KGB, there was another who admired them. My generation was brought up on tales of Soviet secret agents carrying out daring missions to protect the motherland; and in many instances, their missions were directed against the malevolent forces of the capitalist West. An iconic television programme of 1973 called *Seventeen Moments of Spring* depicted a Soviet intelligence agent fighting not just against the Axis powers, but battling at the same time to stop Britain and the USA joining forces with the Nazis to undermine the USSR. Another James Bond-like spy series, *The Shield and the Sword*, was instrumental in inspiring a young Vladimir Putin to volunteer for the KGB.

bosses to ensure that outbreaks of violence and disruption were mini-mised. In return, everyone got a share of the profits from the rampant extortion rackets, prostitution and the transport of drugs. The secu-rity officials who policed the Faustian bargain between authorities and criminals were still following orders, but they were viewed as a relic of a past era – men who would be dispensable once the situation in Russia settled down. For a once proud organisation, it was belittling.

The humiliation experienced in the 1990s, and the resentment arising from it, do much to explain Putin's subsequent behaviour. After all, Putin is the man who recalled with pride that, as a child, he had only one poster on his bedroom wall – a portrait of Felix Dzerzhinsky. When Yeltsin appointed him head of the FSB in 1998, his first move was to summon the members of his old St Petersburg crew. These included former KGB men, many of whom had spent a decade in the wilderness or collaborating with the criminal world and were burning for a return to the corridors of power. Putin promoted them to influ-ential positions within the agency and, after his assumption of the presidency, facilitated their appointment to senior posts in govern-ment and commercial organisations with state connections.

The longer the Putin era endured, the more Russia's political and business elites became populated by his former colleagues from the security services. A 2006 report by the Moscow-based Centre for the Study of Elites concluded that while 'in the Soviet period and the first post-Soviet period, the KGB and FSB were mainly involved in security issues, now half of them operate in business, political parties, NGOs, regional governments, even culture. They have started to make use of all political institutions.' The Centre's analysis of 1,016 leading political figures – including departmental heads of the pres-idential administration, all members of the government, all deputies of both houses of parliament, the heads of federal units and the heads of regional executive and legislative branches – indicated that the careers of 78 per cent of them involved past service in or affiliation to the KGB or its successor agencies. Looking back, Putin's boast in 1999 that the FSB had taken control of the government appears to be less of a humorous aside than a declaration of what he was planning for his time in power.

Exactly a year after Putin's Lubyanka speech, Nikolai Patrushev, the man who succeeded him as director of the FSB, celebrated the dramatic turnaround in the agency's standing. 'Our best colleagues, the honour and pride of the FSB,' Patrushev proclaimed, 'are, if you like, Russia's new nobility.' From outcasts one minute to running the country the next, the secret police were back. Putin knew his old comrades and knew he could rely on them. By reinstating their lost prestige and returning to them the power that Yeltsin had taken away, he created a corpus of grateful, dependent people who owed him everything – and would repay him with their willingness to commit any illegal act they were instructed to enact. In the first decade of Putin's rule, the FSB became a favoured elite, with massively increased funding and recruitment, expanded responsibilities and almost total immunity from any official control. Putin's Praetorian Guard, which includes the leadership and the special forces of all the law enforcement agencies, acquired the nickname of Siloviki, literally 'those who exercise force'. Like the tsarist nobles with whom Peter the Great populated the Table of Ranks of his civil service, the Siloviki would gain influence in every sector of the state, ousting the Yeltsinite liberals who once dominated the government and instilling Vladimir Putin's increasingly hardline values.

Under Putin, the FSB enjoys more power than even the KGB in its heyday, exercising effective control over other law enforcement agencies, including the courts, the Prosecutor's Office, the Investigative Committee, the Interior Ministry, the Customs Agency, Border Control and the Federal Protection Service. It has been empowered to play an active role in removing politicians who pose a threat to the leadership, to control the media and repress business figures who challenge the commercial dominance of the Kremlin oligarchs. Its brief covers intelligence, counterintelligence, counterterrorism, economic crime, electronic espionage, social monitoring and control of the country's computerised election system. It is charged with monitoring non-governmental organisations, specifically those with foreign funding, and has the legal right to hunt down and kill suspected enemies overseas.

In the Soviet Union, the KGB was subordinated to the Communist Party, which exercised political control over its activities; but that is not the case with the FSB. Journalists and others who attempt to monitor the security services' activities are met with hostility. When the investigative writer Andrei Soldatov questioned the lack of safeguards against FSB abuse, he himself was taken to the Lubyanka for repeated bouts of questioning. The extent of the FSB's powers and its exemption from the traditional system of oversight mean there is little prospect for anyone from outside the 'brotherhood of agents' to curb its mission creep.

The combination of Vladimir Putin as president and Nikolai Patrushev as FSB director created an echo chamber of self-amplifying paranoia, with each of them reinforcing the fears and prejudices of the other. In his years at the head of the FSB and then as secretary of the State Security Council, Patrushev has displayed a longstanding distrust of the West, opposing integration and cooperation, encouraging Putin to rely on the security services by feeding him lurid 'intelligence' of alleged American hostility. In 2014, Patrushev declared that it was 'the Americans who brought down the Soviet Union' and that the same CIA operation was still being actively pursued, with the goal now of dismembering Russia. The West had deliberately provoked the war in Chechnya, he reported, with 'extremists and their adherents being supported by US and British intelligence services, as well as by their allies in Europe'. Meanwhile, in his view, Washington had spent the quarter-century since the collapse of the USSR laying the groundwork for the crisis in Ukraine. 'A whole generation of Ukrainians,' Patrushev claimed, 'has been poisoned by the West with hatred for Russia and with the mythology of so-called "European" values ... the calamity in Ukraine is another means for them [the West] to intensify their policy of "containing" our country. They have continued unfailingly to follow this course, with only the forms and tactics of its execution changing.' Other claims by the FSB chairman included the assertion that ISIS had been created by the policies of the United States, that the governments of the Baltic countries were supporting neo-Nazis and that Madeleine Albright believed that Siberia should not belong to Russia. When evidence was sought for this surprising assertion, FSB General Boris Ratnikov revealed that it was based on the work of his mind-reading agent who had 'intercepted Albright's thoughts' and discovered that she had a 'pathological hatred of Slavs'.

Joe Biden's assertion in 2021 that Putin is a 'killer' was grist to Patrushev's anti-Westernism. It was, he said, the signal for another Cold War, just as Churchill's Iron Curtain speech had signalled the start of the first one. 'Even Truman and Reagan, the most fanatical opponents of our country, accepted that there were limits on what should be declared in public ... no matter how extreme their Russophobia behind closed doors.'

In Soviet times, the KGB would regularly stoke confrontation with the West, but its aggression would be softened by the Foreign Ministry, whose diplomats had direct contact with colleagues in Europe and North America. The unprecedented dominance of today's FSB, with its exclusive access to the ear of the president, means that the old mediating forces no longer exist. Wild theories of encirclement, danger and Western aggression, propounded by Patrushev and his associates, have become increasingly dominant and influential in the president's circle. The February 2022 invasion of Ukraine was at least in part the result of the Kremlin's distorted view of reality, stoked by this echo chamber of self-reinforcing paranoia.

As for the promises of continuing liberty and democracy made by Putin in his New Year address of 1999, few if any have been kept. The political freedoms of the 1990s have disappeared, and have been replaced by the autocratic control of a small group of crony gangsters clustered around the president and the similarly bandit-like Siloviki, supported by the loyal apparatus of the FSB. Alternative centres of power, including opposition parties, prominent individuals who challenged Putin's divine right to rule, environmental organisations, human rights groups, foreigners, critics and the media have been repressed. The 'group of FSB men despatched to work undercover in the national government' in December 1999 has achieved its goal. Few of us back then foresaw the toxic consequences that would unfold as a result.

PART TWO
ENTER THE STRONGMAN

CHAPTER 6
ALL THINGS TO ALL MEN

When Boris Yeltsin stepped down and Vladimir Putin came to power on the eve of the millennium, everything changed in Russia. In the runup to Yeltsin's resignation, I heard whispers that Putin would be shooed in as president, but I didn't say anything. I neither supported him nor spoke out against him. I just accepted that Putin had been chosen by Yeltsin, and that Yeltsin must have known what he was doing; that he knew better than I did what sort of person Putin was.

For a while, at first, I thought that maybe Putin was a good choice. I had been involved in Kremlin politics on and off for a decade and I was conscious that we were living through one of those great turning points in history when Russia's future is up for grabs: when the nation can go in radically differing directions and that the slightest nudge of events can send her hurtling along the right or wrong path. At all her moments of destiny – the Mongol invasion in 1237, the reigns of Peter the Great and Catherine the Great in the seventeenth and

eighteenth centuries, the Decembrist Revolt of 1825, the liberation
of the serfs in 1861, the revolutions of 1917, the death of Stalin in
1953 and the attempted coup of 1991 – Russia has found herself
at a crossroads between the path of democracy and the continued
domination of autocracy. When such moments occur, the individual
characters of our leaders have had a disproportionate influence on
their outcome. So, I held my breath and hoped Vladimir Putin would
make the right choices.

The first time I met him, I had the impression I was dealing with
a fairly sensible guy, someone who shared the liberal views of Yeltsin
and the rest of us. After that first meeting, he used to call on me at
times when he needed advice or information about the economy or
Yukos and the company's activities. We usually met in his offices, but
one particular meeting stands out, because on this occasion he invited
me and my colleagues to an outdoor barbecue. It was in May 2000,
when he was already president, and Putin used the occasion to suggest
a deal, a sort of nonaggression pact: the state, he said, would promise
not to interfere in our business affairs if we, the so-called oligarchs,
would agree not to use the power of our businesses to put pressure on
the authorities. He wasn't demanding an end to commercial lobbying,
of course – that would have been naive – but, rather, an agreement
not to use the powerful resources of our companies to cause trouble
for the government by inciting protests against the authorities or sabo-
taging deliveries, for instance, and it seemed to me at the time that this
was a fair request. Because of the circumstances of the encounter, it
became known as 'the barbecue meeting' and people started talking
about the 'barbecue agreement' between the two sides. There were
plenty of more formal meetings between us, always in the Kremlin,
sometimes sitting at the large round negotiating table in St Catherine
Hall, often with other members of the Bureau of the Russian Union
of Industrialists and Entrepreneurs.

Putin, without a doubt, has a convincing manner. It's a skill that I think he acquired in the KGB and then developed when he was deputy mayor of St Petersburg, when Mayor Anatoly Sobchak had used him as a go-between in the three-way conspiracy of officials, security forces and criminals that ruled the city, divvying up the loot between them. He acquired a talent for taking people in, and he used it in the first period of his time in power: if Putin needed your help, he would do everything possible to convince you that you shared the same aims and opinions. One conversation I had with him in those early days was in a basement restaurant next to the Cathedral of Christ the Saviour, a few hundred metres from the Kremlin. Putin started by saying 'This is what the state needs …' but immediately corrected himself. 'No, it's not the state,' he said. 'It's the country! The country is much more than the state; it's the country that's the important thing!' And, of course, I immediately thought that he was a right-thinking and well-meaning man. It seemed that he knew the needs of Russian citizens are more important than the interests of a powerful state – he must be one of us. Even Yeltsin didn't really understand that politicians must work for individual rights rather than for 'the state'.

But Putin was dissembling: it turned out he didn't really believe the liberal views he was spouting. He was simply saying the right words to lull me into believing he was a liberal like myself. And for a while it worked. I persisted in giving Putin the benefit of the doubt. Even when he said terrible things – things that showed he really didn't care about the lives of individual Russian citizens – it took me a long time to understand that he was a cunning liar and hypocrite. When Putin responded to the dreadful tragedy of the *Kursk* submarine with an uncaring shrug and a throwaway put-down, 'So OK, it sank', I convinced myself he had just made a slip in the emotion of the moment; and when he was reported as calling the protesting widows of the dead sailors 'ten-dollar whores', I made myself believe it was a fabrication by his outspoken opponent, Boris Berezovsky. When Moscow apartment blocks started to get blown up in late 1999, conveniently just in time for Putin – who was then prime minister – to use the bombings as a pretext for his military intervention in Chechnya, I refused to believe the terrible rumours of a conspiracy. Surely, it really must have been terrorists, I told myself; surely the bags of left-over explosives they found were just dummies from some training exercise … But more and more facts began to accumulate, until in the end I could no longer deny the truth.

In the early part of Putin's reign, my Kremlin connections meant I was on hand when the new president needed guidance. The inexperienced Putin was initially good at asking for and taking advice. He certainly said all the right things, reaffirming his commitment to democracy, internationalism and reform. Looking back, I do wonder how I managed to get him so wrong. Did he genuinely believe in the liberal values he proclaimed, and did he then change as the years went by? Or did he never really mean what he said? If it were the latter – which I now believe to be the case – how did Putin manage to take me in, and manage to convince many others who supported democracy in Russia that he was the man to secure it? My only answer is that I think Putin is very good at being all things to all men. His technique is to look at you and mirror what you are saying. He tells people what he knows they want to hear. If you're conservative, he makes out that he's a conservative, too; if you're a liberal, then he makes sure he comes over as a liberal. He's a chameleon who leaves everyone thinking he's on their side, a powerful trick for a politician determined to get his way at any cost. It goes a long way to explaining why the West started out believing that Putin was going to continue the sympathetic, market-oriented, democratic policies of Boris Yeltsin. But, after a while, it became clear that Putin wasn't the open-minded liberal he'd seemed to be. That is when I began to realise he wasn't a man I could support; and that's what led to the public confrontation between us.

Because I was, first and foremost, a businessman, and my involvement in politics was sporadic, it was no coincidence that my challenge to Putin came over questions of business. After the crash of 1998, I had recast Yukos as an open, transparent, rules-based entity, capable of matching Western standards in all areas. It saved us as a company and brought us considerable success in the years that followed. I came to believe passionately that the same recipe could rescue not just Russian business, but the Russian state itself; and I felt it was my duty to convey the message to anyone who would listen. In numerous speeches and articles, I promoted the need for a new approach to standards of politics and governance, calling for an end to the ingrained practices of economic corruption and social coercion, the pillaging of the national economy for personal gain and the repression of free expression, that Putin's administration had increasingly come to rely on.

Putin took this personally. As soon as he became president in January 2000, he had appointed many of his former KGB and FSB colleagues to senior positions in the Kremlin. The Siloviki, or 'Strongmen', were determined to arrogate all power to themselves, unprepared to countenance other centres of opinion outside of the Kremlin, and resentful of anyone who proposed a different model of behaviour from the one they were intent on imposing. Putin announced that he was going to 'destroy the oligarchs as a class', echoing Stalin's bloody promise to 'destroy the *kulaks* [rich peasants] as a class'. In fact, as later became clear, Putin's actual aim was simply the redistribution of wealth into the pockets of his inner circle, who would themselves become the real oligarchs. Having established his 'nonaggression pact' in May, Putin once again summoned Russia's top executives to a meeting in July, this time to lay down the law. He said we must keep our companies out of politics, but only later did it become clear that he meant much more than that.* What he really wanted was to appropriate the resources of our private companies to serve his own interests and the interests of his friends. He wanted an end to the denunciations of official corruption, because corruption was the business he was in; corruption was the means by which he was planning to rule the Russian state and he didn't want anyone trying to curb it.

Some of those on the receiving end of Putin's lecture reacted with fury. Boris Berezovsky, who believed he had personally helped bring Putin to power, felt insulted by the upstart president and pledged himself to enduring opposition. Vladimir Gusinsky tried to retain the independence of his media empire but was arrested, locked up and driven into exile, where he was soon joined by Berezovsky and others.

As for myself, I took a step back. I soon began to minimise my personal interactions with Putin and work instead with the prime minister and the government. When we needed to interact with Putin, I asked my colleagues to go instead of me. I knew my antipathy would come to the surface and I wouldn't be able to hide my disgust at some of the things he was doing. So, it was better for our company if someone else dealt with the Kremlin.

Soon, Putin began to show his true face, without even bothering to disguise it. He ordered the closure of the independent TV channel NTV, claiming he was doing so for financial reasons, but making little secret of the fact that it was actually because NTV had the temerity to criticise the president. And then there were the bare-faced lies he

---

* Unfortunately, I did not realise the full extent of Putin's mendacity until I was already in jail. Only then did it become clear that this was not just a personal battle between us over the issue of Kremlin corruption – a battle in which I alone was at risk of ruin – but a fight on a national scale, in which Putin was willing to inflict irreparable damage on the nation's economy by destroying Russia's most successful company in order to hand it over as a gift to his cronies.

told about the Nord-Ost theatre siege in October 2002 and the Beslan school massacre in September 2004, when Chechen terrorists seized innocent hostages and the subsequent actions of Russian security forces resulted in many unnecessary deaths.

I look back now on our conversation over the barbecued kebabs in the grounds of the presidential residence with very different eyes. 'Let's stop going back to the past,' Putin said to us. 'Let's build a new life in this country, where the state doesn't try to dominate and control business, and business doesn't use its resources to disrupt the working of the state.' His words completely coincided with my own views. I vividly remembered the difficult days after the collapse of the USSR, when the 'red directors' used to blackmail the government by taking workers out on strike, refusing to deliver supplies and creating artificial shortages of vital goods. Putin told us he didn't want that sort of blackmail from business and I completely agreed with him. But he later claimed that what had been agreed between us was something very different. He started telling people that we business leaders had pledged to withdraw ourselves completely from anything to do with politics – not just from blackmailing the state with strikes and so forth, but from expressing our views or lobbying or supporting political parties and candidates. That, of course, was complete nonsense. Putin knew he couldn't ask us for commitments like that; it just wouldn't have been possible. All big companies have to lobby for their own interests – it's just a fact of business life, in Russia and in the West.

Throughout all his lying and deceit, and even after those moments when the mask fell, Putin carried on pretending to be a man of principle. He was good at pretending; people found it hard to see through him. It was a crucial time for Russia and I wanted to ensure our country took the path of legality, transparency and Western standards of integrity. If Russia were to founder in the old, familiar ways of corruption, cronyism and patronage, it would be impossible for Yukos to continue to function as an open, Western-style corporation; all sorts of doors would be closed to us and things would start to get worse. It was Putin who had to make that crucial choice for Russia's future. And when I saw he was going down the wrong path, I knew I had to go on the offensive. Sooner or later, I would have to challenge the hardline Siloviki who were surrounding him and try to turn the tide.

• • •

By the early 2000s, it became clear that many of Vladimir Putin's closest aides were no longer interested in democratic freedoms, but were instead determined to return Russia to the old ways of corruption and personalised autocracy. My first reaction was to tell Russians – and, in particular, young Russians – that things don't have to be this way. I knew Russia could still take a different course from the one the Siloviki were proposing, and I believed Putin himself had not made a final decision. I believed he could still be persuaded to take the path of freedom and democracy. With the benefit of hindsight, it is evident that I was wrong; but in the early 2000s, I and those who shared my values campaigned with genuine optimism to promote the ethos of unfettered liberal thinking.

When I founded my educational and philanthropic organisation Open Russia in 2001, I took my inspiration from George Soros's Open Society Institute (now Open Society Foundations) and its mission statement of 'building inclusive and vibrant democracies ... changing the way we think about each other and the way we work together.' I wanted Open Russia to effect real societal change in our country, not just to patch up the failures of the current regime. And back then, I was full of optimism. In 2002, I gave an interview to the *Washington Post*, in which I laid out my hopes for how we could improve Russia's future: 'We believe the key point here is education, and that's why we give money for education in various aspects – teaching kids how to use the internet, establishing contacts between young people in the UK, the US and Russia, training young journalists etc. The aim is very simple. Twenty years have passed. Another twenty or thirty years and we might become a normal country.'

We were prioritising young people because they are the way forward; their thinking has not been colonised by the old spirit of cowed conformity. They are the future 'elite policymakers' identified by the Chatham House think tank on international affairs as necessary for 'the emergence of advanced democratic institutions after Putin leaves'. So, Open Russia ran summer camps where children would camp in tents, play games and learn the basic tenets of a democratic society. We called it 'New Civilisation' and we cheekily copied the outdoor learning activities from the American Scout movement. The children played the roles of businesspeople, workers, state officials and politicians. For the duration of the camp, they were asked to run their own society in microcosm, setting up businesses, hiring and firing workers, collecting taxes and providing pensions, calling elections and running campaigns, and having votes. We were showing Russia's young generation how a free-market democracy can and should function, opening their eyes to another, better way than Putin's 'managed democracy' in which they were growing up – where the hand of the state was guided by the criminal group in the Kremlin.

Open Russia supported Schools of Public Politics in regional centres around the country that would take in youngsters interested in a political career and teach them the values of multi-party democracy. We supported schools for young journalists, helping them realise the importance of the profession and master its secrets. Our Federation of Internet Education trained more than 50,000 teachers and promoted opportunities for access to alternative sources of information and communication, to challenge the monolith of media narratives propagated by Putin's state.

Our ideas and achievements would all subsequently be appropriated by the Kremlin's own youth movement, Nashi, which espoused very different aims. Like the Young Pioneers before them, Putin's Nashi has taken a hold on young people's minds, inculcating the statist, anti-Western values of the Kremlin. Putin's methods of shaping people's thinking – young and old – are powerful and are supported by all the resources of the state. Does that mean he is certain to win? Maybe, or maybe not.

There is undoubtedly a section of the Russian population that is inclined to support his hardline values. This was strikingly evident in the large number of people who gave their unconditional backing to Putin's invasion of Ukraine in February 2022. Older people, in particular, can fear societal change and wish to cling to a regime that claims it is protecting them from hostile outside forces. But I think things are very different where young people are concerned. Young people have more hope for the future and are less scared of demanding individual rights and liberties – all the things that a backward-looking autocracy cannot offer. Youngsters have dreams and ambitions; they want to make the world a better place. It's the same in the East and in the West. If a society doesn't offer its younger generation a positive dream of hope for the future – something other than just 'work hard, do what you're told and save up for your old age' – then they are going to find that dream somewhere else: in superstition, fanaticism or even religious extremism. The aim of Open Russia was to offer young Russians a real way forward. We wanted to give people the choice of how they would like to think and how they would like to live their lives.

To make informed choices, people need information and they weren't getting it from the Kremlin. So Open Russia tried another initiative, called 'Help and Advise'. It was a volunteer service run by youngsters that resembled a sort of do-it-yourself network of Citizens Advice Bureaus. Anyone with a practical problem involving access to public services, difficulties obtaining medical help or complaints about the performance of local authorities could ring a telephone number and speak to a volunteer. The volunteer would then find out the right person for the client to contact and put the two of them in touch. Our 'People's Verdict' programme offered a basic level of assistance for people unable to afford legal representation or – more likely – unable to afford the bribes needed to get justice from the courts. It offered victims help in finding lawyers and advice on how to insist on their legal rights and a fair hearing.

Open Russia funded an orphanage, Korallovo, outside Moscow for the sons and daughters of parents who had died in the service of Russia. It was run by my father, Boris, and my mother, Marina. It, too, was used to teach social values to the younger generation. Conditions were not luxurious, but there was a sports hall, a swimming pool and reliable medical care. When the Beslan school massacre happened in September 2004, a number of injured children who had lost their parents were taken to hospital in Moscow. I was already in jail at the time, but when I heard what was happening, I took an active role in trying to help. It seemed to me that some of the orphaned children were in danger of being abandoned, so we offered them places in our boarding school. While the massacre was in the headlines, the state made a show of caring for the children; but a month later, when they were released from hospital, they were forgotten. That taught me a lesson.

All the orphans and children from broken families who came to us at Korallovo were given a proper education that prepared many of them to go on to university. Every child was given access to the internet, encouraged to explore a diverse range of opinions and to look critically at official propaganda. We wanted to roll out the internet programme to schools across the country to help children think for themselves, instead of just accepting what they were told by state television and newspapers. I gave many public lectures about the work of

Open Russia, and reading them now makes me realise how optimistic we were at that time about the impact education could have on the generation that would decide Russia's future.

> We consider that our own mentality, the mentality of the older generation is very difficult to alter. But if our work with the youth of Russia is successful, then in 15 or 20 years they will start to determine the politics of our country. They will have been born in the new Russia and they will turn Russia into a normal country. The size of our big companies will no longer be dwarfed by those in the West; our pensions will no longer be smaller; things here will become normal.

By 'normal', I meant a turn away from the distorted model of social values that Putin had imposed on Russia and a move towards Western standards of openness, pluralism and enterprise.

> The economic growth of Russia depends on its intellectual potential – the scientists, scholars and entrepreneurs, our intellectual elite ... who are the active, driving force of our society. Our task is the production of highly qualified individuals; so, how do we do that? Most importantly through education and the cultivation of initiative ... And equally importantly, we must ensure that it is attractive for these people to remain in Russia and not go abroad ... The state should serve the interests of the people. The state should not be some great idol that they have created ... An individual's responsibility is first to serve his own interests, those of his family and then those of the society he lives in. The state should be there to serve the interests of the individual. We need to work hard so that these values become natural for

our young generation. That is the work that Open Russia has
been trying to do.

Open Russia's emphasis on changing mindsets and its prescrip-
tions for civic government and free-market capitalism were in stark
contrast to Putin's model of 'managed democracy'. That was a
model that had failed; it had destroyed the initiative and the origin-
ality of thought that underpin a thriving civil society, and I felt it was
my duty to point it out.

We don't even need to go back as far as Carnegie and Rockefeller
for the example I was following; one needs only to look at Bill Gates,
Warren Buffett and George Soros and the importance they have
attached to education and the development of civil society. Our goal,
like theirs, was helping people to be free, creating equal conditions for
people to get quality education and build a normal future. The difference, of course, was that the Americans were operating in an open
society, while we were attempting to produce free people in a country
of restricted freedoms, in a nation whose leaders feared and opposed
what we were doing and took every opportunity to try to foil us.

I have always said that I want my children and grandchildren to
live in a democratic Russia. If I live to see the day that Russia gets
a new political system, I will feel my life has been a success. But for
that to happen, Russia needs to do more than just replace Vladimir
Putin. If we do not make fundamental changes to the system, if we
do not bring governance under the control of society as a whole, I
fear that whoever takes Putin's place will become another version of
him. We need to remake our state into a parliamentary republic; we
need this parliamentary republic to be based on democratic, feder-
alist principles, similar to what took place when the United States
was founded. And, like America, we need talented young leaders to
take us forward.

Open Russia did much to develop these young leaders, working in political education and participatory electoral democracy, providing legal support and information to society. Our organisation had a presence in 40 of Russia's largest regions, with more than a thousand associates. But today Open Russia has been declared 'undesirable' by the state, a completely senseless designation that exposes anyone who cooperates with it to civil and criminal charges. Because of her membership of Open Russia, Anastasia Shevchenko has been under house arrest for more than two years, charged with participating in an 'undesirable' organisation; when her daughter died, she was prevented from sharing her final days with her. Open Russia's executive director, Andrei Pivovarov is now in prison on the same charge and other activists have been arrested or put on wanted lists. As a result, we have been forced to announce the cessation of our activities in Russia, although a large number of activists is continuing to work, either in secret or from exile abroad.

The aim of Open Russia is to give the Russian people the information they need to make decisions about their lives; to encourage free debate; to provide the means for people to think for themselves. In the West, none of these things is in any way controversial – they are the accepted norms of a free society. But Vladimir Putin sees things differently. When a ruler is so afraid of scrutiny by the people, it can mean only one thing: that he knows the legitimacy of his rule is tenuous, and he knows his power depends on deception and coercion, without which his authority would collapse and he himself would be in the dock.

CHAPTER 7
THE CONFRONTATION

In the early 2000s, Vladimir Putin and the Siloviki consolidated their power – and one method they chose was to crack down on independent critics and businesses. They wanted to seize the property of Russia's leading industrialists because they wanted the cash, and because they wanted to show the country who was boss. Renationalising firms that had been privatised under Yeltsin would send a strong message that the era of liberal capitalism was over and the age of state power had begun. It would also allow them – and this was undoubtedly their main motivation – to take over confiscated assets and place them under their own control, just as they did in their criminal racketeering youth, with all the potential for self-enrichment that implied.

For Putin, the most important and attractive target was oil. He tasked Igor Sechin with bringing the privatised oil companies back under Kremlin control and gave him free rein to do so. Sechin had been in Putin's service for many decades: he was Putin's bag carrier in their home town of Leningrad, a KGB functionary who would become a leading member of the Siloviki. After Putin became president in 2000, he had made Sechin his closest adviser and now he appointed him chairman of the board of the state oil corporation, Rosneft, with the brief of taking over the companies that had been transferred to private ownership. Having gained control of Rosneft, Sechin was ruthless in pursuit of assets that would enrich himself and his Kremlin colleagues, including Vladimir Putin. The potential prize money amounted to billions of dollars and Sechin was not going to be deterred.

By now, Yukos was doing well. We had worked hard to transform the company from a polluting, loss-making dinosaur into an efficient modern business; we had battled through the perils of the 1998 crash and I was in no mood to hand over the firm we had created. Boris Berezovsky and Vladimir Gusinsky had been threatened with arrest and worse, intimidated into relinquishing their businesses and moving abroad, but I was not inclined to do so. The Kremlin's response was to mount a series of threats against me and my colleagues.

In June 2002, I was asked by the newspaper *Kommersant* if I felt safe in Russia and I had no hesitation in replying, 'Of course not. As an individual – absolutely not … The risk that I, Khodorkovsky, could be made to disappear? Yes, of course that could happen. But I don't think they could make Yukos disappear. Society understands that the loss of such a major business would be an unacceptable loss for every single Russian person … That is why even if Putin does not like our company, he still talks to us …' My optimism, as events would prove, was hopelessly misplaced. Within months, the talking would stop and the repression would begin.

In January 2003, we were considering making a bid to buy an oil extraction business in northern Russia called Severnaya Neft. The owners were asking for $200 million, which was well over the realistic asking price. No oil company was willing to pay it. But then we heard that Rosneft had bought the firm for a ridiculous $600 million, at least three times its real value. The deal had the hallmarks of corruption and it was likely that the excess $400 million of public funds furnished by Rosneft had simply gone into someone's pocket. For me, it was the last straw, the final confirmation that the Siloviki were pushing Putin away from leading Russia on the path of transparency and integrity towards the old ways of cronyism and corruption. As for Putin himself, despite all his ills, I thought that maybe he was still undecided about which way to go. I would soon realise that I was mistaken.

On 19 February 2003, Putin summoned the country's leading businessmen to another meeting in the Kremlin. It was one of a series of widely publicised forums that were designed to show the people that the president was taking seriously the problems of ordinary Russians. Recordings of the meetings were shown on national television and reported in the press. The subject of this particular meeting was 'the fight against corruption'. The participants were expected to talk about the need to tackle corrupt practices and we thought the presence of television cameras would ensure that the president would express his determination to do something about it. We thought he would give the green light to us and our political allies in the government and the administration to take practical measures to change things for the better.

After a series of speakers had mouthed meaningless platitudes, the microphone came to me. I had prepared a speech, complete with slides, that would deliver a stinging rebuke to those who perpetuated corruption in Russia, up to and including the president himself. When the moment came, I was nervous, but I pressed ahead. 'Corruption in Russia – a brake on economic growth' flashed up on the participants' screens, followed by a damning series of statistics. According to opinion polls, 27 per cent of Russians believed corruption to be the most dangerous threat to the nation; 49 per cent believed corruption had spread to the majority of state officials, including the police, the tax and customs agencies, the security services, the judiciary, the traffic police and *the highest levels of federal power*. The finding that almost half of the Russian population believed the president and his closest allies to be corrupt sent a buzz around the table. Putin was listening and staring at the slides, but like the trained KGB man he was, he betrayed no sign of emotion.

The next statistics were about people's views of the Kremlin's relationship with corruption: 32 per cent of Russians, reported the pollsters, believed that the Russian leadership would like to tackle corruption, but was powerless to do so; 29 per cent believed our leaders could tackle corruption but chose not to do so; and 21 per cent believed it neither wished nor was able to tackle it. The meeting had moved from the empty expression of pious hopes to something much more concrete: evidence that one third of Russians believed their president to be powerless in the face of organised corruption, while another third believed he was complicit in it.

I could see that Putin's patience was running out. He was looking at me with steely eyes, a tense, fleeting smile on his lips, ready to cut me off. But I had something more to say, this time about a specific instance of corruption involving one of the president's own sidekicks. 'We need to make corruption something that everyone is ashamed of,' I said. 'Let us take for example the purchase by the state oil company Rosneft of the firm Severnaya Neft ...' There was silence in the room; all those present knew I was accusing the president of Russia's inner circle of personal involvement in a crooked business deal. I forced myself to continue. 'Everyone knows the Severnaya Neft deal had an ulterior motive ... I have to tell you that corruption is spreading in our country. You could say that it started *right here* – and now is the time to end it!'

Unbeknownst to me at the time, the beneficiary of the Severnaya Neft deal was not merely a sidekick of the president, but the president himself. I was told later by sources close to Putin that the missing $400 million had gone directly into his personal account, so I was in fact accusing him personally of sitting at the centre of the web of corruption. His response was telling. Instead of denying the charges, he retaliated with a not very veiled threat against me and my company.

'You mentioned Rosneft,' Putin said, 'and the deal to buy Severnaya Neft … The first things to say about that are clear: this is the state oil company and it needs to increase its stocks of oil, which are currently inadequate. But some other oil companies, including for instance Yukos, have got excess reserves. The way it got hold of them is a question that forms part of the theme we are discussing today. And that theme also includes questions about the payment or the non-payment of taxes. You and I have at times talked about the problems your own company has had with tax payments, although, to be fair, the leadership of Yukos reached an agreement with the tax office and dealt with … or is dealing with … all the charges against it, all the problems with the state. But nonetheless, one has to ask, "Why did these problems arise?"'

Putin had evidently been taken aback by my words. Unusually for the calculating KGB man that he is, he was shocked into an unguarded response, first raising the question of Yukos's own oil reserves, then muttering darkly about an alleged underpayment of taxes – an issue that he and I had discussed and resolved to everyone's satisfaction several weeks earlier. After this initial outburst, he forced himself to regain control, even acknowledging that we had in fact settled the tax issue, which is pretty much Putin's modus operandi – attack, then take a step back. It allows him to observe a person's reaction, affording him time to plan his follow-up, then launch his deadliest assault when his target is thrown off guard.

His anger was clear, and so was the threat. He was horrified to have the business machinations of his close entourage exposed to the Russian people. I had challenged him and he came out against me. The way Putin responded to my challenge was the clearest possible signal of where he would take the nation in the years ahead. Since then, Putin has taken Russia down a route that is a dead end; a dead end for the economy, for society, and the wellbeing of the Russian people. As part of his programme to replace liberal market democracy with centralised state autocracy, Putin would need to crush all those who had other ideas. I came away from the meeting satisfied that I had not shirked my duty of speaking out against institutionalised corruption, but I was also convinced that punishment would not be long in coming.

· · ·

The months that followed my confrontation with Vladimir Putin were actually good for me and for Yukos, though my meetings with him became scarcer. In the spring of 2003, we announced that we would build a pipeline to carry oil from our Siberian fields to the fuel-thirsty industries over the border in China. We were closing in on a major takeover of the Russian oil company Sibneft and we were in negotiations with two American oil giants – ChevronTexaco and ExxonMobil – for one of them to become a partner in the new conglomerate we were about to create. The oil price, extraction rates and refining capacity were all rising and our profits rose with them. In the first nine months of the year, we netted just over $3.5 billion, compared to $2 billion for the same period in 2002, while turnover jumped from $7.95 to $12.2 billion. In April, Vladimir Putin formally congratulated Yukos on the tenth anniversary of the company's founding, sending us a gushing message of encouragement. 'The effective organisation of work,' Putin wrote, 'high professionalism and responsibility of employees allow the company not only to maintain, but to expand its position on the domestic and foreign market.' But his praise was through gritted teeth – our workers didn't receive any of the usual congratulatory state bonuses – and just two months later, Putin began his campaign to destroy the company.

The early months of 2003 were dominated by the build-up to the American and British invasion of Iraq, a move the Kremlin was convinced was motivated by the desire to seize Iraqi oil. The Russian ambassador to the UN opposed the planned invasion, announcing that he would veto any resolution that declared it legal. Iraq had been an ally of the Soviet Union and Putin was desperate to maintain the Kremlin's influence there. But I looked at it in a different way. It was clear that if George Bush wanted to invade Iraq, he would do so whatever the Kremlin said. So, instead of opposing the US, I argued that Russia should take the opportunity to forge an alliance with Washington. If Russia were to support the US on Iraq – and offer to shore up America's oil supplies with Russian oil in the event of a lengthy conflict in the Middle East – it would foster a 'special relationship' between the two countries, similar to the one enjoyed by the UK.

On 13 March 2003, a week before the invasion began, I gave an interview to *BusinessWeek* magazine, entitled 'A Russian's plea to back America'. In it, I said it would be foolish to let the opportunity for a long-term strategic partnership with the US slip through our fingers. 'For economic development, Russia needs investment, Russia needs highly trained people, Russia needs markets, Russia needs technologies. When we take a look and see who would be the greatest benefit to us in all these directions, the answer is clear: America. Then there's the matter of security, which has nothing to do with business. We've got a lot of regional problems and our only realistic ally is America. So if we're going to prioritize things, then we have to say the most important relationship is with America.' When the interviewer asked me if I had conveyed my views to President Putin, I answered, 'He knows where I stand. It's not a secret … I am well known in Russia for my pro-Americanism.'

I had invited world-class Western experts, including American specialists, to help improve the way Yukos was run. I had brought in US technology and know-how and had promoted the US as a vital market for Russia's oil exports. I had founded the philanthropic foundation Open Russia, which at various times had Henry Kissinger, Jacob Rothschild, Lord David Owen and the former US ambassador, Arthur Hartman, on its board of trustees. Our negotiations with the American oil companies were a big part of our long-term business strategy to operate in the global market, as attracting American investors would be good for Yukos and for Russia. I had always kept Putin informed of our plans, with regular updates of what we were proposing. His replies were encouraging: he told us we were right to go in this direction.

My last face-to-face encounter with Vladimir Putin took place on 26 April 2003. I had asked for a private meeting, because the talks on our takeover of Sibneft and the negotiations with the American oil companies were at a delicate stage. Putin listened carefully and indicated that he was supportive of our plans. He did not mention the clash between us at our confrontation in the Kremlin the previous February. Only at the very end of the meeting did he raise a note of caution. There were parliamentary elections scheduled for the end of the year, Putin said, and he did not want Yukos to play any role in the campaign. He asked me to pledge that we would not support or finance the efforts of any opposition parties. I answered that Yukos was not involved in any political financing, but that individuals in a free parliamentary democracy must reserve the right to donate to any party of their choosing. I heard later that after I left,

Putin flew into a rage and accused me of defying his commands.* Coming after our public confrontation in February, the meeting was another blow to our relations.

In retrospect, it may seem as if I was naive to believe the reassurances I was receiving from Putin, but I also had other highly placed contacts in the Kremlin who were giving me the same encouraging signals. These were the remaining liberals in the leadership, men who had served under Yeltsin – the so-called 'Family' – who, I believed, still carried the torch of freedom and democracy. They included the prime minister, Mikhail Kasyanov, and the Kremlin chief of staff, Alexander Voloshin. The fact that they had stayed in high office after Putin replaced Yeltsin in 2000 indicated to me that there was still a faction in the leadership who believed in liberal values and were doing their best to resist the domination of the hardline KGB operatives of the Siloviki.

My clash with Vladimir Putin had brought to a head the battle between the liberals and the hardliners in the Kremlin and, with it, the battle for the future direction of Russia. While Kasyanov and Voloshin were defending the interests of private business and a free market, Igor Sechin and his cronies were telling the president to act against Khodorkovsky and Yukos. Putin's decision would determine which Kremlin faction emerged victorious.

An unmistakable indication of Putin's intentions came in June 2003, when a detachment of special forces stormed into the office of Yukos's head of internal security, Alexei Pichugin, and ransacked his filing cabinets, impounded his safe and informed him that he was being arrested on charges of attempted murder. It was the Kremlin's

---

* I heard this from my former business associates, who conveyed the information to my lawyers when I was already in prison. They got their information from Vladislav Surkov in the presidential administration, who had heard it at first hand.

opening shot in a war that would not be long in coming, the first clear signal that the liberals had lost out to the Siloviki in the battle for the president's ear.

Alexei Pichugin's job was to protect Yukos's real estate and crack down on theft within the organisation. He was a professional operator, tough but fair, and a family man with a wife and three young sons. But the Russian Prosecutor's Office was making out that Pichugin was a ruthless killer, hiring hitmen to intimidate and eliminate business rivals. His arrest was a signal to us that Yukos was in their sights, that Putin and Sechin were intent on intimidating us into becoming another feeding trough for Putin's cronies.

When we refused to knuckle under, the arrests continued. On 2 July 2003, the chief executive of Group Menatep, Platon Lebedev, was taken from his hospital bed, where he had been recovering from cardiovascular dystonia and chronic hepatitis, by police with guns and handcuffs and led to a waiting prison van. Lebedev was my long-time business partner and friend, involved in all our investment decisions, financial reporting and legal affairs. He was a key figure in the hierarchy of our holdings and his arrest was a dramatic escalation in the Kremlin's assault against us. Lebedev's arrest was a naked act of intimidation. The charge sheet that was eventually drawn up against him involved seven separate articles of the Russian penal code, ranging from 'Grand theft of property by an organised criminal group' to 'Malicious non-compliance with a court ruling' to 'Conspiracy to evade corporate tax obligations' and 'Evasion of personal tax and social security obligations'. I spent the next 48 hours on the phone, trying to get an explanation of what was going on. Kasyanov told me he had spoken to Putin, who had asked him to relay the message that the arrest was 'not political'. Voloshin rang to say he was working on Lebedev's behalf. But the situation was serious. No one had any doubt that this was deliberate intimidation.

The news from prison was that Lebedev was refusing to cooperate with the investigators and had been involved in an angry confrontation, accusing them of violating his civil rights and using false pretences to keep him in custody. As the stand-off escalated, Lebedev was moved to Moscow's high-security Matrosskaya Tishina Prison, where he was held in harsh conditions. I was next on the list.

CHAPTER 8
AN ANATOMY OF CORRUPTION

The actions of Putin and his cronies against Yukos were an indication of the criminal nature of the regime he leads, a criminality that has become ever more flagrant in the two decades since. I have no hesitation in saying that Russia today is a mafia state. But I do not want an English-speaking reader to misunderstand what I mean by that. It is a subtle linguistic point, but when a Western person says 'state', he or she means all the institutions and state bodies that govern the running of her country. For a Russian speaker, the word 'state' means something different. The Russian term for the Western concept of the state would be the judgementally neutral 'state apparatus' or the more negatively coloured 'bureaucracy'. So, when we talk about a mafia state, there is room for misunderstanding between us.

Ordinary Russians, when they are on the receiving end of ill-treatment from dishonest or incompetent local officials, or think of the lack of respect they receive from the healthcare or education systems, may well grumble that 'the whole state' is corrupt. But that would be to overstate the case. No one, least of all me, would argue that the whole Russian 'state apparatus' – which is manned by something like one or two million people – is a gigantic mafia operation, a sort of Corleone clan expanded to the millionth degree. There is undoubtedly poor governance, corruption and other bad things going on throughout the country. In some places, such as Chechnya or Ulyanovsk, it is quite bad, while in, say, Moscow or Novosibirsk it is less so (I know that might sound surprising, but the Moscow authorities do quite a lot for the people of the city, even if they look after their own interests at the same time). If we talk about the state apparatus as a whole, then I would say it is getting on with things to the best of its ability. Allowing for the shortcomings and inefficiencies endemic in the overall system, it seems to be performing the sort of tasks that are the responsibility of any state apparatus.

It is a very different matter when we come to the top of the state pyramid: to the relatively high ranks of the FSB and the presidential administration, and in particular to Putin's inner circle. These people rule by whim and coercion. If they take a dislike to someone, if someone won't knuckle under and do their bidding or, even worse, tries to expose their misdeeds, they get fired, or beaten up, or thrown in jail, or simply eliminated. You don't even need to fall out with them to be targeted: they can simply take a fancy to your business or your property, or they can destroy you for show, just to demonstrate what they are capable of. And once they have you in their sights, there is no way out. You have no one to turn to, no one to help you – not the law, not the courts, not the media, not your bosses or your neighbours. Your only choice is to give them what they want or the consequences will be dire for you; and not just you – nowadays your family may be victimised, too.

You may ask what interests these Kremlin mafiosi. It's the same as the regular mafia – they are after your property or your business, as in the case of Bill Browder, the British-American businessman whose Russian company was stolen from him by crooked officials. They will want you to hand over a significant share of your earnings. They will be embroiled in a power conflict with other members of the mafia or their family. They'll try to force you to collaborate on their projects, such as – crucially – the falsification of election results. Or they will prevent you from using your public position to blow the whistle on their activities, as happened to me, and to the former liberal politician Boris Nemtsov and journalist Anna Politkovskaya, both of whom were eventually assassinated.

How did Russia come to this? As we know, Putin and almost his entire inner circle are former KGB/FSB men, a secretive, closed caste, a tightknit clan that 'protects its own' and resolves disputes 'in house'. The template was already there; but back in Soviet times the KGB was reined in by its subservience to Party control and the demands of communist ideology. In some areas, the KGB was pretty effective, such as its work in intelligence and counterintelligence conducted by ideologically committed people. In other areas, such as the bureau's regional networks, things weren't quite so rosy, but in general the system worked. With the difficult perestroika years of the late 1980s, though, the KGB consolidated its links to organised crime. They moved into racketeering and drugs, smuggling illegal goods, seizing people's property, but they had to be quite careful because the state apparatus was still functioning: the security forces didn't yet control the institutions of civil society, the courts and the Prosecutor's Office, so they could still be called to account with serious consequences. But once Putin came to power, they were in clover.

Putin himself never got very far in his KGB career. He spent his time in middle-ranking posts and even his top job, as director of the Soviet cultural mission in Dresden, was a disappointment. The real shift in his fortunes happened once he had endeared himself to the pro-perestroika mayor of St Petersburg, and under his guidance the city was turned into a stronghold for organised crime, with its historic port acting as the principal gateway for huge volumes of drug-trafficking.

In 1992, Putin was in charge of a deal to trade raw materials for supplies of food that were urgently needed by the hard-pressed St Petersburg population. An official commission of inquiry, led by the St Petersburg deputy Marina Salye, would later discover that the raw materials were duly handed over, with documents bearing Putin's signature, but that the food did not arrive. The money paid for the raw materials, reportedly $100 million, was never found. The deputies demanded Putin's resignation and called for him to be brought to justice, but the findings of the investigation were ignored. In 2001, after Putin had become president, Marina Salye fled from St Petersburg to a village 400 kilometres away, explaining that she was leaving because she was 'in fear for her life'.

Another investigation, closed 'for lack of evidence' during Putin's time as prime minister, involved the activities of a St Petersburg construction company called Twentieth Trust, which appeared to investigators to have been the beneficiary of substantial funds from the city budget, despite being in debt and close to bankruptcy. No explanation was given for why the company received such favourable treatment, but the former Investigator for Serious Crimes in the Fight against Corruption, Lieutenant Colonel Andrei Zykov, later alleged after he had been removed from office that Twentieth Trust had built a dacha for Putin on the outskirts of the city and a villa in Spain. Twentieth Trust is today under different ownership and management.

Many of those involved in the corrupt world of St Petersburg in the 1990s would later rise to prominence in Putin's Kremlin, following the mafia principle that the family looks after its own. Politicians who were foolish enough to attempt to expose the corruption found themselves threatened.

As president, Putin has not only continued to rely on this model of governance, he has taken it to new levels. He rules through patronage, personal connections, corruption and the brazen manipulation of the state apparatus. So, if you want to get an important post, you have to be anointed into the mafia clan – you have to show that you know how to elicit bribes, how to steal and pass on the cut to the bosses upstairs. And even then, you're not safe. As soon as they have got what they wanted from you – or if you fail to carry out their orders – you may find yourself arrested on trumped up charges and facing jail.

Of course, Putin's system of rule through cronyism and personal patronage isn't new. Tsars as far back as Ivan the Terrible ran Russia as a capricious autocracy, with the tsar at the top, the people at the bottom, and no effective civic institutions to mediate power and justice between them. The tsar simply appointed his favourites – corrupt, often uneducated men, who gained advancement through connections and grift – to positions where they wielded unchecked authority over justice, taxes and daily life. The system was known as *kormlenie* – literally 'feeding' – because the appointee would receive no salary, but he would have the right to enrich himself from the cashflow his position generated, taking his cut from the money raised from the people. It was an unfettered licence to steal from the country and its people, and it fostered resentment and unrest.

Russia today is run by what can best be described as a neo-feudal model where the regional elites, Putin's placemen, undertake to provide votes and revenue for the centre and in return get a free hand to run the finances of their region as they see fit. To be more precise, these elites have free rein to pursue personal financial incentives and the Kremlin turns a blind eye, so long as it receives its cut. The mechanism goes something like this: 60 per cent of the revenues that are collected from the population go to the centre, which leaves 40 per cent for the region's spending. But that isn't enough to keep the regional elite happy, so the centre then funnels them another 10 to 20 per cent of the money (in the case of Ramzan Kadyrov in Chechnya, the figure is more than 90 per cent of the regional budget) in return for their unwavering loyalty and political support.

That's one mechanism that the Kremlin uses to maintain its grip on the country. Another is to make sure that all officials are forced to take bribes. If you don't take bribes, the centre simply removes you from power. And if your loyalty at any point starts to waver, they have evidence of the previous bribes so they have a cast-iron criminal charge on which they can lock you up.

There is also a third mechanism that Putin uses, which involves the maintenance of a shifting balance of power between groups of officials whose interests may potentially conflict. The central economy continues to be administered by the so-called liberal group – they are by no means liberal, but that's what it has become accepted practice to call them. On the other side are the Siloviki – the people from the military and enforcement agencies. The Siloviki are constantly in search of money, so Putin plays a game. On the one hand, he instructs the liberal group not to give one kopek more to the Siloviki. On the other hand, he complains, I'm barely holding on to them, these guys are champing at the bit. From time to time the two groups lock horns and the odd one of them is sent to jail. At other times, Putin sets sub-factions within the Siloviki against one another, with similar results.

Putin needs these Machiavellian mechanisms to maintain his grip on the system, to prevent the administrative machine falling apart. He needs to do things this way because Russia under his rule does not have the formal structures and institutions that usually keep societies functioning properly, with civic integrity and the rule of law. Apart from the fact that this makes Russia look like a third world country, it also creates a potentially very dangerous situation. This is because the continued existence of the whole Byzantine apparatus depends exclusively on Putin being there to keep pulling the levers. If one were to remove Putin from the equation, the system would lose its equilibrium and the country would enter a catastrophic state of clan fragmentation. This, of course, is no accident: Putin has arranged things that way with the deliberate intention of making it impossible for him to be removed.

How many people are there in today's Kremlin mafia? It's hard to give exact figures, but at the top are Putin's favoured associates, made up of people like Igor Sechin, Gennady Timchenko, Arkady Rotenberg, the brothers Yuri and Mikhail Kovalchuk, and Nikolai Patrushev. I will say more about most of these in a moment. But there are also further circles, including the 'overseers' in the presidential administration, such as Putin's chief of staff, Anton Vaino, and his deputy, Sergei Kiriyenko; and the top guys in the FSB, Alexander Bortnikov, Sergei Korolev, Ivan Tkachev, Alexei Sedov, whose job it is to persecute the political opposition, and Oleg Feoktistov, who is nominally retired, but is still hard at work. Then there are the regional bosses, men like Alexei Dyumin and Sergei Sobyanin, who do the president's bidding in big cities and regions; plus, of course, the Kremlin's 'oligarchs', such as Alexei Miller at Gazprom and Andrei Kostin at VTB Bank; and the heads of some courts, certain judges and the directors of the Investigative Committee and the Prosecutor's Office; and, finally, their henchmen who do the dirty work.

All in all, there are a few thousand people working for the Kremlin mafia, but between them they control a huge proportion of the nation's wealth. They don't keep the money in their own names and their own bank accounts – that would be far too obvious – but assign it instead to other people, who are told they need to keep silent or face serious consequences. The men Putin trusts with his money come from a small retinue of old friends, most of whom he now keeps at arm's length. By maintaining a low profile, they are able to stay out of the spotlight, while holding the vast wealth that Putin can't keep in his own name. The Panama Papers investigation of 2016 revealed that Sergei Roldugin, a professional cellist whom Putin has known since the 1970s, is the front-man for companies worth in excess of $2 billion, rather more wealth than most classical musicians have access to, with the money widely considered to be part of the cash Putin has plundered from the Russian state. Arkady and Boris Rotenberg, childhood friends of the president (Arkady is his former judo sparring partner), have been handed lucrative contracts from the state energy giant Gazprom and for infrastructure projects such as the bridge connecting Crimea to the Russian mainland. It's made both of them billionaires and Arkady a 'Hero of Labour', an honorary title left over from the Soviet period. Gennady Timchenko, a Russian businessman and long-time ally of Putin who was formerly based in Switzerland but is now back in Russia because of international sanctions, is rumoured to hold billions of dollars on behalf of his old friend. Timchenko's oil distribution business, Gunvor, served for many years as the conduit for overseas revenue from Russia's energy sector, with the US Department of the Treasury claiming that 'Timchenko's activities in the energy sector have been directly linked to Putin, that Putin has investments in Gunvor and that he may have access to Gunvor funds'. A claim which Guvnor denies. Putin's cronies all benefit from their association with him. They benefit from the commercial opportunities that he bestows, and they benefit knowingly from the criminal activities of the Kremlin mafia. The Siloviki occupy the commanding heights of power in politics, the economy and national institutions. They have at their disposal all sorts of powerful resources, including the FSB and the GRU, the foreign military intelligence agency. And they support each other as members of the same organisation. Their ideology is best described as *nash-ism* ('ours-ism'), because it opposes 'us' and 'ours' to 'them' and 'theirs'. They are beyond the reach of the law, so they are free to use violence against anyone who challenges them in any field – political, financial, journalistic. Their rule is, 'if someone touches one of ours, he must suffer'. Because Putin and the Siloviki wield power on a personal and clan basis, public and state institutions have become irrelevant. The civilian oversight and control of the security forces that exists in much of the West is absent in Russia. The Siloviki are far from being a united group, however, and they encompass various cliques and groupings of shifting loyalties.

Of all the Siloviki, one of the closest to Putin – and the one with the most influence over him – has long been Igor Sechin. As Putin's deputy chief of staff since 2000, Sechin oversaw the recruitment of KGB men to positions in the Kremlin. His position as Putin's gatekeeper, in charge of the president's diary, deciding who should be seen who should not, allowed Sechin to influence the direction of the country. He was a pragmatic hardliner who despised the civil liberty, free speech, pro-business policies of the liberals who had run the country under Boris Yeltsin. The Siloviki came from the security services, with a lifetime's indoctrination that made them instinctively antagonistic towards the West; many of them regarded Yeltsin as a stooge of Washington. Once in power, Sechin's behind-the-scenes influence helped to persuade Putin to ditch any remaining liberal sympathies and adopt the repressive, nationalistic policies that would come to define his presidency.

Before he became the CEO of Rosneft, Sechin worked for the KGB, notably in the late Cold War hot spots of Mozambique and Angola. As noted above, he consolidated his alliance with Putin during Putin's time as deputy mayor of St Petersburg, becoming his devoted secretary and bagman, rarely leaving his master. Putin has kept Sechin close to him ever since, making him one of the most trusted representatives of the Siloviki clique. Despised and feared in equal measure,

Sechin was instrumental in convincing Putin formally to renationalise firms, including Yukos, that had been privatised under Yeltsin, while in fact putting the whole of the oil and gas sector under the control of his own inner circle. Sechin was described by the former US ambassador, John Beyrle, in confidential cables released by Wikileaks, as the 'grey cardinal' of the Kremlin, 'who has sought to break the power of the oligarchs, confiscate and amalgamate their assets into state companies under Siloviki control and to limit Western influence'. The damage he has inflicted on the Russian economy is incalculable.

Sechin is notoriously territorial, willing to go to great lengths to protect his position as Putin's chief adviser. His anti-liberal convictions pitched him into conflict with Dmitry Medvedev, once regarded as the leader of a liberalising tendency in the Kremlin. In 2016, Sechin moved against his rival by entrapping Prime Minister Medvedev's ally and minister of economic development, Alexey Ulyukaev, in a sting operation that led to the latter becoming the first serving minister to be arrested in Russia since the reign of Stalin. The move was a risky powerplay that could have backfired, but Sechin was secure in his position. The men he called upon to make the arrest were operatives from the Sixth Service of the FSB's Internal Security Department, an elite unit that Sechin himself had created back in 2004 and knew he could count on. He had used them previously to carry out delicate operations, including the arrests of regional governors who refused to toe the Kremlin line. On 14 November 2016, Sechin invited Ulyukaev into his office and presented him with a suitcase that was later found to contain $2 million, as well as ordering a basket of sausages made from fresh game personally shot by himself to be loaded into Ulyukaev's car. Unaware that Sechin was recording their encounter, Ulyukaev gratefully accepted the gifts, claiming later that he thought the suitcase was full of wine. All this 'evidence' would be used to charge him with corruption, backed by a sworn statement from Sechin that the money had been 'extorted' from him as a payment for Ulyukaev's rubber stamping of a deal to transfer the Bashneft oil company to Rosneft.

At his trial, Ulyukaev denied all knowledge of the money and the recording produced by Sechin was remarkably unconvincing. Ulyukaev's defence lawyers suggested that the prosecution was politically motivated, arising from a disagreement between the two men over the shady dealings of Rosneft. They summonsed Sechin to appear in person to be cross examined, but his office replied that he was too busy. When the court sentenced Ulyukaev to eight years in a strict regime labour camp, he compared the proceedings to the Stalinist show trials of the 1930s.

In all the Kremlin infighting, Putin has feigned the role of the 'good tsar', ostensibly holding the ring between his competing courtiers, while in reality he has played them off against each other. In the rivalry between Medvedev and Sechin, Putin has favoured the latter, possibly because of Medvedev's performance during the time he served as stand-in president between 2008 and 2012. Putin had put him in the post merely to keep the seat warm for his own return to the job, but Medvedev let power go to his head, developing aspirations to hold on to the presidency, an uncalled-for show of ambition that angered Putin. As soon as the two resumed their proper offices in 2012, with Medvedev as prime minister, Putin responded by using Medvedev as a lightning rod against the people's anger at falling living standards and making him take the blame for unpopular pension reforms. When Medvedev was confronted in 2016 by OAPs demanding pension increases, he made a run for it, muttering, 'There simply isn't any money at the moment … Hang on in there, all of you. I wish you all the best and hope you have a nice day …' His vanishing act inspired a rush of comic songs and sketches viewed by millions on social media.

Sympathy for Medvedev was short-lived. In 2017, Alexei Navalny's Anti-Corruption Foundation released video evidence that suggested the 'simpleton' was also involved in crooked schemes. 'Even this incompetent,' Navalny alleged, had been able to pilfer millions of dollars from the country's coffers. 'Far from being a simpleton who falls asleep during important events, [Medvedev] is one of our country's richest people and one of its most corrupt politicians', Navalny claimed. Money that should have been spent on improving living standards and urgently needed infrastructure projects had gone instead, it was said, to help Medvedev and his associates accumulate real estate at home and abroad, funding luxurious lifestyles unimaginable to the millions forced to survive on threadbare state pensions. 'They have palaces, residences and country estates, yachts and vineyards in Russia and abroad,' said Navalny, 'not to mention smartphones, gadgets and personalised Nike trainers.' The photos of Medvedev's interior-designed homes with one-of-a-kind architectural features were accompanied by screenshots of receipts, all of which were printed in someone else's name, and evidence shown of vast wealth secretly held for him by fake charities and willing pals from his schooldays. Such is the nature of Putin's inner circle that there is simply no place in it for anyone who is alleged to be mired in corruption.

Despite its devastating effect on his reputation, Medvedev responded to Navalny's exposé by saying that the corruption evidence was 'from weird stuff, nonsense and some pieces of paper'.* Others have been less restrained. In 2018, Putin's bodyguard, Viktor Zolotov, announced that he was challenging Navalny to a duel, with the intention of 'pounding him into a nice, juicy cutlet'. 'You know what your

---

* Medvedev response: "Медведев о фильме Навального: это попытка добиться шкурных целей". ria.ru (in Russian), 4 April 2017.

A screengrab of Viktor Zolotov making a speech, during which he threatens Alexei Navalny

problem is?' Zolotov asked Navalny rhetorically. 'No one's ever given you the beating you deserve. But now you're going to find out! You libelled me in your internet report, so you and I are going to fight it out – in the ring, on the mat or wherever you choose. An officer doesn't forgive that sort of insult; his honour demands he slap down the scoundrel who insulted him.'

Like Sechin and Medvedev, Zolotov's friendship with Putin began in 1990s St Petersburg. He was serving as a bodyguard to Mayor Sobchak, then transferred his services to Putin, and has accompanied him across the globe ever since. In 2016 it was announced that Zolotov would take charge of a new army unit that would answer directly to the president. The unit, known as Rosgvardiya, has subsequently grown to several hundred thousand troops, meaning that Putin now commands his own Praetorian Guard. When asked about the constitutionality of such an arrangement, the Kremlin maintained that the unit's purpose is to provide a defence against terrorists – but the real motivation seems to be Putin's fears for himself. Ever since Ukraine's Orange Revolution of 2004 and the overthrow of the corrupt Kremlin-ally Viktor Yanukovych a decade later, Putin has fretted that the same fate may lie in store for him. Images of angry demonstrators breaking into Yanukovych's palatial residence provided a chilling foretaste of what could happen. Videos uploaded by the protestors showed them swarming through Yanukovych's private golf course, his ostrich farm, the museum he had built for his luxury automobiles and his full-scale mock galleon decorated with marble, crystal and gold leaf. The thought of the Russian public invading the palaces and mansions that Putin and his associates have constructed for themselves at the expense of the Russian people is one he dares not countenance. It is no coincidence that Zolotov's troops have controversially been given express permission to fire into any crowds that threaten 'important state facilities'.

The number of top Kremlin officials who are former members of – or have connections with – the KGB has reached alarming proportions. Putin's close advisers since he came to power in 2000 have included Viktor Ivanov, a former KGB agent and long-time Putin associate; Sergei Ivanov, one of Putin's oldest friends since their days as KGB officers in Leningrad; Mikhail Fradkov, who reportedly served in the KGB while working at the Soviet embassy in India in the 1970s; Viktor Cherkesov, another former KGB officer who specialised in persecuting Soviet-era dissidents; Sergei Chemezov, who lived in the same KGB apartment block with Putin in Dresden; Alexander Bastrykin, the head of the Investigative Committee and a former Putin classmate; Sergey Naryshkin, the head of the Foreign Intelligence Service and a contemporary of Putin's at the Dzerzhinsky KGB Higher School; and the career KGB-man, Nikolai Patrushev.

Patrushev is now approaching 50 years in the security services, having begun his KGB career in the 1970s. After succeeding Putin as director of the FSB in 1999, he held the post until 2008, when he was appointed secretary of the Security Council of Russia and makes no secret of his admiration for Putin, whom he described as 'a true statesman and a representative of the country's strategic elite, who put national interests above all else.' Under Patrushev's watch, the FSB achieved Andropov's dream of placing its people across all sectors of government and business, with the result that the bureau has been able to play a decisive role in removing politicians who pose a threat to the leadership, strangling the media and neutralising those who push for transparency in public life. Even Patriarch Kirill, the servile head of the Russian Orthodox Church who relentlessly instructs the faithful to support Putin, is rumoured to be a former KGB agent. In return for his unwavering loyalty, Kirill is invited on skiing holidays with the president and has appeared in public wearing bejewelled watches worth tens of thousands of dollars.

Because Putin's Kremlin today is so stuffed with hardline anti-liberals, it can be tempting to assume it has always been so. But as noted above, when Putin came to power, he inherited Boris Yeltsin's team of ministers and officials, who were overwhelmingly reformers. Putin's first government was led by the pro-Western Prime Minister Mikhail Kasyanov and most of its members shared his political views. But the team Putin brought with him from St Petersburg were preponderantly KGB men who coalesced into the Siloviki clique and very soon came into conflict with the Kremlin liberals. The battle-ground on which they clashed was the economy, specifically the results of Yeltsin's privatisation programme of the 1990s. Igor Sechin and the other Siloviki argued that the privatised industries should be renationalised as a signal that the era of liberal free enterprise was over and that the state would henceforth call the shots. The liberals, led by Kasyanov, continued to fight for a free market and economic integration with the West; they argued that wealthy businessmen were a natural part of a properly functioning economy. But by 2003, their opponents were gaining the upper hand.

As I would soon find out.

CHAPTER 9
PUTIN UNBOUND

The arrest of Yukos's head of security, Alexei Pichugin, in June 2003 and then our chief executive, Platon Lebedev, in July was a declaration of intent. Putin had taken offence at my denunciation of official corruption at our February meeting in the Kremlin; he disapproved of our plans to take Yukos on to the world stage in partnership with the Americans and he was alarmed by reports – not all of them accurate – that I was planning to go into politics to champion a pro-Western, liberal democracy. The fact that Putin opted to arrest my colleagues rather than come directly for me indicated that there were still some restraining influences in the Kremlin, that the old-guard liberals who shared my commitment to free-market democracy were still striving to mitigate the predations of the Siloviki.

It has been suggested that Putin was giving me a warning, hoping to persuade me to back down over Yukos's collaboration with the Americans and eat a good helping of humble pie. This was something

I was not prepared to do. It would have meant renouncing everything I stood for – the freedom to conduct business, to express independent views, to stand against the restrictive, stultifying model of xenophobic autocracy that Russia was being drawn into; and it would have meant abandoning my comrades who were now bearing the brunt of Putin's anger. Pichugin and Lebedev were in jail, later to be joined there by another eight Yukos employees, and our lawyers were being physically threatened by the FSB. The pressure was being ratcheted up and there was much anxiety among Yukos employees and their families.

Meanwhile, Pichugin had been transferred to the infamous Lefortovo interrogation centre, where he was pressured to give false testimony implicating the Yukos management in plots to intimidate business rivals. Pichugin refused to perjure himself, so the interrogators injected him with a psychotropic drug that left him disoriented and confused. Despite all the intimidation, the Kremlin was unable to substantiate any of its allegations. When the Moscow Basmanny Court announced that proceedings in the Pichugin case would be held behind closed doors and that defence lawyers would be barred from revealing the contents of the hearings, over a hundred members of the Russian parliament signed a petition of protest, something that would be hard to imagine today. It was becoming a very public dispute with battle lines drawn on both sides.

The Yukos case was of vital national importance for Russia. It was not just a business dispute, a legal battle or a clash of personalities; it was a battle between two diametrically opposed, mutually exclusive ideologies, from which only one could emerge victorious and become the master of the nation's future.

The schism in the Kremlin could hardly have been clearer. On the one hand, liberals like Prime Minister Mikhail Kasyanov were backing business and enterprise, a free-market economy and good relations with the West; on the other, hardline Siloviki such as Igor Sechin and

Viktor Ivanov were attempting to return Russia to a centralised, statist model where strategic industries were controlled by the government and used to challenge the West rather than cooperate with it.

On 8 July, Kasyanov gave a press conference in which he denounced the trumped-up charges against Lebedev. 'It isn't right to arrest [him] for these alleged economic crimes,' Kasyanov said. 'There are enough real crimes being committed that actually threaten people's lives … this is producing an adverse effect on the country's image and a negative impact on the mood of investors.' An anonymous government source, most probably the Kremlin's chief economic adviser, Andrei Illarionov, was quoted by newspapers as saying 'the sensible part of the presidential administration and the government believes that [this case] is inflicting damage on the Russian economy. Regardless of what happens to Lebedev, the negative consequences of what is happening now are already obvious.'

The 'damage' included a $20 billion fall in the Russian stock market in the space of two weeks; the 'negative consequences' would grow and grow until the international community would lose faith in the reliability of Russia as a place to invest. The newspaper *Novaya Gazeta* warned that Putin was now in thrall to the former KGB men who made up the Kremlin Siloviki. Referring to the Siloviki as 'KGB Inc.', the newspaper said they were exhibiting the security services' traditional mistrust of the West and that 'Khodorkovsky's Western-friendly beliefs' were perceived as particularly threatening. By crushing Yukos, they claimed to be combating Western influence. The Yukos arrests had triggered a showdown that would determine not only the fate of the country's business model, but the future of Russian democracy.

On 3 July, I was summoned by the Russian State Prosecutor. I was told I was being questioned solely as a witness, but the threat was palpable. Afterwards, when I was asked by journalists if I was planning to leave Russia, I said I wasn't. 'I do not plan to leave Russia.

I should have travelled to London today, but I decided to stay right here ... I am not hiding and I don't plan to become a political émigré. If it's a choice of forcing me out of the country or putting me in jail, then they'll have to put me in jail.'

A month later, FSB troops raided Yukos's offices, seizing documents and computers. In September, they stormed into the boarding school for orphans that the Open Russia foundation ran outside Moscow. Armed men in masks ripped out the IT system and seized the children's laptops. I asked for a meeting with Putin to seek an explanation, but was told this was not possible. In the past, I had been granted access to him whenever I needed it, even after our relationship had soured, so his refusal to see me now was the clearest possible signal that things were serious. I had instead a meeting with the FSB director, Nikolai Patrushev, whose offer to me of a 'compromise' settlement with terms he knew would be completely unacceptable confirmed that the crisis was reaching a head. I told my colleagues and fellow directors at Yukos that they should leave Russia while they still could, but that I had taken the decision to stay. At the beginning of October, I was a guest of the US–Russia Business Council in Washington, DC, and used the occasion to tell the world about the critical struggle between democracy and tyranny, between liberal reform and a return to repression and isolation, that was being played out in my homeland:

You have no doubt heard that one of the reasons for all this happening may have been my political activism ... But the question before us right now is much bigger, a much more far-reaching choice: is Russia going to become a democratic country for the first time in our thousand-year history, or are we going to continue along our thousand-year path of authoritarianism? Russia has no hope of becoming a modern society in the economic sense without becoming the same in the democratic sense.

I paused, and then sought to clarify the stakes:

> So, right now is a critical moment for Russia. Russian society is about to resolve the question of which path our country is going to follow. Which model of development are we going to choose for our country: the authoritarian one, or the model of a civilized modern state? I very much hope that we will make the right choice. And foreign investment is a great help to us in this. When we meet to celebrate the next ten years in 2013, we will already know the answer to the question of which path Russia took. I very much hope – and this is in all our interests – that Russia will have taken the right path.

• • •

I was arrested on 25 October 2003, on a scheduled airport stopover during a business trip to Siberia. On my last day of freedom, I had been asked by a journalist in Tomsk what lay behind the Kremlin's attack on Yukos and I tried to explain that this was a proxy battle between two factions of powerful men with very different visions for Russia's future. 'We are being attacked not because of something we did. It is the very existence of an independent force like Yukos that they see as a threat to them. And by "them" I mean those [politicians] who are still stuck in the old ways of thinking. I don't want to get into naming names, but I firmly believe this whole affair is the result of a struggle for power taking place between the different factions in Vladimir Putin's entourage.'

The proceedings against me became a political trial of strength between two ideologies; I was supported by the remaining liberals in the Kremlin, including Kasyanov, Voloshin and the chief economic adviser Andrei Illarionov, who believed in the values of free-market economics. They staked their credibility on exposing the ludicrousness of the trumped-up charges against me and against Yukos, but they were outmanoeuvred by the Siloviki. The politically motivated guilty verdict in my trial, and the prison sentence which I later discovered had been personally decided by Vladimir Putin,* signalled the rout of the Kremlin liberals: to a man, they either resigned or were fired, and – with their departure – what may turn out to be the last chance of a liberal future for Russia was gone. From now on, strategic industries would be controlled by Putin's cronies; they would be used for their personal enrichment, to challenge the West rather than to strengthen cooperation with it, and certainly not for the good of the Russian people. Putin's mission to 'make Russia great' would lead to a new toughness in international relations; Moscow's rhetoric would become ever more strident and Russia's neighbours would be held to ransom by cutting off – or threatening to cut off – oil and gas supplies. The Kremlin would become tougher in its attitude towards domestic opposition; the spectacle of my show trial would deter independent figures from entering the political arena; and ordinary citizens who tried to protest or organise opposition would find themselves on the wrong end of police batons.

The events of October 2003 confirmed the triumph of the Siloviki. Spurred on by Sechin and Viktor Ivanov, Putin would move to reimpose the deadening model of state control that had darkened Russia's past, subordinating the position of business, subverting democratic freedoms and individual rights. Not only would Yukos be destroyed, but also its charitable foundation Open Russia, along with many other

---

* I learned this from the words of one of Putin's friends, conveyed to me by my lawyers when I was already in jail.

charities and non-governmental organisations that aroused the suspicion of the Kremlin. Civil society would be reduced to a minimum; the press, including, in time, social media, would be brought under state control; a meaningful parliament and gubernatorial elections would be abolished. At the end of Yeltsin's term in power, business did not depend directly on the Kremlin; after Yeltsin, it became a necessary condition for the normal functioning of any company.

Yukos was chosen as the vehicle by which the Siloviki engineered all these changes. It was chosen because the spoils were so immense, and because it represented everything the Siloviki hated. It was an open, transparent company, operating to Western standards of probity; it had no hidden depths of corruption and it strove for integration into the Western economic system. Like Yukos, I too adhered to Western values. I had founded charitable organisations; I had promoted education and the preservation of Russia's intellectual potential, including the modernisation and computerisation of the country; I was proposing to strengthen relations with China by building a pipeline from Yukos's Siberian oilfields; and I was partnering with American companies to expand Russian business in the West. Putin didn't like any of this. His model was to keep business, the individuals who run it and the whole of the rest of the country on a short leash.

The FSB commandos who arrested me in Novosibirsk, the officials who arraigned me in the State Prosecutor's Office and the jailers who hosted me in Moscow's Matrosskaya Tishina prison were unfailingly polite, at times mortified by the pantomime they were obliged to act out. The junior prosecutor who read me the charge sheet seemed embarrassed by the ludicrousness of the accusations – theft, fraud, tax evasion, both personally and by the company I led, 'amounting to damage inflicted on the Russian state in the extent of $1 billion'.

It was the first step on the road towards a trial, in which the charges would become ever more absurd. Before October was out,

Arriving at my trial in Moscow surrounded by prison guards

the Energy Ministry had announced it was investigating the validity of all Yukos's oil extraction licences and the Prosecutor's Office had frozen 44 per cent of the company's shares. It was the first time private assets had been seized by the post-Soviet state and it was a harbinger of a disturbing new era in Russian politics. A flood of protests from pro-business figures in Russia and abroad warned that the Kremlin was turning back the clock to the old days of Soviet repression. The US Senate passed a unanimous resolution demanding that Russia guarantee the full legal rights of the imprisoned Yukos directors. The American ambassador in Moscow, Sandy Vershbow, warned that the arrests would 'negatively affect foreign investment in Russia' and, bang on cue, the stock market lost a tenth of its value in one day.

In October 2003, I was Russia's richest man. I ran the most important corporation in the most important sector of Russia's economy. I was a prominent philanthropist, socially active and well known in Russia and abroad. I am not saying this to boast, but rather to give you an idea of what it meant for Putin to have me locked up. It was personal for Putin, but most importantly, it was political.

• • •

I knew exactly why Putin was doing it. I had challenged his authority, and that is the one thing that autocrats cannot allow to happen. The authority of dictators lies not in the legitimate conferral of power by the freely expressed voice of the people, but on the maintenance of the myth of their invincibility. So long as Putin is able to convince the Russian people that his rule is unassailable – and he does this through threats, manipulation and increasingly through brute force – he can hope to remain in power. But once he permits his infallibility to be questioned, he risks undermining the aura of omnipotence that guarantees his survival.

My arrest therefore did not come as a surprise. What did surprise me was the inexplicable sense of relief that came over me as I was led away. Looking back, I can see why I felt that way. Over a span of several months, there had been an inexorable expectation that this arrest was about to happen. I was resisting the political drift of my country at that time. I wasn't the only one, but I was the focus. The Kremlin had allowed me time to leave the country and hoped that I would stay away. But I felt I had to return, and once I did, the count-down started. So, you could say a certain weight lifted off my shoulders. I knew they were coming for me; it was time to stop the charade and move to the endgame.

The hardest thing in the first few weeks after my arrest was the uncertainty. I didn't mind sharing a cell with hardened criminals – most of them were nice to me and curious to hear why someone like me had turned up so unexpectedly in their jail. I didn't mind having my hands cuffed behind my back every time I was taken for ques-tioning, and I didn't mind the prison food and the bedbugs, or even knowing that there were stoolpigeons constantly spying on me. But I did resent the strain it put on my family and friends. Inna stood in line to bring me parcels of food to supplement the prison porridge. My mother, Marina, and my father, Boris, stood for hours outside the courthouse on days when I was due to appear there, hoping to touch me in the brief moments as I walked from the prison van to the entrance. Inna and the children were living in our family home in Zhukovka outside Moscow and she was struggling to convince the kids – and herself – that I was all right and would soon be released. I asked my parents to move in with her to lend a hand.

At first, I had a large cell all to myself, but I was soon joined by other prisoners. They immediately established a supply line through which mail, vodka, food and cigarettes would appear. I ran into a few acquaintances, including one in the cell opposite mine. I was amazed

Arriving at the courthouse once again

to learn how many people with whom I had lost touch had not actually gone abroad, but were here in jail.

I wasn't nervous, but I was concerned about what might be put in my food – I remembered Pichugin's experience with the psychotropic drugs – so I refused to eat or drink anything that the jailors gave me. I drank water only from the tap, until I got my head around the situation. It took me three weeks. Now, I would say that knowing how to behave if you get arrested or taken hostage is a useful skill to learn. I recommend that anyone engaged in business, politics or social activities in Russia should learn it, because it can happen to you.

It is vital not to torment yourself with hopes of early release or worrying about what you left unfinished while you were free. It is important to say only what you consciously want to say – to speak only for your own benefit and nothing beyond that; it is astounding how things you say inadvertently can be turned against you as soon you are arrested. I can't remember much of what I asked to be brought from home. I could easily get by without most things, but I had books, pens and notebooks brought in as fast as possible. I was preparing for a long fight and a long time inside.

My arrest triggered ructions at the highest levels of the Kremlin. On 30 October, Alexander Voloshin resigned from his post as Putin's chief of staff in protest at my detention. He was swiftly replaced by Dmitry Medvedev, then a largely unknown young technocrat, whose first act was to criticise the freezing of Yukos's assets. Medvedev said on national television that law enforcement agencies were sometimes prone to an 'administrative frenzy of zeal, with ill-thought-out consequences that affect the economy and cause outrage in national politics'. Medvedev questioned whether the seizure of Yukos's shares was 'legally effective', giving rise to hopes that the dispute might still be settled amicably. It sounded to me like an olive branch and I decided to take it. My overriding goal was to save the company I had built and to protect the people who worked for it. If my resignation could help to achieve these things, it was my bounden duty to do so. I issued a statement from my prison cell.

> I had set myself the goal in the years ahead of building an international energy company – a leader of the world economy. But the situation that has developed today forces me to set aside my plans to continue my personal involvement in Yukos's development. As a manager, I have to do all I can to pull our workforce safely out from under the blows that are being directed at me and my partners. I am leaving the company … We were the first Russian business to consistently implement the principles of financial transparency and socially responsible business behaviour. We introduced international standards of corporate governance. We were able to achieve absolute recognition and trust on the Russian and global markets … Taxes paid by the company to all levels of government will be in excess of $5 billion this year. Over $100 million is spent annually on philanthropic programmes … I shall now devote myself to building in Russia an open and truly democratic society through my continuing work as chairman of Open Russia. … Wherever I may work, I shall give my all for my country, my Russia, in whose great future I firmly believe.

As well as resigning as head of Yukos, I also gave up my stake in the company. I transferred all my shares to my deputy, Leonid Nevzlin, who was by now in Israel, and informed the Kremlin that I would be happy for the whole of my personal fortune to be used to pay off any bill for Yukos tax arrears, if that would help to save the company.

Putin was playing a devious game. He continued to send conciliatory messages via Mikhail Kasyanov and others, suggesting that the whole affair was a mistake and would soon be sorted out. But he was toying with us. At the same time, Igor Sechin was showing no mercy. Sechin and the Siloviki were intent on destroying Yukos for their own reasons. They wanted to put an end to the era of free markets and private ownership, to return to state dominance or, rather, their own control of the economy; to humiliate the remaining liberals in the Kremlin by publicly demonstrating their impotence to stop this happening; and, most importantly, to satisfy their own personal greed. Putin directed the operation personally, using Sechin and Viktor Ivanov to do the dirty work. He crushed Yukos and handed its assets to his cronies as a reward. Yukos was gobbled up by the state oil company, Rosneft, shortly after Sechin was appointed its chairman. Absorbing Yukos made Rosneft a giant in the industry and Sechin had ultimate control over where its profits went.

But the importance of the Yukos case was not just the great financial interests at stake, the vast fortunes lost and gained; not just the personal dramas, the years wasted in the jails and prison camps, the loss of health and happiness and even, on occasions, lives – it was the pivotal role it played in the battle between the liberals and the new hardliners in Russia. It was the test case that demonstrated the annihilation of the former and the apotheosis of the latter. From Yukos onwards, the country would increasingly turn its back on the Yeltsin years of liberalisation and opening to the West; it would see the inexorable rise of nationalist, conservative forces who believe that economic freedoms and individual rights must be subservient to the interests of the state, that America and Western Europe are natural enemies, not natural collaborators. In February 2004, four months after my arrest, Putin announced that he was firing his Prime Minister Mikhail Kasyanov and the whole of his government. He said he wanted a clean break with the old administration in advance of the following month's presidential elections.

CHAPTER 10
THE TRIAL

For a thousand years, Russia has vacillated between two distinct models of society and governance. Geographically split between Europe and Asia, the Russian mentality has been torn between East and West, between the European template of liberal, market-oriented openness and the 'Eastern' model of coercive autocracy, which places the wielders of power above the law, allowing them to rule by divine right or 'by the dictatorship of the people', but almost always by brute force. Educated Russians – the intelligentsia – have traditionally looked to the West, but the forms of governance that the nation imbibed in the early years of her history, what Russians refer to as the *silnaya ruka*, the iron fist of centralised power, have remained a powerful presence.

The intelligentsia of the nineteenth century were repelled by the authoritarian nature of tsarist autocracy. The writer Pyotr Chaadayev attributed Russia's failure to emulate Western democratic principles to the baleful legacy of the Mongol occupation, which lasted from 1237 to 1480. Chaadayev's arguments for a decisive turn towards Western values of law and social justice coalesced into a powerful school of so-called Westernisers. But an equally vigorous movement emerged, in stark disagreement with Chaadayev's solution and proposing instead a return to the supreme 'Russian values' of Orthodoxy, collectivism and nationalism. These were the so-called Slavophiles, nationalist conservatives who supported tsarism and autocracy.

The Slavophiles saw Russia's strength in its unique historical mission and communal institutions that gave Russia an advantage over the decadent, individualistic West. Dostoyevsky summed it up in the 1870s: 'Our land may be destitute and chaotic ... but it stands as one man. All eighty million of its inhabitants share a spiritual unity which does not, and cannot, exist anywhere in Europe.' The Slavophiles were anti-Western in the sense that they rejected European social values and lamented Peter the Great's attempts to introduce them. They believed in the old social model of an autocratic, Orthodox society in which everyone knew their place and did not challenge the power of autocracy. The Slavophiles proclaimed Russia's moral superiority and need to avoid contamination by the West, reviving the old myths of 'Holy Rus' and Russia's divine mission to save the world. The crusading conviction that Russia's destiny was to teach the rest of humanity how to live would characterise Slavophile teachings in the nineteenth century and surface again in the messianic communism of the twentieth.

In 2003, we clearly saw the pendulum swing precipitously from one historic model to the other, an epochal political pivot from the Westerniser ideal of openness, participatory government and social guarantees to the Slavophile glorification of Russian nationalism, isolationism and quasi-feudal authoritarianism. The Yukos managers who took control after my resignation came up with a jolt against the new despotism that had taken hold in Putin's Kremlin. Despite knowing that the demands for tax arrears against the company were bogus, they engaged with the authorities and made constructive offers to resolve the standoff, spending months trying to negotiate with the Kremlin. But the charges of tax evasion, which had begun at $1 billion, mysteriously escalated to $3.5 billion and then, ludicrously, to $5 billion or even $20 billion. When Yukos agreed to pay $1 billion, then $2 billion, then $20 billion and more, the prosecutor simply thought of a higher number. It was clear that Putin had no intention of resolving the dispute.

The Tax Ministry, directed by the Kremlin, justified all the additional taxes and fines by inventing entirely new legal concepts, which were applied only to Yukos, and by misapplying Russian tax law, notably by retroactively assigning profits made by Yukos's trading subsidiaries to the parent company at a higher tax rate. Yukos's alleged back-tax bill for 2000 to 2004 ended up exceeding $30 billion. According to an analysis by the Parliamentary Assembly of the Council of Europe, published in January 2005, 'the total tax burden for Yukos, including the retroactive reassessments, is indeed about triple that of its Russian competitors' and 'the tax burden for 2002 exceeds Yukos's whole turnover for that year'.

In April 2004, Yukos was given just two days to pay all the 'reassessed' additional tax for 2000. But the tax authorities did not even bother to wait: they froze all the company's assets, making it impossible for Yukos to pay even while simultaneously challenging the legitimacy of the reassessment. The spurious back-tax claims, asset-freezing orders and absurdly unrealistic payment deadlines ultimately led to the seizure of one of Yukos's crown-jewel production assets, Yuganskneftegaz (YNG), in June 2004. In November 2004, the Russian authorities announced that an auction of YNG would take place the following month. This contravened Russian law, which requires the sale of non-core assets before core assets for the settlement of tax claims.

Yukos had proposed to the tax authorities that the company would sell its shares in Sibneft, which would have allowed it to pay off most of the tax liability without affecting its core operations, but the tax authorities ignored the proposal.

At the time of its seizure, YNG was responsible for over 60 per cent of Yukos's total output. It had been valued by management at between $16.1 billion and $22.1 billion, and by the Russian state-appointed evaluators Dresdner Kleinwort Wasserstein at between $14.7 billion and $17.3 billion. Nonetheless, the Russian Ministry of Justice announced that the value of YNG for the purposes of the auction would be no more than $10.4 billion.

In an effort to block the sale of YNG, Yukos filed for bankruptcy protection in December 2004, in the United States Bankruptcy Court for the Southern District of Texas. The Texas court agreed to issue a temporary restraining order, according to which, 'the weight of the evidence supports a finding that it is substantially likely that the tax assessments of Yukos and the manner of enforcement regarding taxes were not conducted in accordance with Russian law'. The court also found that 'the evidence supports a finding of the likelihood that the Plaintiff's shares of YNG will be sold for approximately half the value estimated by two different investment bankers'.

In spite of the court order, the auction went ahead on 19 December 2004. The only bidder was a mysterious company called Baikal Finance Group, which was completely unknown in the industry and appeared to have been founded just two weeks earlier. Its total share capital was declared at $300 and its registered company address turned out to be a liquor store in the city of Tver. President Putin nevertheless gave Baikal Finance his enthusiastic endorsement, stating that its shareholders were 'individuals who have been in the energy business for many years ... and who intend to build relations with Russia's other energy companies interested in this asset'. Despite its lack of capital, Baikal

Finance Group was somehow able to put up the $1 billion deposit needed to participate in the auction and then another $8.8 billion to make good on its successful, uncontested bid to purchase YNG. The mystery was explained two weeks later, when it was announced that Baikal Finance Group was itself being purchased by the state-controlled Rosneft, chaired by Igor Sechin, for an undisclosed sum.

The chief Kremlin economic adviser, Andrei Illarionov, who was still in his post at the time, described the unlawful expropriation of YNG as the 'scam of the year', stating that there was 'no free economic space remaining anywhere in Russia' and that Russia now qualified as 'a politically unfree country'. When he resigned 12 months later, he amplified his remarks. 'Russia has become a different country,' he said. 'It is no longer a democratic country. It is no longer a free country.' Illarionov confirmed that his resignation was in protest against the embezzlement of billions of dollars out of Rosneft's profits by Putin's inner circle. Russia, he said, was now run by an authoritarian, corrupt elite. 'It is one thing to work in a country that is partly free. It is another thing when the political system has changed, and the country has stopped being free and democratic.'

In June 2006, the Kremlin appointed a bankruptcy receiver for the remaining Yukos divisions and a creditors' meeting was called. At the meeting, a restructuring plan was presented by Yukos that would have allowed the company to settle its liabilities and continue operating in light of rising oil prices. The plan was rejected by the Kremlin, as the Russian authorities again demonstrated that they were not interested in settling with Yukos. In August 2006, a Russian court declared Yukos insolvent. The rejection of Yukos's restructuring plan forced a fire sale of the company's remaining assets, which included the production facilities Tomskneftegaz (including the Angarsk and Achinsk refineries) and Samaraneftegaz (with a further three refineries). The majority of the assets were acquired at well below market value by Rosneft.

Rosneft then included its stake in YNG in its IPO for flotation on the London Stock Exchange. As the *Financial Times* pointed out, the state-controlled company's expropriation of all of Yukos's production units and refineries transformed Rosneft from Russia's number-eight oil major, worth just $6 billion, into the country's biggest producer, with a market capitalisation of $90 billion. Rosneft itself described the purchase of YNG as 'the most monumental bargain in Russia's modern history'.

Yukos investors received no benefit from any of the auctions, as Yukos's liabilities were artificially calculated to match exactly the fire sale prices of its assets, leaving no balance to be distributed to the shareholders. American investors in particular lost nearly $7 billion. In November 2007, Yukos's liquidation was complete and the company was removed from the Russian register of enterprises.

· · ·

I was put on trial, together with my friend and business partner, Platon Lebedev, at the start of summer in 2004. There was a widespread acceptance in Russia and abroad that the charges against us were a legal farce, and that this was a politically motivated show trial. The Parliamentary Assembly of the Council of Europe, which oversees the European Court of Human Rights, had appointed a commission to investigate the legality of the case. Its chairman, the former German Justice Minister Sabine Leutheusser-Schnarrenberger, was outspoken in her assessment:

> There are many circumstances which lead us to believe there must be a political motivation in this case. Khodorkovsky is the only oligarch who sits in prison since October last year. There are massive claims for back taxes directed against him. And this is not happening to any other large

company in Russia. These are all circumstances where one can say there is politics involved, not the rule of law. There are significant accusations that human rights have been violated around the arrest and also in prison, especially concerning the medical treatment of some of the Yukos detainees. That a businessman manager is held in pre-trial detention for nine months although he is highly unlikely to flee abroad, that he is held like an animal in a cage during court hearings, all this is alarming.

The commission highlighted the wider threat to democracy posed by the Yukos case:

I am very concerned about the developments as far as the rule of law is concerned, democracy in general and the strengthening of civil society. In summary, I believe we are really faced with a very dangerous development here, a move away from democracy and the rule of law.

I believe we must tell Putin: If you are going to continue like this, with the cloak of justice but with political reasons in the background, then we won't be able to continue business relations in this way.

Leutheusser-Schnarrenberger issued a formal report documenting Russia's 'gross infringements' of the European Human Rights Convention and concluded that the Yukos executives had been 'arbitrarily singled out ... in order to weaken an outspoken political opponent, intimidate other wealthy individuals and regain control of economic assets'. I had been arrested because I was perceived to be a figurehead for the democratic, Western-friendly, internationalist

Behind bars in the courtroom, surrounded by the press and media

future that many of us wanted for our country, while Putin and his ex-KGB colleagues were plotting a return to authoritarian rule.

At our televised clash in the Kremlin in February 2003, Putin had responded to my exposé of the huge scale of government corruption by implying that I myself had improperly benefited from the privatisation of Yukos. Yet nowhere in any of the charges against me was there any mention of the Yukos privatisation. Instead, there was a grab bag of indictments relating to long-forgotten business deals that Group Menatep had completed in the 1990s, including the privatisation of the Apatit mineral fertiliser company; the sales of Apatit production; the privatisation of the Research Institute for Fertilisers and Insecto-Fungicides; the use of a specially legislated zone for reducing Yukos's tax burden; the tax implications of registration as private entrepreneurs; and the investment of Yukos funds in Media Most Corporation.

The prosecution's case was conspicuously light on facts and figures, relying instead on misrepresentation and misinterpretation of the law, demanding a conviction based on untenable declarations and ominous insinuations rather than relevant evidence or cogent analysis. None of which mattered in the slightest, of course, because the judges were never going to decide the case on the facts; their role was simply to play the part of an independent judiciary, while waiting by the telephone for the Kremlin to ring and dictate their verdict. The prosecution knew before the trial began that it would be triumphant, yet even with all the advantages it enjoyed, it still managed to demonstrate its professional incompetence and woeful lack of understanding of the fundamental concepts of business law. The judges showed themselves to be equally clueless, making unsubstantiated pronouncements that simply parroted the prosecution's lines, ignoring obvious violations of Russian law and refusing to consider even the most irrefutably well-founded arguments from the defence. Extensive defence evidence was simply discarded, while the judges copied vast tracts from the text of the prosecution's indictment directly into their verdict.

Independent observers from European institutions catalogued the court's violations of due process. Sabine Leutheusser-Schnarrenberger wrote:

> The sheer number and seriousness of procedural violations in my view exceeds a mere accumulation of mistakes that could be explained by a lack of experience or professionalism. During my mandate, I have been confronted with a number of examples of the serious problems from which the Russian judiciary suffers in general, including its notorious openness to corruption, lack of respect for the rights of the defence, and, in particular, the overwhelming influence of the procuracy, which in turn is a tool in the hands of the executive.

The list of due process violations reported by observers at the trial was extensive:

- The court did not treat the prosecutors and the defence equally.
- The defence was not provided sufficient time to present its case and the overwhelming majority of defence motions and requests were denied.
- The prosecution was allowed to introduce impermissible evidence, including unauthenticated documents and materials obtained illegally.
- The defence was denied the opportunity to introduce exculpatory evidence, including key expert reports.
- The scope of direct questions to defence witnesses and of defence cross-examination of prosecution witnesses was restricted.

- The defence was denied cross-examination of prosecution expert witnesses.
- The defence was denied requests to subpoena prosecution expert witnesses.
- Witnesses were harassed and improperly influenced, including through continued investigation and interrogation; threats of searches, arrests and prosecution; and improper questioning during trial.
- The court made motions on behalf of the prosecution.
- The court questioned witnesses on behalf of the prosecution.
- The defendants were denied effective assistance of counsel, including through interference with access; interference with confidential communications; and harassment of counsel.
- The prosecution failed to disclose exculpatory evidence.

Further legal abuses included the selective and retrospective application of laws – selective because such sanctions were never invoked against any entity other than Yukos, and retrospective because the law in question did not exist at the time of the alleged offence. For instance, the prosecution charged that Yukos had used a specially legislated low-tax zone to reduce its tax burden, a fact we never hid, and a scheme of which other Russian oil companies also took advantage. Indeed, the Kremlin itself had encouraged the creation of low-tax zones in order to boost economic activity in areas that were suffering through the post-Soviet transition. The Russian tax authorities had explicitly approved Yukos's use of such mechanisms for reducing the company's overall tax burden. Yet, the prosecution now sought to class this usage as a crime. The tax authorities reopened Yukos's tax returns from previous years that had already been signed off and accepted. They ruled that the use of regional tax shelters was illegal – despite the Russian Audit Chamber having declared them legal just a few months earlier. A representative of the tax authorities specifically confirmed that, at the time of the supposed infringements, the tax reduction methods in question were widely used and considered legal, while the legislation was only changed thereafter, with new rules entering into force shortly before my trial began. Other oil companies operating in Russia used the same methods to reduce their overall tax burden, but only Yukos was subjected to a tax reassessment and prosecution. The Organisation for Economic Co-operation and Development (OECD) concluded that the proceedings against Yukos were therefore 'a case of highly selective law enforcement' which demonstrated how 'Russia's courts are subservient to the executive ... and its prosecutors highly politicised'.

We knew full well that the court would find Lebedev and myself guilty on all counts, so the nine-year prison sentences we were handed in May 2005 came as no surprise. We appealed, because there was no reason not to appeal, but we didn't hold out great hope. In September 2005, in a one-day hearing, the court rejected the arguments put forward in our application, while reducing our sentences from nine to eight years in a show of simulated magnanimity. The fact that the judges could review hundreds of bound volumes of evidence from a case that had lasted a year in the space of just a few hours might have surprised outside observers; but it was entirely understandable to Russians. The appeal was rushed through, ensuring a conviction in time to prevent me filing papers to register as a candidate in the forthcoming parliamentary elections, which would have placed me firmly in the public eye during the campaign. When I politely pointed out to the appeal judge that I was by law permitted to address the court and to be represented by my own lawyer, I saw the panic in his eyes, before he denied my requests with a witty legal quip, 'You're not in Strasbourg here!'

Counting the prison time we had served since our arrests in 2003, Platon and I were scheduled for release in 2011 – but this evidently did not suit Vladimir Putin. In 2009 he ordered us to go on trial again. This time, we were accused of embezzling the entire oil production of Yukos over a period of six years leading up to 2003, around 350 million metric tons of oil worth over $25.4 billion, and of laundering all the proceeds from the sale of this oil to the tune of over $21.4 billion. We were found guilty once more and ordered to remain in prison until 2016. We appealed to the European Court of Human Rights and won favourable rulings that had no effect whatsoever on the Russian authorities.

I had assumed at the outset that I would spend two to four years in jail. It's not that I was looking forward to it, but I was ready to do that. It turned out to be more than ten. I suppose my assessment of how far the justice system could be perverted was naive. But, even after losing a decade of my life, I continue to believe that freedom, democracy and civil rights cannot be contained by even the harshest of jailors.

CHAPTER 11
ARRESTED DEVELOPMENT

Putin's anti-Westernism, his wanton confiscation of private property and the corruption that flows from the highest levels of the Kremlin have devastated the prospects for any renewal or progress in the Russian economy. Why would anyone trust a mafia state that appropriates the resources of the nation and seizes the businesses of individuals solely to enrich itself? Why would global investors choose to invest their money in a country run by such a treacherous regime, and why would the Russian people continue to accept the abuses to which their leaders subject them?

The last question is perhaps the easiest to answer. Historically, the iron fist of Russian authoritarianism has crushed expressions of popular discontent, but it has not dispelled the mistrust that attaches to a system of governance which claims all power for itself and refuses to respect the rule of law or the rights of its citizens. I wonder if you can guess who wrote the following – and when it was written:

The fundamental principle of Russian government has always been the autocratic ruler who combines all legislative and executive powers and disposes of all the nation's resources. There are no limits placed on this principle. When the powers of the ruling authority are unlimited – to such an extent that no rights are left over for the subjects – then such a state exists in slavery and its government is despotic.

It is a description that could accurately be applied to the autocracy of the Communist Party or that of Vladimir Putin, but it was actually written in 1809 by Mikhail Speransky, an adviser to Tsar Alexander I. Speransky lamented that Russia had never been a law-governed country, in words that describe perfectly the state of affairs today.

Under autocratic rule there can be no code of law, for where no rights exist there can be no impartial balance between them … there is nothing but the arbitrary decisions of the ruler, prescribing to the citizens their bounden duties until such time as the autocrat decides to change them. The law is completely dependent on the autocratic will which alone creates it, alone establishes the courts, names the judges and gives them their rules … as the fancy strikes it.

Speransky concluded that the absence of justice, law and protection from capricious authority stifles initiative and progress, with the result that the country remained mired in primitive backwardness. Today, in Putin's Russia, the law continues to be trampled on and bypassed in favour of the dictatorship of the men who occupy the Kremlin. For them, laws exist merely to cloak despotism in the trappings of legitimacy, a fig leaf for the political coercion that makes the system incapable of constructive evolution.

A country's legal system should not be the expression of the sole will of the ruler; it should be the consolidated will of civil society as a whole. That is what allows a state to function on the basis of consent, where citizens obey the law because they respect its foundations. Such laws must be built upon unchanging principles, ones not subject to alteration on the whim of the moment, and they must be passed by an independent, freely elected parliament. So long as personalised autocracy remains the only political configuration known in Russia, there is little prospect of progress.

The lack of legal protection for private possessions in the face of a rapacious, grasping state continues to undermine confidence in Russia. 'What is the use of laws assigning property to private individuals,' Mikhail Speransky wrote, 'when property itself has no firm basis in any respect whatsoever? What is the use of civil laws when their tablets can at any time be smashed on the first rock of arbitrary rule? How can finances be set in order in a country with no public confidence in the law!'

Lack of belief in the protection of the law has caused an outflow of capital and people from Russia, a fall in the number of long-term projects financed outside of the state budget, and the insane corruption and embezzlement of state property that eat up more than 10 per cent of GDP.

Under Putin the state has not only neglected to develop the country's intellectual potential; its predatory policies towards business and its trampling on individual rights have also contributed to a massive flight of human talent, including the cream of Russia's young entrepreneurs. These are people who need to feel independent and safe in conditions of democracy, so the statist ideology that pervades our country has prompted them to emigrate. You can imagine the harm this has done. If a 25-year-old entrepreneur decides to leave Russia, the country loses millions of dollars in potential revenue back into the economy. And a hundred thousand such entrepreneurs and highly qualified specialists are leaving Russia every year.

Official figures record that 4.5 million people left Russia in the two decades following the collapse of the Soviet Union and experts agree that the real number was much higher. A 2016 report revealed the damage this brain drain has inflicted. The majority of those who emigrated to the West were people with potential who felt unable to develop in their homeland – scholars, college students, entrepreneurs and business leaders. The number of independently wealthy émigrés, including former government officials, families of politicians and members of the financial and bureaucratic elite, has escalated since 2000. The reasons they gave for leaving ranged from low salaries and the lack of funding for science and education to the volatile business environment, widespread corruption, fears for personal safety and business assets, the weakness of public institutions, and a lack of confidence in the law enforcement and judicial systems. The exodus, says the report, not only deprives the country of the most active members of society but condemns the remainder to slower development.

A country as richly endowed with human and material resources but with such a level of national poverty as Russia should be achieving 6 to 7 per cent growth rates. All that is needed is a commitment to legality and business integrity for Russia to attain Canadian standards of living within a decade. Two centuries ago, Mikhail Speransky explained to Tsar Alexander how the deadweight of Russia's autocratic past could be thrown off and the door opened to a better future. He drew up plans for freely elected local councils, a national parliament and a remarkable draft constitution guaranteeing civil rights and the separation of powers, an end to the police state and freedom of the press. But Alexander refused, and in the third decade of President Vladimir Putin's rule, the prospects for political reform and economic modernisation are still remote. Trust between Russia and Western governments is at an all-time low. This is bad for the wellbeing of the Russian people, and the safeguarding of their human rights. It tarnishes Russia's attractiveness as a destination for Western investment. And it carries the risk of political mistakes and gambits that may lead to conflict. As a business leader, I am acutely aware of the way Putin's leadership stifles economic prosperity. But it is more than that. It has a noxious effect on the moral welfare of the country. It stifles our nation's present, our people and our future.

As for meaningful economic change, several obstacles stand in the way. The first is domestic investment. Not only is a lot of state expenditure unproductive, the authorities also withhold investment essential for modernising the economy. Apart from the banal purposes of theft and self-enrichment, the rationale for this policy is to accumulate reserves and avoid dependence on Western countries.

Second, Western sanctions, imposed in response to Putin's military and sabotage activities abroad, had already restricted the flow of investment and technologies into Russia, even before the increased measures enacted after Putin's invasion of Ukraine. The involvement of high-level foreign professionals and entrepreneurs in the economy has been reduced almost to zero by the international isolation of Russia after February 2022 and a large part of the Kremlin's aforementioned financial reserves has been frozen. This situation is unlikely to undergo radical change, for no one wants to strengthen a Kremlin autarchy prone to exporting violence.

Finally, there is the question of Russia's institutions and the rule of law. The state under Putin continues to demonstrate its high-handed attitude to private property and the decisions of international courts. Its own parliament, courts and other institutions are not independent. Russia today is simply not a good place to invest your energy, acumen and capital. Regular scandals erupt in the form of corruption, money laundering and even violent crimes – explosions, poisonings, murders.

By now, everyone should understand that the Kremlin sees the economy as a tool of politics. Simply put, one can achieve and hold on to economic success in Putin's Russia only by agreeing to engage in corruption or by becoming an agent of Kremlin policies. This is what Western investors should keep in mind. The Washington-based think tank, the Atlantic Council, wrote in 2020 that 'a "state–criminal partnership" developed in Russia, in which the shadow financial services market was monopolized by the SEB/FSB under the leadership of current FSB Director Alexander Bortnikov. Since then, SEB [the FSB's Economic Security Service] employees control the entire chain, from schemes for withdrawing money from the budget to cashing out these funds and laundering them abroad.'

Putin wants to see himself as a full-fledged player in the 'big game' of global geopolitics, but the state of the Russian economy and society does not afford him that opportunity. Therefore, he claims his seat at the table by using other methods – by playing against the rules. Western leaders seem to have had enough. The Biden administration has promised that, from now on, such games will cost the Kremlin dearly. For his part, Putin has vowed to draw a 'red line' in defence of Russian interests, warning that those who cross it 'will regret what they have done in a way they have not regretted anything for a long time'. Matters might be different if there were a genuine prospect of political change. But Putin's regime in its current state is not ready for reform. Its laws completely rule out the possibility of changing the power structures by means of elections.

Combined with torrents of state propaganda, school education, orchestrated political processes and outright violence, this has contributed to a sense of hopelessness in society. At the same time, the authorities intentionally keep income levels within a range where people scrape along from pay cheque to pay cheque, keenly aware of the total dependence of themselves and their families. All this reduces Russia's economic growth rates, but serves to preserve the political status quo.

Public attitudes to Putin's regime reflect the structure of Russian society. Perhaps half the population would not mind keeping Putin in power for a fifth presidential term after his present six-year spell ends in 2024. The same half thinks that the sentence imposed on Alexei Navalny, the opposition activist ailing in prison, is appropriate. Among the other half, there are many critics of the system, but also many others who are not ready to take an open stance.

Russian society is heterogeneous. About 25 per cent of people are educated residents of big cities, where opposition to Putin is strongest. About the same amount, maybe a little less, live in 'electoral sultanates', or territories where feudal and even tribal orders rule. The remaining 50 to 60 per cent live in the industrial society of the mid-twentieth century – in so-called 'mono-cities' and other urban areas of central Russia that have only two or three large enterprises. Meanwhile, the population of big cities has changed greatly because of the influx of migrants from Central Asia. For all these reasons, I am not sure we can expect early positive political changes in Russia driven by public pressure.

Under Putin, the authorities have consciously sought to revive the imperial reflexes of the Russian population, and this includes the inculcation of a mentality that can perversely equate business success with foreign encroachment. It was an argument that was used to justify the Kremlin's attack on Yukos and there are countless other examples, including the infamous Magnitsky case that brought the practice of state-sponsored corporate raiding – called *reiderstvo* in Russian – to the world's attention.

In June 2007, armed police raided the Moscow offices of the thriving investment fund, Hermitage Capital, run by the British-American financier, William Browder. The police identified themselves as members of the FSB's Economic Security Service and claimed they had authority to confiscate documents and computers as part of a tax probe. In fact, they were perpetrating a classic *reiderstvo* operation, which would result in three of Hermitage's subsidiary companies being seized on bogus charges.

The FSB officers who carried out the raid were not acting alone; they had enlisted the help of corrupt law enforcement officials and judges, who were all part of the scam. Using the corporate registration documents that they had seized, the FSB men and their associates were able to perpetrate a fraud, in which they claimed (and received) a refund of $230 million in taxes that Hermitage had paid to the Russian state. When the company's lawyer, Sergei Magnitsky, discovered that the raiders were claiming bogus tax refunds in Hermitage's name, he made an official complaint, only to find himself arrested by the very police who were involved in the plot. In November 2008, he was brought before a judge and charged with tax evasion. On remand in jail, Magnitsky was pressured to make a deal and testify against Browder. He was threatened and denied medication for serious health problems, but he refused to perjure himself. On 16 November 2009, after 11 months of imprisonment, Sergei Magnitsky died in a cell in the prison hospital, having been handcuffed in a stress position. The European Court of Human Rights would later rule that he had been held in conditions that amounted to 'inhuman and degrading treatment' and subjected to negligence and lack of adequate medical care in breach of Article 3 of the European Convention on Human Rights.

The Magnitsky case provoked international outrage, prompting the US Congress to pass legislation targeting individuals directly or indirectly involved in his arrest and death. The Magnitsky Act, signed into law by President Barack Obama in December 2012, named a series of Russian officials who would henceforth be prohibited from entering the United States or using the US banking system. Canada, the United Kingdom and other European countries followed suit with their own sanctions.

In evidence to the US Senate Judiciary Committee in July 2017, Bill Browder testified that the Magnitsky Act restrictions were having an effect on those it targeted, including Putin himself. 'President Putin is … the biggest oligarch in Russia and the richest man in the world,' Browder said. 'I estimate that he has accumulated $200 billion of ill-gotten gains from these types of operations over his 17 years in power. He keeps his money in the West and all of his money in the West is potentially exposed to asset freezes and confiscation. Therefore, he has a significant and very personal interest in finding a way to get rid of the Magnitsky sanctions.'

Inside Russia, the Magnitsky case changed little. The Kremlin's failure to act against those responsible for Magnitsky's death was a signal to foreign businesses that they would not be treated differently from domestic firms. Kowtowing to the authorities, paying kick-backs and bribes, would remain the cost of doing business there. Entrepreneurs have continued to be targeted and cases of *reiderstvo* are now estimated to account for one in seven of all business takeovers, involving funds in the tens of billions of dollars.

The *reiderstvo* pandemic began almost as soon as Putin came to power in 2000, when the Siloviki were given free rein to carve up Russia's strategic assets and share the proceeds between themselves. Their first targets were the industries that had been privatised in the previous decade, which they picked off one by one. As scions of the security forces, the Siloviki held sway over the key state institutions, including the tax authorities, law enforcement and judiciary, fashion-ing them into a biddable machine that they deployed to plunder their hapless victims.

Under Putin, *reiderstvo* itself became a business, with specialist companies offering professional analyses of potential targets, teams of bent lawyers ready to rubber stamp the theft and detachments of corrupt FSB operatives to carry out the physical seizure. The Moscow magazine *Ogoniok* even produced a standard price list for the services on offer, ranging from $1,500 per day to tap a mobile phone to $20,000 for surveillance of the target enterprise, while suborning the police and Prosecutor's Office costs between $30,000 and $60,000.

Because speed is of the essence, the raiders usually arrive in force, overwhelming the company's security men and intimidating employees with threats of violence. The owners are either removed from the scene or bound and gagged and held in a storeroom. The police are then called, by which time the new 'owner' has his feet under the desk, armed with fraudulent company papers and forged share registers. If victims appeal to the courts, they invariably discover that the judge has been bribed by the raiders and consequently refuses to hear their case.

Just as in some third world countries, the law in Russia can be hired as a tool for profit. Judges can be bought; courts are not independent of the will of their political masters; the judiciary knows full well that its judgements must conform to the wishes of the Kremlin. Opposition activists, including Alexei Navalny, who have tried to pursue cases of official corruption through legal channels have been uniformly rebuffed. In the single instance when a court did agree to consider a lawsuit alleging financial impropriety by the president, the Kremlin moved swiftly to shut the procedure down. Judge Tatyana Leskina of the Saratov Court of Arbitration received a motion in April 2016 calling for Vladimir Putin to be tried as 'an enemy of the state, due to his plunder of Russia and impoverishment of the Russian people'. When she imprudently agreed to hear the case, Leskina was fired from her position and her decision quashed on the grounds that the courts have no right to interfere with the activities of the president.

The constitutional immunity from prosecution that Putin enjoys has facilitated his acquisition of the fabulous levels of wealth referred to by William Browder and his gracious distribution of largesse to his friends and family. *Forbes* magazine has published an annual list of those who benefit most from Putin's patronage, a remarkable number of whom have turned out to be his own relatives and childhood chums. Arkady Rotenberg, Putin's judo partner, figured in every edition of *Forbes*'s 'Kings of State Contracts' roster from the year it first appeared, receiving annual orders from the Kremlin worth over $7 billion for his engineering and construction companies. Another fixture on the list, Kirill Shamalov, improbably became deputy CEO of SIBUR at the age of 30. The petrochemical conglomerate was the recipient of multibillion-dollar state contracts. Shamalov's own company, Yauza 12, was reported in the media to have received a $1 billion loan from the state-backed Gazprombank (where his brother Yury happens to be the deputy chairman), which he used to buy 17 per cent of SIBUR from Putin's old pal Gennady Timchenko. It was perhaps no coincidence that Kirill Shamalov was Putin's son-in-law, married to his second daughter, Katerina; or that when relations with the president's daughter faltered, he was forced to sell out to Leonid Mikhelson. Both Timchenko and Mikhelson also feature prominently on *Forbes*'s 'Kings of State Contracts' list. Helping to keep things in-house, Katerina herself, having achieved some success in the little-known discipline of acrobatic rock 'n' roll, was appointed to head a $1.7 billion publicly funded project to build a new science hub at Moscow State University. Arkady Rotenberg's son, Igor, whose assets have included the drilling company Gazprom Bureniye and power generation company TEK Mosenergo, has also powered his way up the *Forbes* list, underlining the extent to which people close to Putin now run Russia's key industries and are passing down their wealth to sons and daughters.

Putin and his cronies have acquired a fondness for building themselves luxury residences – palaces, according to some reports – a trend that has been exposed and lampooned by Alexei Navalny's

Anti-Corruption Foundation (FBK). In January 2021, Navalny released a video titled *Putin's Palace: The World's Biggest Bribe*, which broke all records for social media views in Russia. The film showed footage of an opulent coastal property near the Black Sea resort of Gelendzhik that has been built for Putin by the grateful recipients of his state-funded business deals. According to Navalny, $1.35 billion of illicit funds went into the construction of the palace, which extends to more than 17,000 square metres, making it the biggest private residence in Russia. Putin can enjoy the services of a private port, a vineyard, a chapel, a casino, an indoor hockey rink and toilet brushes costing $850 each. Among those reported to have funded the president's gift was Nikolai Shamalov, who worked with Putin during his time in the St Petersburg mayor's administration in the 1990s and who had benefited from lucrative Kremlin contracts following Moscow's annexation of Crimea. Nikolai also happens to be the father of Kirill, who married Putin's daughter.

When other members of Putin's inner circle, including Dmitry Medvedev, State Security Council chief Nikolai Patrushev, former Russian Railways boss Vladimir Yakunin and even Putin's press secretary Dmitry Peskov, were all revealed to live in multimillion-dollar homes, the response was swift and indicative: Putin decreed that property ownership records would henceforth become classified information, no longer available to the general public. 'They want to hide the truth about their homes and yachts,' declared Alexei Navalny, 'but our investigations will continue – we can still take photographs ...'

Navalny's videos of the luxury lifestyles of the Kremlin elite hit a national nerve. While Putin and co were getting ever richer, the Russian economy was going from bad to worse. Early in his reign, Putin benefited from high prices for Russia's oil and gas, boosting GDP and lifting living standards. But, instead of using the breathing space to diversify the economy and develop other streams of sustainable revenue, the Kremlin marched blindly on towards the precipice. When global energy prices collapsed in 2014, Russia slid inexorably into recession. Putin's response was to annex Crimea, a manoeuvre that succeeded in shoring up his domestic poll numbers, but brought Western sanctions and a further, inevitable decline in national prosperity. Putin has stifled market competition by shrinking the private sector and bringing more and more of the economy into the hands of the state or, to be more precise, into the hands of his inner circle. Since 2000, the share of GDP controlled by state-owned (and crony-controlled) firms has risen from 35 per cent to 70 per cent, a deadening influence that has reduced enterprise and innovation. With the exception of the arms industry, Russian goods have become dishearteningly uncompetitive on the world market; technological research and development have dwindled and the much-touted creation of a Russian Silicon Valley at Skolkovo, near Moscow, ended in fiasco. Putin's promise of 25 million new jobs in the IT field was a farce. 'Russia,' goes one popular joke from Soviet times, 'now boasts of producing the biggest nanochips in the world.' The Kremlin has subsequently dropped any serious attempt to modernise the economy, with the result that it has been left behind by the developed nations of the West. Russia's GDP is considerably smaller not only than that of the US, but also of Germany, Britain, France and Italy.

If the definition of a third world kleptocracy is a country where the leaders get fat at the expense of the people and the nation, Putin's Russia fits the bill.

CHAPTER 12
GULAG

The Kremlin took a rather touching amount of care in picking the labour camp to which I would be assigned. Despite having 766 penal colonies to choose from, and notwithstanding a provision in Russian law that prisoners should serve their term in a facility close to their home town, I was sent to camp IK14/10, 3,000 miles from Moscow, in the Chita region of Siberia. Chita has average temperatures of plus 45°C in summer and minus 45°C in winter. Our prison barracks were built next to the slagheaps of a uranium mine, where radiation levels were high. In Russian prisons, nine out of ten inmates suffer from at least one chronic disease, with one in three displaying symptoms of serious contagious infection. Platon Lebedev, if this were possible, had things even harder, being despatched to a remote prison colony near the town of Kharp in the Arctic Circle, where the distance from Moscow made it almost impossible for his family and legal team to visit him.

For the first few months, while we were awaiting our trial, I was held in remand prison 99/1 in Moscow. For much of the time, there were just three prisoners in a cell that was built for four. The cell was 4 metres by 5 metres, including the toilet area, which was separated with a partition and a curtain, although it didn't reach up to the ceiling. As well as the toilet bowl, we had a sink with hot and cold water. Our cell was quite new and clean, with a small television, a fridge that was old but usually worked, and a fan. There were four bunks on two levels – like in a train compartment, only made of metal. The window was covered in non-transparent tape, and there were two metal grilles on either side of the glass, with a small ventilating window that we could open. We were taken to have a shower once a week.

There was a kiosk that we could visit once a month. It didn't have any delicacies, but the essentials were all there – milk, kefir, sour cream, apples, carrots, oranges, etc. We also got parcels from home, but these didn't help much. The prison authorities inspected everything and didn't let much through; whatever did get through would be cut up into little pieces. The main thing was that the parcel came from home, which psychologically was very important and counted for a lot.

We were allowed out for exercise once a day for one hour. I used to take walks on the roof of the building, like a cat, because it was the closest to fresh air – but you never got to see the sun because there was a canopy over it. The radio was played all day and that drove me crazy – with pop music and the endless 'letters from listeners' that they broadcast. The light was kept on at night, but that's something you get used to. Jail food is awful. I don't doubt that the fat and carbohydrate contents match the officially prescribed norms, but the way it is cooked – I don't even want to think about it.

I was allowed to work on my defence papers for our court appearance – the only problem was getting access to data and information.

On days when I knew I was due in court, I wouldn't eat anything before I went, as I didn't want to have a problem during the endless hours they kept me in the prison van and then in court, when the guards often neglected to provide toilet breaks; I would eat in the evenings instead. There were searches every day, both personal and in the cell. The guards were polite, but thorough. Four to six searches every day – at least it provided a diversion.

Once we'd had our day in court and got our expected sentences, Platon and I were sent our separate ways to the camps. Where you're going, and how you're going, are kept secret. The guards put you in a special railway carriage, a sort of prison on wheels, divided up into cells with guards patrolling the corridor, and it's only at some station stop en route that you hear an announcement, 'The Moscow to Chita train will be leaving from track two.' That's when I knew where we were going. Six days later, having read a whole bag full of books, we arrived. I say 'we', but in fact I was the only prisoner in the whole carriage. They took me out of the train and bundled me into a paddy wagon to take me to the camp. There, I was made to walk the gauntlet between two lines of barking mongrels with soldiers holding them back. A group of officers ordered me to doff my hat. I knew the order was illegal, because I'd had plenty of time to learn the law, but I did it anyway. There was no point picking a fight over nothing. They confiscated all my possessions that they said were 'not allowed' and, again, I didn't protest. The main thing was that they left me my books and notebooks, having had a good rummage through them.

Life in the camp is better than in prison. In prison, you're locked in a small room with the same people all day; in the camp, you can walk around as much as you want. The sun, the sky, greenery in summer, which in prison you can't see, is all important for a person's wellbeing. After a year in prison, you really suffer from the lack of such simple things. And your health, of course, is undermined: your eyes, your muscles, your immune system. Human beings are not designed for a prison cell: your body protests.

A few days after arriving in the camp, I was called before a committee headed by the camp commander and was told that I had been assigned to work in the sewing workshop. I was immediately suspicious. Sewing professionally requires training. As soon as I saw the equipment, I knew it was a trap. It was simply impossible to meet the required production standards on such machines. Later, the young staff in the administration section told me they had actually been planning to put me in the bakery, which is considered safe, but they had received a phone call from Moscow telling them to put me in sewing.

I wrote a complaint – the first of several[*] – claiming I had poor vision, and deliberately failed the workplace exam, having warned them that if they falsified the exam results, I'd kick up a fuss. My engineering training had allowed me to spot so many safety breaches in the way the camp workshops were run that they filled two whole sheets of paper, with a list of the most serious violations that legally require production to stop until they are rectified. I politely gave the list to the boss and two days later I received a notification: I was being transferred to work as a porter.

Shortly afterwards, the camp commander invited me in for a 'talk'. He didn't say so explicitly, but it was clear that he had received an order to treat me harshly. To put it bluntly, he'd been told to treat me 'like dirt' and it seemed like he wanted my help to show he was doing his job. He was on the point of striking a deal with me, but at the last minute he couldn't bring himself to do it and we parted with matters unresolved.

---

[*] Three years later, at a farcical parole hearing, the commandant told the judge that he'd been 'instructed to put Khodorkovsky in strict confinement', but that the prisoner 'kept complaining and getting the courts involved'.

The upshot was that they started giving me spells in a cramped punishment cell where the bed is lowered from the wall only at night. I responded by going to court. The administration were stunned, but I had learned my way around the judicial system and I was granted a hearing, right there in the camp. The chairman of the city court announced that he was going to take evidence, but the camp authorities were prepared and had a trick up their sleeve. They summoned a 'witness' from among the prisoners, someone they had evidently lined up to make accusations against me that would send me back to the cooler for an even longer period. But, unexpectedly, the 'witness' couldn't go through with the lies. He turned around and pointed at the head of department. 'He forced me to lie,' he told the court. 'He gave me cigarettes. Here they are – you can have them back; but I'm going to tell the truth.'

Everyone was taken aback. I pulled myself together, just in time to hear the chairman of the court say to the camp commander, 'Cancel the defendant's punishment! And as for the witness, if you punish him, I will personally lay charges against you.'*

That's how things went on from that time forward: I would be given a punishment; I would be put in the cooler; I would complain to the court and the court would cancel the punishment. In between times, I worked and got to know my fellow prisoners. We had illiterate shepherds from 'nearby' villages (meaning only 300–400km away) and miners from the uranium pits; we had ordinary, law-abiding citizens and we had big bosses from the criminal world. We had normal people and we had complete villains, young men who had been

---

* I should note that a year later, the chairman of that court got a summons to go to Chita to appear before the President's personal representative, who accused him of having 'helped a state criminal' and fired him shortly afterwards. My local lawyer told me the story – in a town of just 50,000 inhabitants, there aren't many lawyers and they all talk to each other.

sentenced to ten years as minors for serial murder and were serving out the end of their sentence in an adult camp, without understanding that their next murder would mean life imprisonment. There simply were no constraints on these men.

It was a strange mixture, with all of us kept in a single pot, corralled by the prison authorities or by the leaders of the criminal gangs that ruled the roost in the camps. We all shared a common understanding of how we should deal with each other, of the limits of acceptable personal behaviour, and an acute awareness of interdependence. A truly antisocial personality in the camp was a rarity, and they were quickly dealt with by the administration or by the other prisoners. The methods varied from confinement in a specially created 'ghetto' to full 'serious bodily harm'.

My position was a bit of an anomaly. For the first year, prison society couldn't fit me into any of the usual categories. The criteria for these are clear: if you collaborate with the camp authorities, you are a 'red'; if you stand up for yourself and suffer for it, you are 'black'; if you work and you bow the knee to the criminal kingpins, you are a 'peasant'; if you refuse to work, make people pay attention to your views and defend the idea of individual freedoms from the yoke of the state, you are an 'authority'. As for me, I worked and I interacted with the authorities; but I also spent considerably more time in the cooler than anyone and I certainly wasn't a 'squealer'; I conversed with the career criminals who ran camp life, but I never kowtowed to them in any way.

At the end of my stay in Chita, I had an interesting conversation with one of them. He was one of the more respected gang bosses in the criminal hierarchy and he had just been told he was being transported to the fearsome Blagoveshchensk camp, where people of his kind are taken to be broken. He knew what lay ahead and awaited it with open eyes, defending his individualistic world view, which I would describe as close to nineteenth-century-style anarchism. This was a very deep person, a man of strong will and convictions, despite not yet being 30 years old. He told me that in ordinary life, he and I would certainly have been enemies since my goals were the opposite of his, but now we were both battling against an unjust and oppressive state, simply using different methods to do so. I would say that his assessment pretty much summed up people's attitude towards me in the camp: I was an outsider, but one deserving respect.

In the hut where I was assigned a place, there were anywhere from 70 to 150 people at different times. Most didn't stay long – around three to six months before they were transferred. If someone came up to me openly and didn't get punished, I knew he was a 'spy' for the administration who wrote reports for the Security Section; anyone else would get sent to isolation. That was the way the camp administration thought they could 'keep me under control', by deciding who I could speak to and who would be allowed to be in my social circle.

In April 2006, two-and-a-half years into my sentence, I was woken in the night by the blow of a knife striking my head. I jumped up with blood flowing on to my mattress in time to see the man running away. He had wanted to stick the knife into my eye, but in the dark he missed and just slashed my face. He soon was transferred closer to the city of Chita where his family lived.

The prisoners who did the administration's bidding and came to spy on me were flawed people who had problems, real or imagined, with the rest of the inmates – and that meant they could be easily manipulated. One of these 'agents' was very afraid of another prisoner who was menacing him with terrible threats, including bodily harm. The authorities used this to blackmail him. The prisoner figured that the only way to get himself transferred to another camp was to try to stab me.

As for me, the authorities spotted their opportunity: this was the perfect pretext to put me in permanent solitary confinement. They made a camp announcement that Khodorkovsky was in fear for his life and had asked to be transferred to 'a safe place'. Of course, solitary is the opposite of a safe place; it is the direct road to the cemetery, both literally and figuratively. I knew I couldn't afford to let it happen so I decided to go down fighting.

I went on a 'dry' hunger strike – no food, no liquids – the second time I had done so. The first had been in the Matrosskaya Tishina prison in Moscow, after Platon Lebedev had been taken to the punishment cells and told he would never get out alive. I had fasted for six days before Platon was released and by then I was on the brink. When you go 'dry', your blood thickens and your blood pressure shoots up. Mine reached 180 and the doctors said the next thing on the horizon would be blood clots and a stroke. But the advantage is that this forces the authorities to make quick decisions. You're at risk of dying as early as the third day and almost no one survives more than ten, while the usual 'wet' hunger strike gets dangerous only after 30–60 days.

This time, I found it particularly tough going. Evidently, my health wasn't that good any more. By the fourth day, I couldn't walk and I was fainting. When the doctor came, he informed me that the camp commander had accepted my demand. I was transferred to the infirmary, where I spent several days trying to put my body right.

When Putin brought new charges against me in February 2006 and I was recalled to prison, the head of the camp operations department personally carried all my belongings to the transport. He even brought a mattress and a blanket. We parted on companionable terms. His last words were, 'Just don't come back!'

The overall changes to the gulag system since the days of Stalin are enormous. For a start, no one is deliberately starved any more. There were and are still instances of people dying from lack of food; in the early 2000s, there were even entire de facto 'hunger camps', but these are the result of conflicts on the ground, mismanagement or corrupt officials stealing supplies, rather than official government policy.

Prisoners are not worked to death through slave labour any more. Sometimes there's even the opposite problem of camps with no work at all. In these places, prisoners become stupefied, like animals, and lose all their social skills (if they had them in the first place). Nowadays, no one is punished for not working, but attempts at escaping are punished very harshly.

The camp bosses can no longer kill a prisoner out of hand, as they used to in the past. Beating and torture can and does happen, but killing is prohibited. Doing so would require a massive amount of paperwork. This ban on killing, of course, gets broken just like any other ban, but the situation is very different from when camp officials had the unfettered right to kill their prisoners.

The living conditions are hard, but they are no longer murderous. For example, in winter they try to stop the temperature inside the barracks dropping below zero and they supply water, albeit cold, so prisoners can wash themselves and their clothes. It is 'trifles' such as these that make the difference between life and death.

But other things in the gulag have remained very much the same. In the camps, a prisoner is not a person; he is an animal, even though his value to his owner has increased significantly since the Stalin years. You can't kill him, but you can, and should, beat him. You can't starve him, but neither do you have to worry about the quality of his food. Neither do you need to worry about ethical considerations in the way you treat a prisoner: you can and should lie, deceive, play prisoners off one against the other and routinely show contempt. As always, there are exceptions. There are officials who wouldn't allow themselves to bully prisoners and there are prisoners who wouldn't allow themselves to be bullied. But it was like that in the old gulag, too. Back then, a prisoner's life was at stake, while now it's 'merely' his health and his chances of early release.

Health remains a 'second tier' priority in Russia and the quality of healthcare in society as a whole leaves much to be desired, so you can imagine how much worse it is in the camps. Personally, I was lucky on the two occasions when I needed healthcare. The first time I went under the knife, I had a military surgeon with a steady hand. The second time, when I needed to be sewn up after I was stabbed, by good luck the man who was listed as a dentist turned out to be a facial surgeon and now, thanks to him, the scar on my face is not noticeable. But my experience is the exception. More typical is the experience of a prisoner I knew who was viciously beaten. He was taken to a medical unit, which was just the other side of the fence from our hut, so in the evening I shouted through the barbed wire to ask how he was. Someone shouted back that he was not doing well and would probably die. The paramedics had applied first aid, but no one did anything else for him and now he was lying on his back, unconscious. I told the administration that if the man died, I wouldn't keep silent about it. An hour later, a doctor came from town. The telephone in the medical unit was not working, so the whole camp watched as the doctor had to run first to the control room and then wait for an ambulance to move him. We held our breath. He had a ruptured spleen and by the time he was put on the operating table he had lost more than two litres of blood from internal bleeding, but the prisoner was saved.

Today's gulag is survivable, although a person's place in the world of the camps depends on the individual. You mustn't allow yourself to be afraid. The result of doing that is a terrible life, and I am not exaggerating when I say that it can seem a fate worse than death. As for death, people do die inside, although not in alarming numbers.

The camps have their advantages over prison. You get to see the sun and you receive visits. You can have a family visit four times a year, each time for three days, and you spend it in a room that feels a bit like a provincial hotel. In prison, the only visits are by intercom, through glass and bars. In the camps, you get to see your mother, your wife or your daughter, and you can touch them, kiss them, hug them. Such bliss. The time flies by in an instant.

On the other hand, prison can destroy families. Only one in 20 prisoners get regular visits. Wives leave their husbands; children forget their parents. Within five years, most people have lost their support network. Outside the gates is a desert awaiting them, which is why returns are so common. Whoever created and perpetuated this system – their reasons are beyond me. Perhaps it's not done out of malice, simply through inertia, but the consequences are awful. A whole host of discarded people. Millions of families and lives destroyed. There needs to be a humane alternative that keeps hope alive. Everyone knows this, yet nothing changes.

For those inside the camps, there is the problem of the opposite sex. It is hardest for young prisoners aged between 18 and 35, especially those who have come from a camp for minors and have no real experience of a regular sex life. Those who are older don't suffer quite as much from its absence, possibly because of the stressful situation they are in. Inside, you can talk about these things quite calmly. Family is another matter. Family issues are a minefield that you tread on at your peril; talking about them can unleash the cruellest thoughts, depression, even suicide.

By and large, I didn't suffer from obsessive thoughts and memories or the sort of depression that afflicted many other prisoners. I can remember a few nights, though, when I couldn't sleep. This was especially true in the first year of my imprisonment when radio and TV channels were talking every day about my company being wrecked. All the lies and propaganda weighed on me. I had techniques to keep my mind under control. For example, I would start mentally writing a letter or building a house. I took pleasure in slowly 'furnishing' the room with imaginary furniture and appliances. I discovered that the best way to release the tension was by putting my thoughts on paper. I started writing theoretical speeches and letters and complaints. None of it was for public consumption. When you're getting things off your chest, it isn't for other people to read. And when you reread it much later, the writing may not be very good or coherent, but I have got into the habit of putting my thoughts on paper and I've become quite proficient at it. As a schoolkid who didn't like writing and usually asked my favourite girl friends to write my essays for me, this is an achievement.

I also took pleasure in practical things. Household chores are not a problem for me. Until I was 30, I did my own housework and washed my laundry, even when there was no hot water. Prison isn't home, but these skills help; and your relatives support you by sending you things that are allowed. The biggest problem is that you're not allowed to have a computer, so there's a lack of access to information. Not only up-to-the-minute information, but useful information in general. There's a limit on how many books you can take into prison, so having a lawyer coming in from time to time is invaluable.

Another skill that helped me in jail was the ability to concentrate on a task and block out unnecessary thoughts. For the full working day, eight hours or more, I made myself think in a disciplined manner about concrete, practical problems that I could actually do something about, and not to dwell on those I was powerless to tackle. I used to take short breaks and relax by thinking about something pleasant. And at the end of my working day, I switched off my brain by thinking positively about my family and friends. I liked to remember and daydream about seeing them again.

In some ways, prison is like a magnifying glass for observing social processes that are going on outside. When living standards fell sharply in Russia after 1998, prisoners were literally eating grass. Cases of dysentery were reputedly in the thousands. In my time in prison, I was struck by the number of illiterate young people I met, 20-year-olds completely unable to read or write. Then I was a witness to the shift in the population of Moscow's notorious Matrosskaya Tishina prison, when the usual deviants and street criminals were replaced en masse by people whose property had been stolen from them by raiders in uniform. I saw these people forced to sign documents giving up the right to their property and come out with or without sentences. And I saw crooked law enforcement officers who were sent to prison when conflicts broke out between agencies. In jail, despite all the limitations, much of what happens outside is plain to see.

Being in prison is akin to acquiring a sensory disability, where one failing sense is compensated for by the others becoming sharper. In place of absent external stimuli comes a greater sensitivity to the remaining ones, the hidden clues that betray people's real intentions. Those who have been in prison for a long time react more sharply to events and are much more sensitive to those around them. Prisoners released after a long spell inside say that, for the first few months, they can read people like an open book, until this acquired 'super-sensitivity' begins to fade. I experienced it myself.

Prison also distorts ethical standards, especially in young minds. While in normal life 95 per cent of people consider lying to be something that is bad, and cruelty to be abnormal, in prison this is not the case. You mustn't lie to 'your' people and you mustn't steal from them, but otherwise cruelty is the norm. Such rules apply not only in the criminal community; collaborators with the administration and the administration itself operate by the same standards. The camp is a big village, where everyone knows everything about everybody. Nothing can be hidden: the camp authorities divide and rule, setting you up, beating you in the punishment cell, buying services – and it's all done openly. Drug dealing is the only thing that takes place surreptitiously, even though everyone knows about the drugs and who uses what. In the camps, for example, there are bricks of hashish and marijuana, which nearly everyone smoked in season. It has a strange, sweet smoke, which is very particular. When I first arrived, I couldn't understand why people were behaving as if they were drunk.

Prison changed me. I reassessed my understanding of the importance of relationships with my family and loved ones. My understanding of the world evolved, too. I think it's noticeable in the articles I wrote while inside. Prison magnifies emotions, including outbreaks of anger or despair that periodically erupt. The question then becomes: can I control myself? And for me, luckily, the answer was yes. I felt despair and anger, but I kept a lid on it. That's how I am in most aspects of life. I found it helped to pour things on to paper, rather than on to those around me.

I have always found it hard to express my emotions. I was brought up with the belief that it's unseemly for a man to be sentimental. To poke fun – yes; sometimes even very sarcastically, including at myself, and especially at the powers that be. But never to show real, genuine emotions. I show emotions when I interact with my children; perhaps I'm a little more sentimental with my family and friends. But I almost never experience strong emotions outside of that circle. Neither the prosecutors nor Putin nor Sechin trouble my deepest emotions. They're like a rain shower in autumn: an unpleasant natural phenomenon, nothing more.

Some people say I'm a bit of a robot, and there may be some truth in that. My threshold for strong emotional engagement is high. For me to get angry, something really extreme has to happen. But, on the other hand, I am easily offended by cases of manifest injustice, even in small things. The initial hearing in our first trial at Moscow's Basmanny Court was a shock for me. People simply didn't listen.

I wanted to say, 'Wait a minute, where's your evidence for that? Haven't you dreamed it all up? Why does your word count more than mine? Why should I have to go to prison because of your paranoia?' But no one cares about your questions. The law in Putin's Russia consists of meaningless pieces of paper.

That upsets me. Sometimes, you feel as if you have been kidnapped by aliens. They aren't the enemy, they aren't fascists; they're just extra-terrestrials who happen to look like us, but having nothing whatsoever in common with human beings. You just have to accept that there's no way you can talk to them about anything. And that's how you calm yourself down. I started seeing prison, the courts and the investigators as some sort of natural phenomenon that could be studied with an objective eye, but to which it's pointless to respond emotionally.

What was harder to deal with was the unknown. Not what's happening to you personally, but what's going on at home, with your family and friends. Sometimes days or even weeks go by before you receive responses to questions you desperately want to have answered. There are plenty of hidden phones in prison, and for many they're a lifeline, but not everyone has access to them. I never did.

The authorities use psychological ploys. Your own destiny is kept secret from you, even in its tiniest details, which is a form of psychological torture. Why you've been summoned ... where they're taking you – no one will tell you. 'Take your things', 'Don't take your things', 'Bring your papers', 'Leave your papers behind', 'Put your coat on', 'Don't put your coat on'; all that deliberately keeps you guessing. If a document arrives concerning your case, they keep it back from you; you are only given it when the investigator comes to question you or your own lawyer brings it to you on a visit. The purpose is clear – so you don't have time to prepare or consult.

The endless, humiliating searches get you down at first, but you slowly become used to them. They happen up to six times a day and of course it's bad. But the bar of human dignity has been lowered. If you don't want to sink under the weight of it all, you have to make yourself fight in your heart for every little thing. You need to push yourself: regular exercise, cleanliness, daily work, politeness in dealing with every person. It may all seem obvious, but it isn't obvious when the authorities try, year in, year out, to break you through hopelessness and the prospect of oblivion, and the repellent prison practices that wear you down.

Prison makes conversation more important than it is on the outside. Conversation on all manner of topics. There is a premium attached to people who can speak about the law. Very few prisoners have their own lawyers, and the state-appointed ones aren't worth much, so a prisoner who knows the law and doesn't mind sharing his knowledge is much in demand. I did this myself. The 'professional' consultations I used to provide weren't very complicated; they didn't need to be. The majority of Russian judges know the criminal code, criminal procedure and a few Supreme Court rulings. But even this much they don't know very well. It means it's easy to predict their mistakes. Spotting flaws in a prisoner's verdict can give him reasonable grounds for an appeal and make him very grateful. I would say that in two cases out of three you can find something in any sentence that you can latch on to so they can demand a review. Many cases give you a nasty feeling when you read them, while others make you wonder if the people making the judgements are living in another reality. It doesn't take long to figure out what is truth and what is lies. For the majority of professional judges, it's not a secret either; it's just not in their interest to say anything about it.

In prison, you have to put all of this into perspective. And you have to stay calm. Prison allows for introspection and a deeper analysis of external reality. The pace of life slows down. It's a curious paradox – every day drags on slowly, but weeks, months and years fly

In prison, with pen and notebook

Former Yukos lawyer Vasily Aleksanyan sits in court

by. One thing I learned in prison that I did not have before is patience. When I was free, an hour seemed a long time; but in prison, it's a moment. Prison lets you go deeper into your thoughts. The quality of concentration is absolute. My ten years inside were a chance to think, to read and to learn. I thought about myself and my family, my life and my beliefs; I thought about Russia and what my country stands for. I read Solzhenitsyn, but I didn't take any great inspiration from him – I felt these were the writings not of a fighter, but of an opportunist. I would never condemn someone whose aim is survival and who writes about surviving as an achievement. I simply didn't find it inspiring. Vasily Grossman and Varlam Shalamov, on the other hand, I found full of integrity, if also very harsh. You read them and you know that these are people whose example you want to follow; they make you want to keep on fighting.

I felt responsible for my friends and colleagues who were arrested with me and who were suffering in captivity. Vasily Aleksanyan, our former Yukos lawyer, was diagnosed with AIDS in prison and the authorities denied him life-saving drugs unless he agreed to testify against me. Vasily refused to perjure himself and I again went on dry hunger strike to demand he be transferred to hospital. The demand was met after ten days, but it was too late – they let him out just in time for him to die in freedom. Despite the efforts of his family and friends, Vasily Aleksanyan fell victim to the vindictiveness of the system. Just like Sergei Magnitsky, the Hermitage Capital tax adviser who perished in police custody, my friend was the victim of a ruthless state apparatus.

• • •

After an international outcry and the intervention of Western politicians including Angela Merkel and Hans-Dietrich Genscher, I was released in December 2013 and put on a plane to the West. I was able to meet my young granddaughter for the first time and to spend time with my parents. It was an emotional moment. My mother had fallen ill while I was in jail and she died soon after my release.

It is clear that Putin wanted to release me, not least because keeping me in jail was making him look bad in the eyes of the world, but because he also wanted to brush up his image ahead of the Sochi Winter Olympics in February 2014.

How did I feel when I was released? Joy to see my family was the predominant emotion. And it was nice to eat proper food again. As for things that surprised me, I'd say the power of social media was the biggest shock. I read a lot when I was inside, so I had a theoretical understanding of everything that was happening, even of iPhones; but the whole phenomenon of social media in practice was a culture shock. Nothing prepared me for the extent of the influence it has had on humankind. Technology had made communication so fast and so efficient.

I kept a diary while I was in prison, but I don't go back and read it, and I have neither the time nor the desire to continue writing diaries now. I don't have bad dreams and I don't have flashbacks to my time in jail – luckily, I'm calm about it all. Of course, I've read the stories about Putin's FSB assassins coming to the West to murder people that their boss doesn't like. I've never had the sense that I'm being followed, but I understand perfectly well that if Putin gives the order to have me removed, I will be. What else can I say? I suppose that since everyone knows I am one of his most prominent personal enemies, having me killed would be a very obvious and public gesture on his part. I don't know if that would stop him; maybe it wouldn't – he has been pretty brazen about these things. But let's hope that some rules of the game remain in play.

I have made an effort to use my experiences for positive ends. I redoubled my charitable activities and expanded my philanthropic

Reunited with my parents, Marina and Boris, and my son Pavel in December 2013

A woman shows her support for me during a rally in Moscow, 2007

organisation, Open Russia, which promotes civic values and the education of young people. Because Vladimir Putin views these values as a threat, the authorities harassed and threatened Open Russia with increasing vehemence. In the Russian presidential elections of 2018, and in all elections since, Open Russia supporters have played a big part in organising democratic opposition to the current regime.

Through a combination of vote rigging and the repression of independent political activity, including the banning of genuine opposition candidates, Putin has continued to win his Potemkin-style elections. There is anger within Russia and, increasingly, abroad too, at the contempt with which he treats the democratic process. In November 2021, the US House of Representatives bi-partisan Commission on Security and Cooperation in Europe – known as the Helsinki Commission – introduced a Congressional Resolution to end US recognition of Putin as the president of Russia, stating that any attempt by him to remain in office after the end of his current term in 2024 would be unconstitutional and illegitimate. In 2020, Putin rewrote the Russian constitution in order to abolish the legal ban on him serving yet another term as president, submitting the change to a plebiscite of voters that the Congressional Committee described as 'the most manipulated vote in the country's modern history'. 'Any attempt by President of the Russian Federation Vladimir Putin to remain in office beyond the end of his current and final term on May 7, 2024,' concluded the Commission, 'shall warrant nonrecognition on the part of the United States.' It struck a nerve. Putin's spokesman immediately condemned the resolution as 'aggressive meddling' in Russia's affairs and warned that if Congress were to endorse the Commission's wording, it would cause 'a rupture in relations between Russia and the United States'.

PART THREE
EAST AND WEST

CHAPTER 13
ENEMY AT THE GATES

When I came to live in London after my release from Vladimir Putin's prison camps, I knew I would not be returning to my homeland anytime soon. It made me sad, but I have always been a person who tries to make the best of his situation and minimise futile regrets. I already spoke a little English, but now I decided I must properly master the language of my new host country – something I am still working on. Like all students, I regarded television as an important tool. I watched the BBC news, dramas, thrillers, comedies and anything that could help my spoken English. One programme that caught my attention was the weekly quiz show *Have I Got News for You*. Some of the jokes between the panellists were hard for me to understand, but they were discussing the events of that week's news, which gave me the key to what was going on. Having arrived from a country in which criticism of the authorities leads to unfortunate consequences (a similar Russian TV show was banned for mocking

Putin), I was glad to see the freedom with which *Have I Got News for You* poked fun at the people in power. But what really struck me were the programme's opening titles, in which cartoon figures acted out recent news stories.

About halfway through the titles, they showed an evil-looking Russian man in a fur hat and military greatcoat grinning wildly as he closed down a pipeline carrying gas and oil to the West, followed by a sequence in which Western Europe is plunged into darkness. It was so far removed from the self-image that Russians have of themselves that I jumped out of my chair.

The vast majority of Russians regard their country as peaceful and well-intentioned, a force for goodness and moral behaviour. In their eyes, the villains and aggressors, the real culprits behind the deteriorating global situation, are in the West. It was the West that historically invaded Russian lands; and the Russian people have been constantly told that the West has now pushed NATO military forces eastwards to the Russian frontier.

At his annual news conference in December 2020, Vladimir Putin was asked if he, as president of Russia, bore any responsibility for the dangerous state of East–West relations. Asked if he felt Russia was 'whiter than white' in terms of culpability for the 'new Cold War', he replied angrily, 'By comparison with you [the West], yes we are! We are indeed whiter than white. We agreed to release from Soviet domination all those countries that wanted to live and develop independently. We heard your [the West's] promises that NATO would not advance eastwards to our borders, but you did not keep your promises!'

It can be shocking to discover that the other side has a very different view of us from that which we have of ourselves. It is a feature of the East–West standoff that we have developed distorted images of each other – stereotypical views that categorise others as villains while we ourselves are the 'good guys'. If we are ever going to break down the psychological barriers between us, we need to overcome these stereotypes, to replace prejudice with open-mindedness and blinkered thinking with greater self-awareness. We need to look at ourselves with the same fierce glare that we shine on 'the other'.

Is Russia Europe? This is an important issue that has been outstanding for several centuries. Geographically, Russia is undoubtedly Europe – 120 out of 144 million Russians live in the European part of our country. But from a cultural point of view, the answer is not so obvious. The question is an important one, because I believe the twenty-first century is an age of competition between civilisations: Euro-Atlantic, Islamic, Confucianist and so on. I happen to think that competition is good for the human race – it stops us stagnating and resting on our laurels. But competition also means struggle, the defence of one's own interests and the choice of allies.

In this context, Russia is the last undecided country with a kindred European culture. Note that I say 'kindred' – perhaps even sisterly – but not totally the same. We are part of the European family, and inter-family conflicts are often the most difficult. Russia has always felt an ideological threat from Western Europe, which, given other geographical realities, means the threat of destruction and chaos. At the same time, Western Europe was and remains for us the model of an ideal future, which we sometimes try to adopt for ourselves. Suffice it to say that the ideologies of socialism and communism came to Russia from Germany, Great Britain and France. In Russia, they resulted in a tyrannical socialist state, while Western Europe also adopted them to some extent, but without the tyranny. Throughout the eras of tsarist autocracy, Soviet rule and now the two decades of Putin's criminal gang, the West has been both an ideological enemy and the standard by which we measure ourselves. Every Russian recognises the old Soviet exhortation to 'catch up with and overtake the West' as the expression of our national inferiority.

Western Europe, on the other hand, has always felt threatened by Russia's huge size, by its incomprehensible vastness and its disorderly nature. The West has tried to organise us in its own way or to distance itself from us, always without success. The West created strange images of the Russians: Western intellectuals saw us as terrifying Dostoyevskian characters, unaware that many Russians regard Dostoyevsky as a depressive outsider with psychological problems and his characters as incomprehensible in their sufferings, about which we have no desire to read. On the contrary, anyone who is familiar with popular Russian art and crafts – Khokhloma wood painting, Palekh lacquer miniatures, Gzhel ceramics – knows that they are distinguished by their cheerfulness and romanticism.

The psychological conflict between our branches of the common European civilisation did not begin with Putin, and his departure will not in itself put a stop to it. Up to the end of the Soviet era of stagnation, the government was promoting anti-Westernism, so the Russian people naturally regarded being pro-Western as a sort of protest. But Russians have made the usual error of psychological transference, assuming that because we love the West, the West must love us, too. That was bound to be a mistake. The West was busy with its own problems and the reduction of the threat from the east was simply seen as an opportunity to do business without interference. Western speculators and failed businessmen came to Russia, projecting their own problems on us. Russians took them to be examples of what all Western people were like (just as the West took us all to be Dostoyevskys).

The love began to fade. The symbolic turning point in the relationship was when Primakov decided to turn back his plane over the Atlantic after the NATO decision to bomb Yugoslavia in 1999. Those bombs hit us Russians in our hearts and created Russia's version of our own Versailles syndrome. When Putin came to power, it allowed him to revive an anti-Western trope – that 'the only thing the West understands is force'.

For a few years during his internal evolution, Putin understood the danger of such an approach, but his desire to get re-elected for a third term – and the need to keep Medvedev in his place – made the perpetuation of the image of a Western 'enemy' inevitable. Putin's speech to the Munich Conference on Security Policy in 2007 was aimed at alarming the West, and also the Russian people: 'the enemy is at our gates', was his message to the domestic audience, 'This is no time for thinking about democracy.' The seed fell on fertile ground. The 2008 war with Georgia was the litmus test of this. The annexation of Crimea in 2014 and the invasion of the rest of Ukraine in 2022 signalled the beginning of a hybrid war with the West. It is no coincidence that Putin, according to several sources, chose Kiev at the start of the past decade to proclaim to his entourage that a Third World War was now inevitable, and he made the fateful decision to embark on a grandiose rearmament programme. The Russian economy and Russian society are now predicated on this concept. Russian foreign policy has been reoriented towards the east. Putin, in the spirit of Alexander Nevsky, is ready to sacrifice Russia's political independence in order to enlist China in opposing Western ideas. But there is a massive gap between the interests of the ruling criminal gang in the Kremlin and the interests of the country. The Russian people and Russia herself have no antagonistic conflicts with the West. There is competition and a desire to preserve our own identity, but there is a clear understanding that historically we belong to a common civilisation, and an acceptance and willingness to draw on it to define the vision of our future.

The problem is that Putin and his entourage are unable to accept this vision. Democratic values, human rights, transparency of business, compromises and the refusal to use force as a tool of coercion and competition – all this is not just ideologically unacceptable to them, it objectively jeopardises their power and therefore their existence. The current generation of Russians have a choice of what relationship we wish to build when Putin is gone. We must decide if we perpetuate the insane paradigm of the Cold War, the paradigm in which 'the only good [Russian] bear is a dead bear', or whether we find a way to live together; perhaps not even together, but at least in friendly proximity …

CHAPTER 14
MANAGED DEMOCRACY

People in the West are sometimes puzzled about the nature of power in Russia. There is a lack of clarity about how the political system works and whether Russia is a democracy. The Western media carry reports of votes and elections, opposition candidates and campaigns and debates; yet Vladimir Putin appears to go on and on, seemingly wielding power in the style of a tinpot dictator. Because of the confusion about these conflicting perceptions, it may be worth mentioning a few things that help to explain the reality behind the appearance.

Boris Yeltsin retained and expanded the democratic institutions introduced by Mikhail Gorbachev, including broadly free elections and an (initially) independent parliament. The 1993 constitution declared Russia a democratic, federative, law-based state with a republican form of government. State power is divided among the legislative, executive and judicial branches. Diversity of ideologies and religions is sanctioned, and a state or compulsory ideology may not be adopted.

The right to a multiparty political system is upheld. The content of laws must be approved by the public before they take effect, and they must be formulated in accordance with international law and principles. But the economic chaos of the 1990s led many Russians to lose faith in the free-market democracy Yeltsin had developed. He acknowledged this in his resignation speech, when he handed over the baton to Vladimir Putin in December 1999. As I touched on earlier, first indications were that the new man would continue to uphold the democratic values of his predecessor, as Putin pledged to preserve free and fair elections, freedom of speech, freedom of conscience, freedom of the media and private ownership rights.

An early sign of what Putin was actually planning came with a manifesto he published in 2000, titled *Russia at the Turn of the Millennium*. In it he pays lip service to democratic principles, but his warmest words are reserved for the personalised model of state power that he would go on to introduce in Russia. He describes the liberal reforms of the 1990s as a Western imposition that must be overthrown. 'The experience of the 90s vividly shows that our country's genuine renewal cannot be assured by an experimentation with models and schemes taken from foreign text-books. The mechanical copying of other nations' experience will not guarantee success … Russia cannot become a version of, say, the US or Britain, where liberal values have deep historic traditions.' Putin's questioning of 'liberal values' was contrasted with his praise for statist autocracy: in place of individual rights, a strong state and centralised authority. 'Our state and its institutions and structures have always played an exceptionally important role in the life of the country and its people … a strong state is not an anomaly to be got rid of. Quite the contrary, it is the source of order.'

To correct the mistakes of the 'Western' experiment, Putin said there would need to be a return to traditional 'Russian' values. Some of the values he listed evoked elements of Russia's authoritarian past.

Patriotism: Patriotism is the source of the courage and strength of our people. If we lose patriotism and national pride and dignity, we will lose ourselves as a nation. Belief in the greatness of Russia: Russia was and will remain a great power.

Statism: The Russian people are alarmed by the weakening of state power. They look forward to the restoration of the guiding and regulating role of the state.

Collectivism: Cooperative forms of activity have always prevailed over individualism. The collectivist mindset has deep roots in Russian society. The majority of Russians believe that the support of the state is the key to improving their prospects, not individual effort and entrepreneurialism.

The New Russian Idea: The New Russian Idea will come about as an amalgamation of universal principles with traditional Russian values.

When I read Putin's manifesto in 2000, I was struck by the similarity of his 'Russian' values to the founding principles of Alexander III, the most repressive of the later Romanovs, who decreed that the state must be built on *Pravoslavie, Samoderzhavie, Narodnost* – Orthodoxy, Autocracy and the Nation. Putin's downplaying of individual enterprise and his insistence on the supremacy of the state appeared to me alarming and backward looking. Even the name he chose for his model of state power – the New Russian Idea – was redolent of old thinking. The 'Russian Idea' was first introduced to the West by the philosopher Vladimir Soloviev at the end of the nineteenth century to denote Slavophile anti-Westernism, and a belief in Russian cultural supremacy. The 'Russian Idea' was one of Russian exceptionalism, the conviction that Russia has been chosen to play a special role in the history of civilisation, with a unique identity that points her to a different path from the rest of the world, in opposition to the liberal, individualistic freedoms of Western Europe.

In Putin's version of 'The Russian Idea', the powerful state is identified with a powerful leader; national unity is embodied in and represented by a single collective spokesperson: the president. His claim that the Yeltsin years had been an unwelcome aberration, and the experiment with Western-style government proof of Russia's unsuitability to such a system, appealed to some sectors of public opinion, including those who recognised Putin's message that Russia becomes ungovernable without a strong state to impose order. A 'strong state' might have been justified in the transitional period needed to build a free civil society, but a free civil society never got built. And Putin's supporters gave 'The Russian Idea' a new, added dimension: the notion that only Vladimir Putin could guarantee stable governance was so widely repeated and promoted that, like Louis XIV, he came to believe *l'état c'est moi* – the state is me. When Putin's chief of staff, Vyacheslav Volodin, said in 2014, 'there is no Russia today if there is no Putin', it was not a joke, but a consecration of the one-man state.

Along with reimposing law and order, Putin pledged to return Russia to her former standing as a world power. Boris Yeltsin had viewed the dismantling of the Soviet empire as his greatest achievement, a liberation of independence-seeking republics that would allow Russia to re-join the global community of nations; but Putin described the demise of the USSR as 'the biggest geo-political tragedy of the century'. He berated the West for humiliating Russia and for expanding NATO to Russia's frontier. He would strive to offset domestic economic decline and his own falling poll numbers by foreign adventurism, including the annexation of Crimea and the fomenting of revolts in eastern Ukraine and elsewhere.

Putin would restore a semblance of economic stability, albeit with sluggish rates of growth and pitiably low income levels. But these modest successes were accompanied by the abandonment of the democratic reforms of the Yeltsin years. It was these reforms that had created the economic growth which, together with the rise in oil prices, allowed Putin to strengthen his hold on power. Having consolidated his position, however, he turned the clock back. Under Putin, the powers of parliament have been weakened and those of the president enhanced. Opposition parties suffer discrimination and harassment; they are excluded from the media; political rallies are broken up and protestors jailed. Freedom of the press has been restricted; the legislature, the courts and most of the media – including television news – are once again controlled by the Kremlin.

This is what Putin calls 'managed democracy'. In reality, it is not democracy at all; Russia is governed by *imitation* democracy. Putin's simulacrum of democracy shows the Russian people and the West the facade of democratic structures, but behind it there is nothing. One of our most perceptive political commentators, Lilia Shevtsova of the Carnegie Moscow Center, describes it very accurately:

The external wrappings of democracy are present: elections, parliament and so on, but the essence is absolutely different. In the Russian case, we are dealing with … the deliberate use of democratic institutions as Potemkin villages in order to conceal traditional power arrangements … The political regime that has consolidated itself resembles the 'bureaucratic authoritarianism' of Latin American regimes in the 1960s and 1970s. It has all the characteristics: personalised power, bureaucratisation of society, political exclusion of the populace … and an active role for the secret services (in Latin America it was the military).

For much of the early 2000s, Putin continued to call himself a democrat, while suggesting that the suppression of some civil liberties was justified by the need to restore state control. 'Russia is in the midst of one of the most difficult periods in its history,' he wrote. 'For the first time in the past two or three hundred years, it is facing the real danger of sliding to the second, if not third, echelon of world states. We are running out of time to avoid this.' Putin's swagger on the international stage won him support from those Russians who yearned for a strong leader to restore national prestige after a decade of weakness. He pandered to nostalgia for the days of Soviet belligerence by reinstating the Soviet national anthem (albeit with new words) and military parades through Red Square with convoys of missiles and tanks and marching regiments shouting 'Hurrah!' to their president. Putin's picture was hung in schoolrooms and public buildings. He acquired a taste for pomp and ceremony, making regal entrances along red carpets with trumpets blaring.

His personality cult has become reminiscent of that of Stalin. He now appears in military uniform at army and naval bases, piloting a fighter plane into Chechnya or standing beside a tank, tranquillising a Siberian tiger, driving a Formula One car, diving to recover antique treasures from the seabed, shooting a whale with a crossbow, scoring unopposed goals in ice-hockey games, even flying a microlight to guide migrating cranes on their journey to the south. When a photoshoot of the shirtless president boosted his standing among female voters, he was delighted; when it was co-opted with ribald comments by Russia's gay websites, he was furious. The newspaper *Komsomolskaya Pravda* splashed the he-man photos under the headline 'Be Like Putin!' and a pop song titled 'Putin Is a Man of Strength' shot up the charts.

Vladimir Putin strutting his stuff in Tuva, 2007

There have been sarcastic suggestions that it might soon be time for St Petersburg to be renamed Putinburg.

The adulation inflated Putin's self-importance; slights to his dignity, even constructive criticism, were met with vengeful punishment. When the *Kursk* nuclear submarine sank in the Barents Sea in August 2000, he didn't return from his summer holiday; when the vessel was finally lifted, all 118 of those on board were dead. When the ORT television channel voiced criticism of the *Kursk* operation, its controlling owner Boris Berezovsky was targeted by the Kremlin and soon found himself in exile. Vladimir Gusinsky, the owner of another independent television channel, NTV, was arrested and held in jail until he agreed to hand over his business interests to the state, and then expelled from the country.

A January 2018 report for the Foreign Relations Committee of the US Senate, titled 'Putin's Asymmetrical Assault on Democracy', summed up the very *un*democratic means by which he gained and now maintains his hold on power:

> Vladimir Putin gained and solidified power by exploiting blackmail, fears of terrorism, and war. Since then, he has combined military adventurism and aggression abroad with propaganda and political repression at home, to persuade a domestic audience that he is restoring Russia to greatness and a respected position on the world stage. All the while, he has empowered the state security services and employed them to consolidate his hold on the levers of political, social, and economic power, which he has used to make himself and a circle of loyalists extraordinarily wealthy … Putin's overarching domestic objectives are to preserve his power and increase his net worth.

The senators describe Putin's model of state power as 'authoritarianism secured by corruption, apathy, and an iron fist'; but they are careful to note that this is not the fault of the Russian people, who should not be tainted by the crimes of the regime that rules over them. Put simply, *Putin is not Russia and Russia is not Putin.*

All anti-democratic regimes fear independent scrutiny; the illegitimate nature of their right to rule makes them unwilling to countenance open debate, so they move to suppress it. Putin has done so through intimidation and violence, backed up by fabricated legal restrictions and administrative penalties. Legislation introduced in 2005, then reinforced in 2012, banned foreign NGOs from operating in Russia, as well as any native organisation deemed by the Kremlin to be a 'threat to the national interest'. Scores of groups have been shut down, including nearly all of those monitoring human rights and democracy.

Civil society activists have been subjected to abuse and physical attacks. Politically motivated prosecutions against myself and other critics of Putin's leadership, with concocted charge sheets, automatic guilty verdicts and 'exemplary' sentences, were a signal to others that speaking out carries great risk to one's personal wellbeing. Smear campaigns, fake sting operations and lies have been used to demonise political opposition figures, with the pro-government media characterising criticism as disloyalty and critics as traitors. In February 2015, the leading political activist and former deputy prime minister Boris Nemtsov was shot dead within sight of the Kremlin walls, following a concerted campaign of vilification against him. Nemtsov had been organising protests against the Kremlin's economic mismanagement and was due to release a report on Russia's interference in Ukraine.

At the same time, Putin has cosseted institutions willing to support the Kremlin and speak on its behalf. While harassing genuine political opposition, he has created 'rubber-stamp' parties that play the game of providing ersatz competition in bogus elections. He has granted the Russian Orthodox Church special recognition under Russian law, while targeting other religions with onerous registration processes and restrictions on proselytising. The Orthodox Church's hierarchy have benefited from presidential grants and the restitution of property forfeited under communist rule. In return, the Church has bestowed its blessing on Putin and promoted his policies as a willing instrument of the Russian state. Patriarch Kirill has declared Putin's reign a 'miracle of God' and given thanks that he has corrected the 'deviation' of Russia's flirtation with liberal democracy. In February 2012, Church and state cemented their alliance with a shared paroxysm of righteous indignation after the rock group Pussy Riot performed their 'Punk Prayer' in Moscow's Cathedral of Christ the Saviour.

Virgin Mary, Mother of God, banish Putin!
Banish Putin, banish Putin!

The priest's black robes have epaulettes,
And all parishioners crawl and bow.

Liberty's a phantom, gone to heaven,
Gay-pride's in chains in Siberia now.

The KGB chief, their holy saint,
Leads protesters to prison vans.

Women, don't offend His Holiness!
Stick to making love and babies.

Shit, shit, this God stuff is all shit!
Shit, shit, this God stuff is all shit!

Pussy Riot perform their Punk Prayer at Moscow's Cathedral of Christ the Saviour

Virgin Mary, Mother of God, be a feminist!
Be a feminist, be a feminist!

The Church now praises corrupt dictators,
A cross-bearing procession in black limousines.

... The Patriarch believes in Putin!
Mary, Mother of God, join in with our protest!

Patriarch Kirill was the first to fulminate against Pussy Riot's lese-majesty. 'The Devil has laughed at all of us,' he thundered. 'We have no future if we allow such mockery ... if people think this is acceptable as some sort of political expression.' In response to calls for mercy to be shown to the women, Kirill refused, saying that hearing Orthodox believers ask for such indulgence made his 'heart break with bitterness'. Putin followed up with more outrage, planting the thought that Pussy Riot were the agents of hostile foreign powers sent to undermine Russia's moral fibre. Russia, he said, must look to its traditional spiritual values, 'to the power of the Russian people with Russian traditions ... and absolutely not the realisation of standards imposed on us from outside'. A couple of months later, he signed a new law that made it a criminal offence to 'insult the feelings of religious believers', punishable by fines and up to three years in prison. The three Pussy Riot women could count themselves lucky that they 'only' got two years in jail for 'hooliganism motivated by religious hatred'.

Pussy Riot's cathedral performance came at a difficult time for Putin. Allegations of fraud in the legislative elections of 2011 had sparked large street protests opposing his return to the presidency, which was scheduled for May 2012. Demonstrations in Moscow, St Petersburg and other cities had coalesced into a self-named Bolotnaya or 'Snow' Revolution, conjuring memories of the successful Orange

Revolution against Ukraine's pro-Moscow government. Crowds chanting 'Russia without Putin!' were an ominous signal of discontent. The Kremlin declared the protesters traitors to the motherland and bussed in pro-government supporters to mount counter rallies. Fast-track legislation was introduced to increase penalties for unsanctioned demonstrations and other infringements of public assembly regulations. Putin's response to the protests was a sharp turn to the conservative right.

The cultivation of the Orthodox Church allowed him to appeal to the anti-liberal values of many believers, while 'Western immorality' was loudly denounced. He pandered to traditional Russian homophobia by passing laws criminalising 'gay propaganda' and to male chauvinism by decriminalising domestic violence. The Orthodox hierarchy – which has no opinion on domestic violence, but considers homosexuality a sign of the Apocalypse – gave him their enthusiastic backing.

Putin framed the measures as a campaign to protect Russia's purity against outside efforts to corrupt her. 'The West knows no difference between good and evil,' he told the Valdai International Discussion Forum. 'They have rejected the Christian values that constitute the basis of Western civilisation. They deny moral principles and traditional identities: national, cultural, religious and even sexual … They are implementing policies that put normal families on a par with same-sex partnerships, belief in God with belief in Satan. The excesses of political correctness have reached the point where people are seriously talking about registering political parties whose aim is to promote paedophilia … And they are aggressively trying to export this model [to Russia]! This would open a direct path to degradation and primitivism, resulting in a profound moral crisis.'

Having served their jail sentences, the Pussy Rioters might have been expected to keep their heads down, but they failed to learn the lesson Putin had taught them and made an unscheduled appearance at the Sochi Olympics. Sochi was one of Putin's many self-aggrandising projects – he had spent over $50 billion of taxpayers' money to put on an international display of his success as Russia's leader – so, in February 2014, it was a natural target for dissent. Wearing their trademark fluorescent balaclavas, Pussy Riot hardly had time to sing the first verse of 'Putin Will Teach You to Love the Motherland' before a detachment of Cossack militia started to lash them with horsewhips.

Successive reports by international monitoring organisations reveal how rapidly the electoral process in Russia has been undermined since Putin came to power. Despite the upheaval of the 1990s, observers from the Organization for Security and Co-operation in Europe (OSCE) described Boris Yeltsin's final set of parliamentary elections, in December 1999, as 'competitive and pluralistic', marking 'significant progress for the consolidation of democracy in the Russian Federation'. Three years into the Putin era, the OSCE reported that the 2003 parliamentary vote 'failed to meet many Council of Europe commitments for democratic elections' and queried 'Russia's fundamental willingness to meet European and international standards for democratic elections'. The 2004 presidential election was marred by problems concerning the secrecy of the ballot and the biased role of the state-controlled media, with OSCE observers concluding that 'a vibrant political discourse and meaningful pluralism were lacking'. For the 2007 parliamentary elections, in which the pro-Putin United Russia party secured a two-thirds majority, and the 2008 presidential race, won overwhelmingly by Vladimir Putin, there was no monitoring because European Instrument for Democracy and Human Rights and OSCE observers were refused visas by the Kremlin. The Council of Europe called the 2008 poll 'more of a plebiscite', or a one-horse race, than a genuine exercise in democracy, because the Kremlin had disbarred Putin's only credible challenger, the former prime minister,

Pussy Riot's Nadezhda Tolokonnikova attacked by a Cossack with a whip during the Sochi Olympics in 2014

Mikhail Kasyanov, who had been dismissed by Putin in 2004. In subsequent elections, the OSCE has noted the increasing move towards a one-party state – 'the convergence of the State and the governing party' – and the absence of genuine choice for voters.

In addition to manipulating the vote, Putin has subverted legal norms to ensure his continued hold on power. Article 81 of the Russian constitution stipulates that the same person cannot hold the office of president for more than two terms. Having come to the end of his second stint in the job in 2008, he declared that the rule actually meant two consecutive terms, so he would temporarily swap jobs with his compliant prime minister, Dmitry Medvedev, before returning to the presidency in 2012. With his second set of consecutive terms due to end in 2024, Putin initially accepted that he would not be able to run for a fifth time, but later changed his mind. In July 2020 he rewrote the constitution and reset his term limit to zero, opening the way for him to appropriate two more presidential mandates and stay in the Kremlin until he is 83.

You will not be surprised to learn that the Russian people have discerned the truth behind the shenanigans and that electoral fraud figures high on the list of topics for the political jokes characteristic of our folk humour. My favourite is the story of the Kremlin lackey who rushes in to give Putin the results of the presidential election.

'Mr President, I have good news and bad news,' the lackey says.

'What is the good news?' Putin asks.

'You won the election,' comes the reply.

'And what is the bad news?'

'No one voted for you.'

CHAPTER 15
INTERNATIONAL OPERATIONS

Among the band of criminals who run Vladimir Putin's Kremlin, some stand out. Yevgeny Prigozhin has something of a personal connection to me. Prigozhin is Putin's trusted counsellor; in addition to advice, he provides many of the technical, logistical and military resources that Putin needs to impose his will. But the way in which Prigozhin attained such eminence is unusual: a street thief who served time in jail, he later became a caterer and food merchant, running a hot-dog stall in St Petersburg in the early 1990s. With the help of friendly local officials, he was able to open a restaurant, then a convenience store, eventually expanding his activities to become one of the city's most powerful operators, providing food for public bodies. This brought him into contact with the first deputy chairman of the St Petersburg city government, Vladimir Putin. Their partnership has endured for over a quarter of a century; and even now, with Prigozhin wielding influence in every area of Kremlin activity, he's still universally known as 'Putin's Cook'.

As I have mentioned, one of Putin's responsibilities during his time in St Petersburg was managing the relationship between the municipal authorities and special services and the city's organised crime groups. The Russian mafia wielded great power in St Petersburg in the lawless 1990s, to the extent that it was impossible for the authorities to control their activities. The only solution was to do deals with them, a task that the mayor entrusted to his deputy. Putin dealt with the worst elements of the St Petersburg underworld, so he probably didn't bat an eyelid when he learned that his associate, Yevgeny Prigozhin, also had a criminal record. Prigozhin served nine years in jail – covering most of the 1980s – for offences including robbery, burglary and fraud. Extracts from some of his convictions suggest a significant level of violence, with charges of assault and battery against young women. 'Prigozhin continued to strangle Ms Koroleva,' runs one graphic indictment, 'until the point at which she lost consciousness …'

It seems prudent to ask why a man with such a chequered past became, and still remains, an adviser to the Russian president. Prigozhin himself has used his position to pressure internet search engines to remove references to his criminal convictions, with some degree of success. In more recent times, his actions have been equally unsavoury, but now they are carried out at the behest of the Kremlin and bring him approbation rather than jail sentences. His Concord Management and Consulting Group has become a multi-billion-dollar company, with deals to provide school meals throughout the country, and to feed conscripts in the Russian army and patients in Russia's hospitals. Periodic outbreaks of dysentery caused by contaminated food have not persuaded Putin to terminate Concord's contracts, and investigations of fiscal impropriety have been discreetly shelved.

More worrying than run-of-the-mill corruption, however, are Prigozhin's international activities. A number of reputable news outlets have reported that Prigozhin finances a group of outfits collectively

Yevgeny Prigozhin serves Vladimir Putin at a banquet near Moscow in November 2011

known as the Wagner Private Military Company (Wagner PMC), a secretive organisation of mercenaries that carry out missions dictated by the Kremlin. Prigozhin has denied any links and gone as far as to use the English courts to try and sue those who repeated and adopted the allegation. Wagner first came to the world's attention in 2014, when Vladimir Putin's illegal seizure of the Crimean peninsula was preceded by the appearance of groups of unmistakeably military men wearing unmarked uniforms and staying largely in the shadows. Their self-effacing behaviour earned them the nicknames 'polite people' and 'green men', but their mission was to prepare the way for a brazen land grab that trampled on the norms of international law. The same 'green men' were later spotted in eastern Ukraine, supporting pro-Moscow separatist rebels, and in Syria, fighting alongside government troops loyal to Bashar al-Assad.

The Kremlin has denied any ties to them, claiming that they were private individuals who happened to be 'on holiday' in Crimea. When investigative journalists established that many of them had served in or had connections with the Russian special forces, Moscow said they were all 'retired' and must have travelled to the war zones off their own bat. Mercenary groups are illegal in the Russian Federation, but Wagner PMC troops have an impressive habit of turning up wherever the Kremlin seeks to exert its influence. And it isn't always the interests of the Russian state that Wagner PMC is sent to support: more often than not, it seems that Putin and his cronies use its resources to further their own venal objectives. Prigozhin is, we are told, the tool they use, not the instigator – his strings, according to some people, are pulled by Putin's 'personal banker', Yuri Kovalchuk.

Not all of Wagner's activities have been successful. In early 2018, a dozen Russian military operatives were killed in US airstrikes against Syrian pro-government forces in the east of the country. The world expected the Kremlin to react with fury at so many Russian deaths; but Moscow was silent, evidently embarrassed at having to admit that 'volunteer' Russian forces were taking part in military operations abroad.

Also in 2018, Wagner PMC mercenaries began work in the Central African Republic (CAR), where Moscow was hoping to extend it political and military influence, displacing the former colonial power, France. Wagner's brief was to train the CAR army, in return for which another of Prigozhin's companies, Lobaye Invest, was granted lucrative diamond mining rights. I provided funding for a group of Russian filmmakers that was travelling to the CAR to investigate Wagner's operations. In July 2018, the TV journalists Alexander Rastorguyev, Orkhan Dzhemal and Kirill Radchenko tried to film a camp where Russian mercenaries were based. Shortly afterwards, their vehicles were ambushed and all three of them were killed. An inquiry by local authorities concluded that the murders were the work of 'robbers', an explanation that was immediately supported by the Kremlin. But investigations by the Dossier Center, my fact-checking media organisation dedicated to probing the Kremlin's illegal activity in Russia and beyond, uncovered a darker story: the journalists had been lured to a secluded spot by a fixer connected to Prigozhin's employees and the alleged robbers had stolen nothing after murdering them. The Dossier Center concluded that 'the murder was premeditated and carried out by professionals … following carefully planned surveillance.' Its report indicated that Wagner employees had obstructed the inquiry into the men's deaths by destroying evidence, and when a CNN reporter travelled to the CAR to investigate further, she too was followed and harassed. There is no evidence to suggest that the murders of the journalists were instructed by Prigozhin.

Western experts estimate that Prigozhin commands a force of around 5,000 troops, former regular soldiers and special forces veterans, who have become Putin's unofficial and usually invisible army.

Funded and deployed by the Kremlin to countries as far away as Libya, Sudan and Mozambique, they enjoy almost total impunity, gaining a reputation for ruthlessness and cruelty. The investigative Russian newspaper, *Novaya Gazeta*, obtained video footage of Wagner operatives torturing and executing a Syrian deserter. And in the CAR, a United Nations report accused Wagner-deployed mercenaries of human rights abuses, including the random shooting of civilians, extrajudicial executions, gang rape and torture. Britain, like several other Western countries, has added Prigozhin to its sanctions list, citing his 'responsibility for significant foreign mercenary activity and multiple breaches of UN arms embargos'.

Rather than deny the charges against him, Prigozhin chooses instead to intimidate and threaten those who question his illegal activities. When Prigozhin was challenged by Alexei Navalny's Anti-Corruption Foundation, he successfully sued in the pliant Russian courts, promising to 'ruin' Navalny as he lay in a coma after a state-sponsored Novichok poisoning.

It was Yevgeny Prigozhin who, in March 2021, offered half a million dollars to any Russian who would kidnap me back to Russia. This action fits the same pattern. Angered by my support for the Dossier Center and its investigation into his African machinations, he made a series of inflammatory public statements about me, none of which bore any relation to the truth. Yevgeny Prigozhin is not interested in the truth, of course, but he is interested in deflecting attention away from himself and – in this instance – from an announcement a few weeks earlier that the American authorities had issued a warrant for his arrest. The FBI had accused him and 12 other Kremlin operatives of 'involvement in a conspiracy to defraud the United States … for the purposes of interfering with the US political system, including the 2016 Presidential Election'. The charges detailed Prigozhin's role in the Kremlin's cyber-hacking campaign to undermine Hillary

Clinton's election bid and the FBI was offering a $250,000 reward for information leading to his conviction.

When I was asked about the case by journalists from the Moscow Echo radio station, I said that Prigozhin seemed to be facing quite serious allegations that should be properly resolved by an open and impartial legal process. I expressed the hope that such issues might one day be addressed by an independent judiciary in the territory of Russia. Prigozhin's response was typical. 'I am a patriot and a good guy; and Khodorkovsky is a villain! He is a former oligarch who bribed the country's top leadership in the 1990s and stole huge funds from the people … The American charges against me are for non-existent crimes, but Khodorkovsky killed people in large numbers!' Asked why he thought it was he, rather than Khodorkovsky, who was being accused by the FBI, Prigozhin gave an enigmatic answer: 'I am a scapegoat for the US authorities to cover up the massive gap between the deep state and the [American] people … the only way I will ever go to jail in the United States is if some traitor in [Russian] law enforcement decides to betray the motherland. Luckily, I don't think that is a real possibility in Russia, because in our country there are many, many more patriots than there are liberals willing to take dirty money from the West.'

Anti-Western invective has become the go-to excuse for anything that reflects badly on Putin's Russia. For many Russians, this rhetoric is enough to convince them that the motherland is under attack from hostile Western forces and that the patriotic response is to rally to the support of the Kremlin.

• • •

In early 2018, I was invited to the hearings organised by the US Republican Party, at which Mark Zuckerberg was asked how Facebook was dealing with the threat of fake news. His answer was that people should be provided with honest information and this would allow them to figure out the truth for themselves.

In his subsequent speech to the US Senate in April that year, Zuckerberg admitted that fake news was being used as a tool by agents acting on behalf of Vladimir Putin's Kremlin to influence people's thinking in the battle between the Kremlin and the West, and that Facebook and other platforms had been hijacked.

> We build technical tools to try to identify when people are creating fake accounts – especially large networks of fake accounts, like the Russians have – in order to remove all of that content ... But it's clear now that we didn't do enough to prevent these tools from being used for harm, as well. And that goes for fake news, for foreign interference in elections, and hate speech, as well as developers and data privacy.

Putin's propagandists were promoting conspiracy theories and anti-Western paradigms, driving them into people's minds by the ruthless use of fake accounts, fake postings and fake activist groups, amplified exponentially through the power of social media. Because Western democracy was itself in crisis, beset by doubt and self-questioning, it proved singularly vulnerable to the Kremlin's subversion. Putin was able to use the disputes and conflicts that were dogging politics in the West, fanning extremist rhetoric and promoting radical views.

In all of this, Putin's chief lieutenant was Yevgeny Prigozhin. In the months leading up to the US presidential election of November 2016, Prigozhin had been orchestrating the Kremlin's efforts to trash Hillary Clinton's campaign and manipulate American voters into backing Donald Trump, who the Kremlin was not convinced could win. The aim was to discredit the US electoral system and, if possible, foment civil conflict by accusing the Clinton campaign of dirty tricks. It was a role in which Prigozhin seemed to take great delight but, as would later become clear, US intelligence officials had been tracking Prigozhin's own dirty tricks and knew full well what he was up to. So, when they switched on their TV sets on the morning of 1 June 2016, they most likely exploded with indignation. Standing in front of the White House, in the very spot where the international press corps train their cameras, an individual was holding up a banner bearing the words, 'Happy 55th Birthday Dear Boss'. The images had already been transmitted worldwide before the DC Police Department was despatched to the scene. According to their deposition, the 'real US person' holding up the banner had been 'informed by the defendants and their co-conspirators' that the sign was 'for someone who is our leader and our boss ... our founder'. Knowing that Yevgeny Prigozhin's birthday was 1 June 1961, and learning that the 'co-conspirators' who commissioned this person to carry out the stunt were Russian, the FBI and the CIA realised that their number one adversary in the murky world of cyber warfare was thumbing his nose at them.

We know about Prigozhin's little jibe thanks to the FBI or, more exactly, the sixth director of the FBI, Robert Swan Mueller III. Bob Mueller was tasked with investigating the covert subversion carried out by Vladimir Putin's Kremlin against the American people and the American system of electoral democracy – and he did his job so well that he uncovered absolutely everything, including the 'real US person' who stood outside the White House with a banner congratulating Yevgeny Prigozhin on his birthday, as well as the 16 'defendants and their co-conspirators', all of whom had Russian names. Chief among them was Prigozhin.

The Mueller Report arose from an FBI investigation of alleged links between Donald Trump and the Kremlin. Operation Crossfire Hurricane had been triggered by claims that Russian agents were offering to supply the Trump campaign with information damaging to Hillary Clinton. The FBI established that the 'damaging information' consisted of emails hacked from the account of the Democratic Party in the same month as Prigozhin's 2016 birthday stunt.

By the end of that year, Trump had won the presidency and did everything in his power to halt the investigation, including firing the FBI's director and deputy director; but Congress voted to pursue the inquiries and Bob Mueller was appointed special counsel in charge of them. In May 2017, the remit of the inquiry was widened to include all forms of Kremlin interference in the presidential election, allegations of coordination between the Trump campaign and the Russian government, and the US president's alleged obstruction of justice. In pursuit of his brief, Mueller would issue 2,800 subpoenas, execute 500 search warrants and interview more than 500 witnesses. His report, delivered in March 2019, resulted in 34 indictments, including against former members of the Trump campaign, and 448 pages of lurid detail of what Vladimir Putin and his agents had been involved in. According to Mueller, the Kremlin's efforts to subvert the US electoral process began as long ago as 2014 and included the hacking and leaking of illegally obtained information, conspiracy-theory disinformation, coercive messaging and psychological operations, paid advertising, false-flag posts and information warfare. The aim of all the operations was to support the Trump campaign and undermine that of Hillary Clinton. Putin and the Russian Government, Mueller concluded, aspired to help President-elect Trump's election chances whenever possible.

I read one particular indictment generated by the Mueller inquiry with especial interest. The defendants in it were named as 'The Russian Internet Research Agency (IRA), its leadership and affiliates'. Issued in February 2018, its 37 pages read like a spy thriller and made clear that the inoffensive-sounding 'Research Agency' was in fact a hotbed of subversion, and it was run by Prigozhin.

Prigozhin's Internet Research Agency was founded in 2013 in a suburb of St Petersburg. It was paid for by money from Prigozhin's Concord catering conglomerate, a business entity described by Mueller as having 'various Russian government contracts' and which, as we have already seen, acts as a conduit for large-scale Kremlin funding of Putin's black operations. The IRA set about recruiting IT-literate employees, mainly young marketing and computer graduates, offering salaries far higher than those available elsewhere, and put them to work producing a flood of pro-Putin, anti-Western propaganda. The online comments of the IRA trolls – attacking foreign and domestic critics of the Kremlin, including myself, and accusing Western countries of repression at home and abroad – hit the internet with a tsunami of disinformation and bile. Putin's political opponents were mocked and slandered; the leaders of Ukraine were described as fascists and Nazis. Using bots and automated delivery algorithms, the IRA became so notorious that by 2014 it was widely referred to as the Troll Factory.

Prigozhin appointed three of his cronies to run the operation. Its chief executive was reported to be a former St Petersburg police officer, Colonel Mikhail Bystrov; its executive director, Mikhail Burchik, was a young tech entrepreneur; and its chief deputy director, Alexandra Krylova, had previously worked at Prigozhin's Federal News Agency. Between them they ran the IRA as a streamlined digital marketing firm, with departments generating editorial content, graphics and search engine data analysis, and trolling targets. They had an HR unit to oversee recruitment, staff incentivisation, finance and budgeting.

By the spring of 2014, the operation had nearly 1,000 employees and was expanding. A new unit, at first secretive but then widely touted within the organisation, was set up. The blandly named Translator Project was tasked with 'focusing on the US population and conducting operations on social media platforms such as YouTube, Facebook,

Instagram, and Twitter'. An internal IRA memo defined its remit as American electoral politics and its aim 'to spread distrust toward candidates and the political system in general'.

The Translator Project conducted research into American voting patterns, political campaigning and the demographics of party affiliation, coordinating with the Kremlin in defining the tasks that Vladimir Putin would set for them. As Robert Mueller would later report, the operation was always focused on the end goal of the 2016 presidential election, the political event that mattered more to Putin than any other: 'The conspiracy had as its object impairing, obstructing, and defeating the lawful governmental functions of the United States by dishonest means in order to enable the Defendants to interfere with US political and electoral processes, including the 2016 US presidential election.'

The Translator Project infiltrated groups dedicated to politics and social issues on US media sites, monitoring the popularity and engagement of online conversations, including the frequency of posts and the nature of comments or responses. Its employees adopted fake social media identities, pretending to be Americans, and the IRA's IT department set up a network of proxy servers to conceal the fact that they were posting from Russia. 'In order to collect additional intelligence,' Mueller reported, 'defendants and their co-conspirators posed as US persons and contacted US political and social activists', communicating with 'unwitting members, volunteers, and supporters of the Trump Campaign involved in local community outreach, as well as grassroots groups that supported then-candidate Trump'.

Translator Project operatives would eventually run hundreds of accounts with fictitious American identities, with the stated aim of becoming 'leaders of public opinion'. Working round the clock to hit all the US time zones, they were instructed to 'inflame political intensity through supporting radical groups, users dissatisfied with the social and economic situation, and oppositional social movements'. To that end, their pages on Facebook and Instagram fomented unrest about the Obama administration. Under the title, 'Secured Borders', one online group strove to fuel voters' anger at the Democrats' alleged failure to curb immigration. Another fanned the flames of racial discontent with a Black Lives Matter-style page titled 'Blacktivist'. Yet others appealed to old north–south resentments with groups named 'South United' and 'Heart of Texas' or targeted religious groups with pages such as 'United Muslims of America' and 'Army of Jesus'. United Muslims of America encouraged Muslims to boycott the elections because 'most of the American Muslim voters refuse to vote for Hillary Clinton'. And an IRA fake Instagram account titled 'Woke Blacks' declared, 'A particular hype and hatred for Trump is misleading the people and forcing Blacks to vote Hillary. We cannot resort to the lesser of two devils. Then we'd be surely better off without voting at all.'

The IRA's Twitter accounts that served as cheerleaders for Trump appeared to be authentically American, with like hashtags like @TEN_GOP, 'Tennessee GOP', and were retweeted by senior Trump officials including General Mike Flynn, Kellyanne Conway and Donald Trump Junior. By having each fake account repost, retweet and promote the content of the others, Prigozhin's trolls were able to amass hundreds of thousands of followers. 'Over time, these social media accounts became Defendants' means to reach significant numbers of Americans for purposes of interfering with the US political system,' Mueller's indictment says. 'They had the strategic goal to sow discord.'

Prigozhin's team decided on key messages and on key targets for their attack bots, pouring vitriol on Hillary Clinton and the Democrats, using all available means to boost the Trump campaign. English language specialists monitored the team's posts to 'ensure they appear authentic' and offered guidance on wording and visual content. A system of bonuses encouraged workers to make extra effort and compete with their peers. The monthly budget of Prigozhin's IRA was now estimated to be around $1.25 million.

When campaigning commenced for the 2016 election, the IRA took out fake political advertisements, paid for via a shadowy internet agency. As many as 10 million people viewed the ads, which promoted divisive political and social messages, supporting Trump and attacking Clinton. Not content with buying their own publicity, the trolls began opening counterfeit PayPal accounts in the names of unsuspecting US citizens, stealing their Social Security numbers and driving licence details to authenticate the payments. The accounts were used to purchase advertisements with messages like, 'Trump is our only hope for a better future', 'Support the Second Amendment', 'Hillary Clinton Doesn't Deserve the Black Vote' and 'Ohio Wants Hillary 4 Prison'. The IRA bosses instructed employees to 'use any opportunity to criticize Hillary and the rest (except Sanders and Trump – we support them) … it is imperative to intensify criticizing Hillary Clinton'.

Not satisfied with sowing discord over the internet, the Kremlin put agents on the ground. In the summer of 2014, Prigozhin instructed Alexandra Krylova and another IRA employee, the data analyst Anna Bogacheva, to apply for US visas, according to the indictment, in order 'to collect intelligence for their interference operations'. The women falsely stated that they were travelling to the US for personal reasons and concealed their place of employment. They equipped themselves with cameras, SIM cards and untraceable burner phones, agreeing on pre-planned 'evacuation scenarios' in case something went wrong. Between 4 and 26 June, Krylova and Bogacheva travelled through Nevada, California, New Mexico, Colorado, Illinois, Michigan, Louisiana, Texas and New York, for the purpose of what the indictment calls 'the collection of intelligence'.

With the election approaching, that intelligence was put to practical use. Pretending to be grassroots US activists, the IRA began organising political rallies in several states, building attendance through fake social media accounts and emboldening the administrators of political activist groups. Using the email address allforusa@yahoo.com, they distributed press notices promoting a 'March for Trump' in New York in June 2016, contacting rally organisers with an offer to 'give you money to print posters and get a megaphone'. The following month, they helped mount a rally in Washington, DC to promote false claims that Hillary Clinton planned to introduce Sharia law in the US, hiring people to carry banners with a picture of Clinton and the slogan, 'I think Sharia Law will be a powerful new direction of freedom.' They supported a 'Down with Hillary' rally later in July, sending out press releases to more than 30 media organisations and paying for Facebook ads. In August, they helped coordinate 'Florida for Trump' rallies, using their fake social media personas to communicate with Trump campaign staff. 'Florida is still a purple state,' they messaged via Facebook, 'and we need to paint it red … What about organizing a YUGE [*sic*] pro-Trump flash mob in every Florida town?' The ads got 8,300 likes, with users being clicked through to the IRA's fake Facebook page 'Being Patriotic.'

Mueller calculates that the IRA posted more than 80,000 items between 2015 and 2017, and that more than 126 million Americans viewed its propaganda. For the Florida rallies, they arranged for a lorry with a prison cage on it to join the parade, paying a local woman to appear as Hillary Clinton in prison uniform. At further events in New York and Pennsylvania, Mueller reports, the IRA paid protesters to join the rallies.

One of the most insidious – and most effective – tactics of Putin's trolls was to spread rumours of voter fraud. As a trial run, at the time of the Democratic primaries, the IRA posted fake reports that Clinton had somehow 'stolen' the Iowa caucuses from Bernie Sanders. Encouraged by signs of controversy and division among Democratic voters, Prigozhin repeated the trick by circulating allegations of illegal mail-in votes for Clinton in Broward County, Florida. The tactic found fertile ground. As far back as 2012, Donald Trump had made unfounded accusations that the election had been rigged by Barack Obama ('This election is a total sham and a travesty! We are not a democracy!') and in the summer of 2016 he was warning that the impending election was going to be rigged by Hillary Clinton. It was easy to prey on the fears of voters and Putin's campaign increased the atmosphere of unease. By the time of the 2020 election, the trope of voter fraud and stolen elections had become so ingrained in the American consciousness that Trump was able to convince many of his supporters that they had been 'robbed'. Putin and Prigozhin could congratulate each other that the group entrusted with sowing doubt and distrust in democracy had succeeded in the first phase of its mission.

It is evident from the Mueller Report that the IRA operated with remarkable self-confidence. Its directors knew from the US media that the FBI was tracking suspicious activity by Russian bots and trolls, but did nothing to scale back its operations. Not until the autumn of 2017, when Congress ordered Facebook, Twitter and Instagram to reveal the identities of suspect groups that had used their services, did Prigozhin's operatives begin to panic. On 13 September, a senior IRA specialist, Irina Kaverzina, emailed a friend: 'We had a slight crisis here at work: the FBI busted our activity (not a joke) … so I got preoc-cupied with covering our tracks, together with colleagues.' As for the successful impact of her work, Kaverzina was in no doubt. 'I created all these pictures and posts,' she wrote, 'and the Americans believed that it was written by their people!' It was a taunt that was echoed by Prigozhin himself in February 2018, when the IRA was indicted by the FBI. 'The Americans are very impressionable people,' he commented

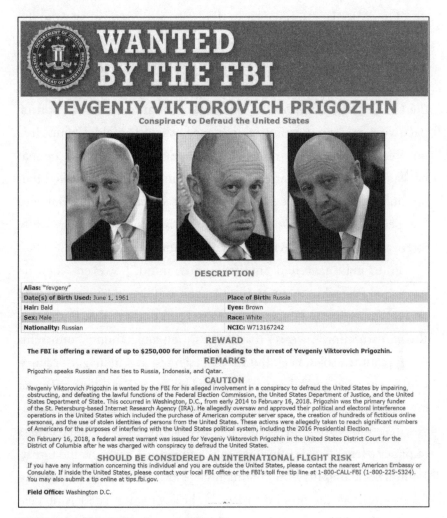

WANTED
BY THE FBI

YEVGENIY VIKTOROVICH PRIGOZHIN
Conspiracy to Defraud the United States

DESCRIPTION

Alias: "Yevgeny"

Date(s) of Birth Used: June 1, 1961	**Place of Birth:** Russia
Hair: Bald	**Eyes:** Brown
Sex: Male	**Race:** White
Nationality: Russian	**NCIC:** W713167242

REWARD

The FBI is offering a reward of up to $250,000 for information leading to the arrest of Yevgeniy Viktorovich Prigozhin.

REMARKS

Prigozhin speaks Russian and has ties to Russia, Indonesia, and Qatar.

CAUTION

Yevgeniy Viktorovich Prigozhin is wanted by the FBI for his alleged involvement in a conspiracy to defraud the United States by impairing, obstructing, and defeating the lawful functions of the Federal Election Commission, the United States Department of Justice, and the United States Department of State. This occurred in Washington, D.C., from early 2014 to February 16, 2018. Prigozhin was the primary funder of the St. Petersburg-based Internet Research Agency (IRA). He allegedly oversaw and approved their political and electoral interference operations in the United States which included the purchase of American computer server space, the creation of hundreds of fictitious online personas, and the use of stolen identities of persons from the United States. These actions were allegedly taken to reach significant numbers of Americans for the purposes of interfering with the United States political system, including the 2016 Presidential Election.

On February 16, 2018, a federal arrest warrant was issued for Yevgeniy Viktorovich Prigozhin in the United States District Court for the District of Columbia after he was charged with conspiracy to defraud the United States.

SHOULD BE CONSIDERED AN INTERNATIONAL FLIGHT RISK

If you have any information concerning this individual and you are outside the United States, please contact the nearest American Embassy or Consulate. If inside the United States, please contact your local FBI office or the FBI's toll free tip line at 1-800-CALL-FBI (1-800-225-5324). You may also submit a tip online at tips.fbi.gov.

Field Office: Washington D.C.

FBI 'wanted' notice for Yevgeny Prigozhin

wryly, 'and they see what they want to see. I am not upset at all … If they want to see the devil, let them see him.' His subversive activities would earn him a place on the US sanctions roster, a criminal indictment and, in February 2021, elevation to the FBI's Most Wanted list.

The Mueller Report caused much indignation among the American public – it isn't nice to learn that a foreign government is sneaking around, trying to mess with your thoughts and opinions. But I do wonder what exactly Putin was hoping to achieve by hacking the US election. It is possible, but unlikely, that he had some sort of pact with – or some means of influence over – Donald Trump. It is possible he thought Trump would be easier to push around, or that he was overcome with hatred for Hillary Clinton, who had called him out on numerous occasions when she was secretary of state. But very few people in Russia would be particularly impressed by or overly interested in Putin achieving that sort of outcome.

Putin may have had another aim in mind, however, when he instructed Prigozhin to stir up trouble, one that would have a big effect on Russian opinion. People in the West tend to think that Putin runs Russia with effortless ease, that he has the whole country under his shiny, platform-soled heel. But he isn't talented as a manager or hardworking or even a good organiser. And he knows that things in Russia are not going well. The US election allowed him to create the *impression* that things are going well, a fantasy of pretence and fake claims to paper over the reality. Just like in the times of Catherine the Great, Putin has created his own Potemkin villages – but instead of erecting fake villages on the ground in Russia, he is creating citadels of fake news and history on a global platform, that is online. He projects a mirage of wellbeing to force the Russian people to believe in it and to stave off the day when they finally realise their emperor has no clothes.

But even Putin's Truman Show falters at times and the parlous state of Russia becomes too big to ignore. At moments like these, he needs a way of explaining to the Russian people why not everything in the garden is rosy. He needs someone to blame. He can't blame the political opposition, because he cleaves to the image of a powerful president who has dealt with internal opposition and crushed them into irrelevance. So, instead, Putin turns to America. In Putin's cosmology, America takes the blame for everything. The US is big and powerful, capable of inflicting all sorts of woes on Russia, a most convenient enemy for Putin to have or, perhaps, for him to invent.

Putin's preoccupation is always with his domestic audience and with how his image will play with the Russian people. Prigozhin's IRA allowed him to demonstrate to the Russian people that American democracy is corrupt. Putin may not have been overly concerned with backing Trump; but he did want to convince the Russian people that the vote was being falsified in favour of Hillary. He wanted to provoke outrage among Trump supporters, so they would proclaim to the world that the US system was rotten.

And he succeeded in spades.

CHAPTER 16
WHAT IS RUSSIAN FOR FAKE NEWS?

For many years, political and media discourse has been founded on an inviolable distinction between fact and opinion: as C. P. Scott, a famous British newspaperman, pointed out, comment is free, but facts are sacred. In the post-truth universe of the twenty-first century, that distinction has been trampled underfoot.

Nowadays, many politicians and journalists treat facts as if they were as inherently malleable as their own personal opinions, fair game to be twisted and moulded to fit the case they wish to make. Donald Trump lived in a different truth-universe from everyone else, believing only the things he wanted to believe and using all methods to force others into agreeing with him. The issue is not the correctness or otherwise of political decisions, but the way that facts are shaped to communicate with society and impose specific views.

But Vladimir Putin trumps even Trump. Putin peddles falsehoods to the Russian people, insisting all the while that his lies are true, that black – despite much evidence to the contrary – is white. When people have the effrontery to stand up for the truth, the Kremlin shows no mercy. A woman whose son died in the *Kursk* submarine disaster of 2000 tried to criticise the inefficiency of the rescue mission at a Foreign Ministry press conference, only to be rendered unconscious by a hypodermic syringe plunged into her arm in full view of the assembled media.

Disagreeing with the Kremlin's version of events is dangerously unrewarding. It behoves the West and the democratic opposition to stand up for those who dare to speak the truth. And that applies not only to politicians, but to the Western media, too.

Since I have been living in London, I have been impressed by British television news. The BBC, ITN, Channel 4 and Sky strive for objectivity and impartiality. The BBC is attacked by politicians from both the left and the right, which suggests to me that its reporting maintains a good standard of balance. Despite being owned by the Fox magnate Rupert Murdoch until 2018, Sky News rejects the political bias that has become the calling card of so many broadcasters abroad. In the US, for example, there has been a marked radicalisation of TV networks, with CNN openly supporting the left and Fox equally siding with the right. This has led US politics to become damagingly polarised and people's prejudices entrenched to extremes. I regret that Ronald Reagan dropped the 'fairness' requirement that up until 1987 demanded balance from the broadcast networks. Now that social networks permit people to close themselves off from alternative opinions and live within a monolithic group, sometimes sharing the most radical and often patently erroneous convictions, this is a question that must be seriously reconsidered.

But in Putin's Russia, the situation is much worse. In the US, there is at least market competition, which ensures most political views are represented by at least one channel. In Russia, the state has a de facto monopoly of the mass media, which guarantees it also has a 'monopoly of truth'. Boris Yeltsin allowed a brief interlude of freedom in the 1990s, but Vladimir Putin is replacing glasnost with a return to Soviet times. The Kremlin has created a dominant information stream that wages an aggressive and permanent information war. The few remaining independent media outlets are harassed and restricted by the authorities.

A popular joke of the past couple of years in Russia asks, 'What is the Russian for fake news?' with the answer being, 'News.' It has become a favourite among those who despair at the mendacity of Vladimir Putin's state media and communications machine. But the truth is more nuanced. People in Russia know what is going on. News is distorted, but it is not always hidden. The insidious thing is the way that Putin's propaganda operation has got inside people's heads and the facility with which it has learned how to make people believe in presumptions. If all the available sources of news keep telling you that a fact should be viewed in a certain way, the majority of us will agree that that is the way it should be viewed.

Psychologists have shown that people are relatively easily persuaded to adapt their opinions to the general view. A series of experiments in the 1950s by the US researcher Solomon Asch investigated the phenomenon of conformity, the process by which a person's opinions are influenced by those of groups. Asch found that people are willing to ignore reality – to disregard the evidence of their own eyes and give an answer they know to be incorrect – in order to conform to the rest of the group. He concluded that individuals have a compulsion to follow the unspoken rules and behaviours of the society in which they live, driven by an innate fear of appearing different, or by a desire to belong.

The Kremlin's propaganda machine is adept at exploiting those fears and desires, and we in the democratic opposition must learn to combat them. Freedom of speech and societal openness have been, and remain, the most important elements of democracy. We know from psychology that social support is an important tool in reducing pernicious conformity; if an individual knows that others in her social group are willing to resist, she too is more likely to do so. Our task is to provide that support, to furnish the factual reassurances that will lead to a critical mass of citizens willing to reject the Kremlin's manipulation. Asch suggests that conformity decreases when people are able to respond privately, without the external pressures of the social domain. This has had the perverse effect that many Russians pretend to accept the 'official' view of things in their public life – to avoid opprobrium or appearing different – while remaining fully conscious that the official version is a lie. As the Polish writer Czesław Miłosz has pointed out, it can be an uncomfortable mental task to live this double life of knowing and pretending not to know. It is a conflict summed up in another Russian joke about two KGB men who are having a drink after work. The first one, Dmitry, says to his friend, 'Tell me, Ivan. What do you *really* think about this regime we live under?' Ivan replies, 'The same as you do,' after which Dmitry thinks for a moment, and then says, 'In that case, it is my duty to arrest you.'

Forcing people to believe in lies is not new in Russia. Joseph Stalin rewrote reality on an epic scale, bigging up his own importance by excising former rivals from the historical record, airbrushing their faces from photographs. 'Who controls the past controls the future,' wrote George Orwell in his novel *Nineteen Eighty-Four*, 'who controls the present controls the past.' The Bolsheviks regarded history as a resource to be reinvented at will to suit the Kremlin's present objectives and justify its promise of an ideal socialist future. 'Communism has made the future certain,' ran another joke, 'but the past completely unpredictable.'

Stalin was punctilious in telling Soviet historians what to write about him. He dictated his own entry in the *Great Soviet Encyclopaedia*, the official version of the country's history. 'Everyone knows the shattering force of Stalin's logic,' Stalin modestly opined, 'the crystal clarity of his intellect, his steel will, his love for the people. His modesty, simplicity, sensitivity and mercilessness to enemies are well known to everyone ...'

Putin is the latest Russian autocrat to mould history to suit himself. In February 2013, he ordered Russian historians to come up with guidelines for new school history books that suggested a portrayal of the past – and the present – more in line with his version of autocracy. Part of his motivation was the fear that gripped him following the widescale protests of 2011 and 2012 and the need to shore up his image before the impending presidential election. But it was also a vanity project. The guidelines were to make no criticism of the president, no reference to any protests against him and no mention of the confrontation over his crushing of Yukos. 'It was a simple political order,' wrote the independent Russian historian, Vladimir Ryzhkov, 'to justify the ruling authorities, to explain that they are doing everything right'. The guidelines reaffirmed the myth that Russia needs strong autocratic rule to protect the nation against its foes and credited Putin with providing it. 'During his first and second presidential terms, Vladimir Putin managed to stabilise the situation in the country and strengthen the "vertical of power",' the guidelines conclude, adding that Putin had fostered stability, economic growth and 'the restoration of Russia's position in international affairs'.

The man Putin engaged to implement his revision of history was Sergei Naryshkin, a former Kremlin chief of staff and senior representative of the president's own United Russia party. Like so many of Putin's enforcers, Naryshkin had been with him at the KGB Academy and would go on to become the director of Russia's Foreign Intelligence Service, the SVR. As the head of the Orwellian-sounding 'Presidential Commission of the Russian Federation to Counter

Attempts to Falsify History to the Detriment of Russia's Interests', Naryshkin was instrumental in moves to whitewash some of the most shameful aspects of Russia's past, including Soviet cooperation with the Nazis and the treatment of 'liberated' peoples after war. Another of Putin's Siloviki advisers, the FSB director, Alexander Bortnikov, made clear that the rehabilitation of Stalin was official Kremlin policy when he declared that 'a significant proportion' of the executions carried in the Stalinist purges were justified, because they were based on 'objective' evidence. Leading academics at the Russian Academy of Sciences warned against the dangers of such baseless revisionism; the Kremlin was rewriting history that it considered 'detrimental to Russia's interests' by besmirching the memory of millions of innocent people murdered by a tyrannical regime.

Glorifying the Soviet past and refusing to express regret for the crimes of the Stalin era appeal to many, mostly elderly, Russians, who wish to look back with pride on the years of Soviet rule. By reviving the Soviet anthem, reinstating Soviet-style military parades and reintroducing Soviet tactics against political dissent, he has won the gratitude of those who felt themselves demeaned by the post-perestroika mood of repentance for past crimes; but to do so, he has had to distort the facts.

At a televised meeting with history teachers in 2007, Putin issued instructions for how his new version of the past should be taught to the young generation whose beliefs will determine Russia's future. 'There is nothing in our history for Russians to be ashamed of,' he told the audience. 'No one must be allowed to impose a feeling of guilt upon us.' The responsibility of teachers was to make students 'proud of the Motherland'. To help them with their task of creating this alternative history – one which overlooks unfortunate episodes in favour of Russia's achievements – the presidential administration produced a handbook of instructions. *A Modern History of Russia,*

A pensioner sheds a tear at Stalin's tomb in Moscow on the 63rd anniversary of his death

1945–2006; A Manual for History Teachers explains that Stalin's purges of the 1930s were necessary because of the need to prepare for war with Germany, while the collapse of Soviet communism in 1991 was a historical tragedy. 'The Soviet Union was not a democracy,' the handbook somewhat understatedly concedes, 'but it was an example to millions of people around the world of the best and fairest society.' The reigns of Gorbachev and Yeltsin, in which the Soviet vassal states of Eastern Europe and then the Soviet republics were granted independence, are presented as a cause for regret, while Putin himself is lauded for pledging to restore Russia's 'greatness'.

In seeking to deploy the past as validation for his own brand of autocracy, Putin is following in Stalin's footsteps. Stalin commissioned his 1938 *History of the Communist Party of the Soviet Union (Bolsheviks): Short Course* in order to enshrine a (fake) version of history, in which he played the central role in the 1917 revolutions, while other Bolsheviks deferred to his leadership. To underline the veracity of the *Short Course*, Stalin obliged the Soviet historical establishment to declare him a great historian, whose judgements were infallible. Putin, too, has set himself up as a scholar of history. At a press conference in December 2013, he praised two historical figures who embody many of the attributes to which he aspires. 'What is the difference between Cromwell and Stalin?' he asked the audience, before demonstrating his historical expertise by answering his own question. 'I'll tell you. There is none. Our liberal politicians think these men were both bloody dictators. But Cromwell was actually a smart man who [like Stalin] played a controversial part in history. And his statue is still standing in London. Nobody is tearing it down. We, too, should treat our history with that sort of care.' The comparison is deeply stretched, and Putin's historiography is alarmingly selective, but his purpose is clear. By excusing Stalin's excesses and rescuing his memory, Putin is placing himself in a tradition of strongman autocrats who saved their nation from chaos.

It is not a narrative that chimes with everyone's view of the past. The human rights group, Memorial, was founded in the Gorbachev years to document the crimes of the Stalin era, honour the victims of political repression, and use education and remembrance to ensure that such abuses never happen again. But to Putin, Memorial was an inconvenience, an unwelcome voice pointing out that historical reality cannot be erased simply to suit the wishes of today's leadership. Instead of listening to the message, Putin attacked the messenger. In December 2008, Memorial's St Petersburg offices were raided by the security forces and archives chronicling hundreds of thousands of individual cases of people repressed or murdered under Stalin were confiscated. Memorial's director, Irina Flinge, said they had been targeted because their work contradicted the ethos of 'Putinism', a strident nationalism that draws strength from the autocratic past. 'The official line now', Flinge concluded, 'is that Stalin and the Soviet regime were successful in creating a great country. And if the terror of Stalin is justified, then the government today can do what it wants to achieve its aims … Russians are told to be proud of their history, not ashamed, so those investigating and cataloguing the atrocities of the past are no longer welcome.' In December 2021, the Russian Supreme Court ordered the closure of Memorial for breaching recently promulgated laws on 'foreign agents' – a catchall instrument of censorship to which I will return later.

By rewriting history, Putin wishes to create a narrative of continuity between the eras of tsarism, communism and the present day, in which Russia appears as an imperial power, equalling and rivalling the West, exerting strength and influence across the globe. That would allow him to place his own imperial dreams in a historical context of heroic expansionism, a narrative attractive to the conservative elements of the Russian electorate and bolstered by the reinvention of the external enemy myth. In the past, it was the Mongols, Napoleon or Hitler; today it is once again the West that fills the role of menacing foe, in the face of which Russian society must forget its differences and unite behind its strongman leader.

More recent times have also been rewritten. The 1990s experiment with market democracy is portrayed by Putin's textbooks as a modern 'Time of Troubles', in which chaos, poverty and violence outweighed any benefits; while the era of communist rule is remembered for its subsidised prices, free housing and education, rather than the political repression, shortages of consumer goods and persecution of free speech. Deploring the 'wild' liberalism of the Yeltsin years allows Putin to make the leap to a blanket condemnation of democracy and pluralism, while the mirage of a glorious autocratic past helps him silence dissent, political opponents and critics.

When, in 2019, the European Parliament issued a resolution condemning the Kremlin for 'whitewashing' the facts of Soviet collaboration with the Nazis, Putin responded angrily. In a lengthy essay published on the 75th anniversary of the end of the Second World War, he defended the Molotov–Ribbentrop pact of 1939, in which Moscow and Berlin agreed they would invade and divide up Eastern Europe between them. The real guilt, Putin wrote, belongs to the Western powers who acquiesced to Hitler's demands to annex the Czech Sudetenland. 'Britain, as well as France … sought to direct the attention of the Nazis eastward so that Germany and the Soviet Union would inevitably clash and bleed each other white.' As for Poland, the country that would suffer more than most from the secret protocol of the Nazi–Soviet pact, Putin argued that Warsaw was to blame for its own misfortune. 'It is clear from examining the archive documents,' he claimed, 'that the Polish leadership of the time was colluding with Hitler … Maybe there were also some secret protocols in there, too.'

Most alarmingly, Putin rewrites the brutal Soviet invasion of the Baltic states, describing it as a peaceful unification of nations. 'In autumn 1939, the Soviet Union, pursuing its strategic military and defensive goals, started the process of the incorporation of Latvia, Lithuania, and Estonia. Their accession to the USSR was implemented on a contractual basis, with the consent of the elected authorities.' Such an explanation is completely false. Latvia, Lithuania and Estonia were subjected to a violent occupation that involved repression and mass murder. His contention that they joined the USSR 'voluntarily' and 'with the consent of the elected authorities' is a fiction that has alarmed other former Soviet states that the Kremlin might once again seek to annex.

For his domestic Russian audience, Putin's manipulation of history has had the desired effect. In a 2012 poll asking Russians to nominate 'the greatest ever Russian', Stalin came top and he has retained his title ever since. In that initial poll, Vladimir Putin finished in fifth place, behind Peter the Great, Yuri Gagarin and Alexander Pushkin; but by 2017, he had risen to second, only a few percentage points behind the man he has striven so hard to rehabilitate and, perhaps, imitate.

CHAPTER 17
STOP THINKING YOU CAN BE SAFE WITH THE BEAR

While in power, Donald Trump used the language of populism to pledge to 'make America great again'. Vladimir Putin continues to use the same rhetoric today. Both of them have stirred up resentment among their own population, insisting that their nation has somehow been demeaned and diminished, while promising a return to what they see as its rightful national glory.

The world would benefit if ideas of 'greatness' were consigned to the past. Russia in particular would gain from an acceptance that the Soviet superpower is no more and that Russia needs to find a new place in the world, a role that corresponds to the real interests of her citizens who, like citizens across the globe, yearn for freedom, security and economic prosperity. Britain in the 1950s and 1960s went through the painful process of relinquishing its great power status and its old imperial dreams, finding itself a new role in global politics. If the Kremlin were to make the same leap, it would strengthen global peace and stability and would permit a new focus on the civilian economy to the immense benefit of the Russian people. Sadly, such a transformation is unlikely to happen under the current Kremlin administration.

Putin's imperial thinking is in part explained by Russia's history. For the last five centuries, Russia has been an empire, an agglomeration of territory invaded and swallowed up by successive tsars, then by the Bolsheviks. Empire has become Russia's default mode; Russian people have grown used to it and come to regard it as a safeguard for national security. In the twentieth century, it encompassed the satellite states in Eastern Europe, which were seen as protection against invasion from the West.

But the world has moved on; empires are a thing of the past. Russia finds herself in thrall to an outdated system and now she must choose between the discredited past and the way of the future. To me, it seems evident that Russia must plump for the latter, for a unified nation of people of different ethnic origins, whose commonalities are more important than their differences. Such a state can exist only as a result of freedom, self-determination and the rule of law, not through compulsion and the force of arms.

Following the collapse of the Soviet Union, there was a lot of ill-considered enthusiasm in the West about the rapid and trouble-free transformation of Russia into a 'junior partner'. The West gave Russia lots of advice, but much less in terms of investment or technology. After the crisis of 1998 and the progressive disintegration of the Yeltsin regime, Western enthusiasm for helping Russia move into the twenty-first century quickly faded and was largely replaced by scepticism. Russia was seen as the new 'sick man of Europe', no longer worthy of interest or attention. It was an attitude that bore real-world consequences. In the early 2000s, Western governmental and quasi-governmental programmes such as the UK's Know How Fund were shut down or refocused on Africa and the Far East. Some Western academics who had previously studied the USSR retrained as sinologists. Only those who really understood Russian history warned against writing Russia off: the Russian bear may spend long periods asleep in its den, but the longer it sleeps, the more serious the consequences.

Even those who recognised that Russia was not about to fall apart lost interest in the idea of Russian democracy. There were two streams of Western rhetoric about Russia: the ritualised speeches about the importance of Russia's transition from authoritarianism and totalitarianism to democracy; and the informal consensus that formed at the end of the 1990s that however much you feed the Russian bear, it will always scurry back to the authoritarian forest. Even worse, there was a growing feeling behind the scenes that, actually, a bit of 'moderate' authoritarianism in Russia is both good for the Russian people and for the West; that a 'moderately' evil ruler is the best way – perhaps the only way – to keep a very evil and unruly nation under some sort of control. Such a ruler, the reasoning went, would keep Russia from rivalling the West in the struggle for the economic future; and since Russians are not suited to living in a democracy anyway, it would be useful for them to have a moderately authoritarian regime that would not frighten the West with Russia's social abominations or provoke mass waves of emigration. Such thoughts, together with simple self-interest, played a part in the rise of Trumpism in America and Schröderism in Europe over the past two decades. If Russia isn't going to fall apart, they suggest, then such an outcome – a sort of enlightened monarchical repression – is not a bad outcome.

Such attitudes are a mistake. Russia can be one of two things: despotic, aggressive and dangerous; or a democratic, strategic ally. The West can never be safe with an authoritarian Russian bear. Such a bear will forever be in search of prey, inventing external enemies on whom to blame internal failures and to rally the Russian people around its leadership. Russian authoritarianism will always be belligerent and aggressive. Its modus operandi will always be messianism, militarism and adventurism. It has no possibility of internal stability; it can be stable only when it is thrusting aggressively outwards. Such is the fate of all empires that refuse to transform themselves into a nation-state.

The paradox is that a weak Russia will seek to assert its strength, to take what it wants by force, to breach the rules of civilised behaviour; while a strong, confident Russia possesses the self-belief to focus on its own problems at home and play by the rules abroad. The security of the West can be assured only if Russia is strong and democratically governed. The West, ironically, needs to encourage a worthy competitor in Russia if it wants to be certain of its own safety. It may seem counterintuitive, but it will be worth it: Europe's choice is between Russia as a difficult but civilised competitor and Russia as an aggressor, threatening the foundations of European civilisation. Despotism in Russia will always be a threat, no matter how much Europe tries to convince itself otherwise. That is why it is in Europe's interest to help Russia become a modern, civilised country with a stable economy and predictable policies.

Russia cannot become a modern country while it maintains its current archaic system of governance. It is a burden that weighs it down, condemning the nation to stagnation in industrial or even pre-industrial conditions, while fostering dissatisfaction among society's most productive forces with their country's lack of development. The exodus abroad of the most active and educated members of Russian society exacerbates the problem, as the economy suffers from their loss. Like all authoritarian regimes, Putin's answer is even more foreign aggression, to keep Europe always on the defensive, and – following the invasion of Ukraine – on the brink of war.

If the West wants to protect itself from the threat from the East, it would be a mistake to try to weaken or break up Russia. The consequences of that would be an internal power struggle in Russia with a predictable outcome – power would be seized by the toughest, most unprincipled autocrat who, in order to maintain his position, would inevitably provoke a confrontation with the West. If this is to be avoided, we need democratic states in the East and West to work together. Competing and collaborating with a strong Russia is a much better solution for everyone. As a geographic neighbour and sister civilisation, a future Russia can either be part of the problem or she can become part of the solution to much bigger problems. The creation of a Russian civic state is the greatest goal towards which the people of Russia have laboured historically, but it is yet to be achieved. With greater informational freedom, the internet, social media, international travel and an increasingly integrated world community, that task is now possible.

CHAPTER 18
EXPANSIONIST DREAMS

Whatever politicians may say, the foreign policy agenda of all nations is based on self-interest. Political leaders may declare they are taking action to support other nations and help right moral wrongs, but altruism is rarely the true motivation.

When the West sent support to the anti-Assad opposition in Syria, it was a gamble aimed at shoring up its own presence there. When Vladimir Putin sent the Russian military to defend Assad, he was doing the same. This was not a moral crusade, but an East–West arm wrestle. The difference was that Putin played things more ruthlessly and with greater purpose, and his aims were less the interests of the Russian state than the venal self-interest of his clique of cronies. Western leaders, on the other hand, were constrained by pressure from parliaments and critical voices at home, in ways that Putin was not.

Putin's aim is always to secure for himself and his entourage a strong position in relations with the West, which will allow him to maintain his grip on power in Russia without criticism of the methods he uses, to legitimise his authority at home through recognition abroad and to persuade Russian citizens that the country is surrounded by hostile forces. The West allowed him to do this. The US withdrew from Syria, leaving the field to the forces of the Kremlin, while American wavering on the future of NATO left the Baltic countries and others in anxious limbo. NATO may have advanced to Russia's doorstep, but it no longer constrains the Kremlin.

Shortly after Joe Biden became president of the United States, I was asked by an American interviewer for my opinion of Vladimir Putin's foreign policy intentions and whether his aggression against neighbouring countries was likely to continue. I could see that my interlocutor was concerned about the damage the Kremlin was inflicting on the prospects for world peace, but I could offer him little in the way of reassurance. My assessment, I told him, is that Putin is a former KGB agent who regrets the loss of the USSR and has set himself the goal of regaining control of as much of the old Soviet Union as possible.

When my interviewer asked me what the West could do to curb an escalation of international confrontation, my response was equally gloomy. The United States, I predicted, would do nothing, except maybe impose a few more sanctions. The Democrats' lack of resolve would give the Trumpian faction of the Republican Party enough ammunition to beat up on Biden and proclaim that the US was now led by a weak and incompetent president. As for Europe, I expected that the EU would do even less than the US, since Germany, the only country whose opinion really matters, does not want to alienate the Kremlin and risk jeopardising its supplies of Russian gas or seeing Russian markets closed to German manufactured goods. The consequence of Western weakness, I concluded, would be to further embolden Putin in his campaign of foreign expansionism. It gives me no pleasure to note that just a year after my remarks to the American journalist, my predictions were borne out by his invasion of Ukraine.

Putin's intentions evidently revolve around the acquisition of control over more and more territory, for reasons which, frankly speaking, make very little sense. Even if he achieves his aim, Russia will be no better off than before: it will have taken on responsibility for more territory, which it doesn't need, and more people, most of whom will be unhappy and resentful, in political, economic and social terms.

Yet, despite all the obvious disadvantages, Putin has clung to his expansionist dreams. In his 2005 State of the Nation address, he called the collapse of the Soviet Union 'the greatest geopolitical catastrophe of the twentieth century'. 'For the Russian people,' he said, 'it has become a genuine tragedy – tens of millions of our fellow countrymen are condemned to live beyond the boundaries of the Motherland ... and the pestilence has spread to Russia herself.' In 2018, he repeated his remarks to an audience in Kaliningrad, declaring that the dissolution of the USSR was 'the one single event of Russian history' he would most like to see reversed.

It is no secret why Putin was doing it. Opinion polls show that 55 per cent of Russian people expect Putin to make Russia 'a great country' again. The older generation have preserved the memory of the Soviet Union as a superpower and there is nostalgia for those bygone days. Many of them say they want Russia to be respected; but being respected is different from being feared. In opinion polls, however, they don't differentiate between the two. Older Russians have been inculcated with the dangerous belief that for Russia to be respected by the world, she needs to be feared by the world. For younger folk, things are more complicated. I would say that maybe half of them share the same dead-end nostalgia for a lost superpower, having imbibed the values of their parents; but the other half genuinely want a Russia that is open and integrated into the global system of values. It is on this section of the population that we, in the democratic opposition in Russia and worldwide, must focus our best efforts to secure a more rational, less belligerent future for the nation.

It won't be easy. Putin has shown himself to be adept at exploiting the politics of aggression abroad in order to boost his standing at home. It is a fact that the Russian economy has deteriorated dramatically since he illegally prolonged his hold on power; in the majority of Western democracies, such a disastrous performance would have resulted in a drubbing at the polls. Putin's approval ratings slipped alarmingly between 2008 and 2014, when Russia officially went into recession, only for the Kremlin to launch its campaign to annex Crimea, followed by military intervention in eastern Ukraine. Almost immediately, Putin's poll numbers soared to more than 80 per cent. But the cost of shoring up his own domestic standing has been to draw Russia into perilous foreign adventures that put the whole country at risk. The Kremlin-controlled media endlessly repeat the claim that Russia is beset by enemy forces, surrounded by a supposedly hostile West bent on destroying the Motherland. In such circumstances, it is little wonder that some people believe Putin is their only hope, a leader dedicated to defending Russia's international clout whom they must trust implicitly.

Just like the Soviet leaders of the 1970s, Putin has increased military spending at the expense of the civilian economy, prioritising nuclear weapons that can destroy cities in Western Europe and North America over investment in health, education and social provision for his own citizens. He has used the narrative of conflict with the West to give lucrative contracts to his cronies who control the state arms industry. He announced that he has developed new generations of weaponry and presented them to the world in menacing terms. In March 2018, he gave a video presentation of what he said were new, 'invincible' nuclear weapons, developed in secret by Russia's scientists.

'No anti-missile system, either now or in the future, has a hope of stopping them,' Putin told his audience. Images of the new missiles were projected on to a giant screen with animations of the destruction they were capable of inflicting. In one sequence, a missile was shown hovering over a map of Florida, a not-too-subtle threat that Washington was quick to condemn. 'It was certainly unfortunate,' said a State Department spokesperson, 'to have watched a video presentation that depicted a nuclear attack on the United States. We do not regard this as the behaviour of a responsible international player.' It was, though, exactly the response the Kremlin was hoping for: Washington's discomfort was widely reported and apparently enjoyed by some Russian voters who were going to the polls just two weeks later. In an election where real opposition candidates were barred from standing, Vladimir Putin was re-elected to a fourth term in office with 77 per cent of the votes (of which only about half were the result of ballot rigging).

Russian military intervention in Syria had a similar effect. The fact is that Russian society *a priori* has very little interest in Syria and the Middle East, which means that Putin has a free hand to do whatever he wants there. The only problem would be if Russian soldiers started getting killed, so Putin has been clever. He has maintained the fiction that there will never be Russian boots on the ground in Syria, while pursuing his goals through the deployment of hundreds of 'private' troops, mainly belonging to the PMC Wagner Group controlled by his associate, Yevgeny Prigozhin.

The fiction of Russian 'non-involvement' was exposed in February 2018, when between 300 and 500 Wagner mercenaries with tanks and field artillery attacked a stronghold of the Syrian Democratic Forces, a largely Kurdish militia with close ties to the US-led anti-ISIS coalition, close to the town of Khasham. American advisers working with the Kurds called for US air support and a full-scale battle ensued. The attacking troops were pummelled by American artillery, fighter planes and helicopter gunships, with the Pentagon estimating their casualties at more than 100 men. It was the first direct confrontation between American and Russian forces since the end of the Cold War, with the potential for catastrophic escalation.

As international tensions rose, Putin continued to deny any knowledge of the operation or, indeed, of any Russian fighters on Syrian soil; but US intelligence reports told a different story. According to the *Washington Post*, covert Russian communications, intercepted by the intelligence services, revealed that Prigozhin had been authorised to carry out the attack by senior officials in the Kremlin. Prigozhin reportedly boasted to Bashar al-Assad's Minister of Presidential Affairs that he had 'secured permission for a ... fast and powerful operation' to be launched in early February. It would, he said, be 'a nice surprise' for Assad; and the Syrians, in return, promised Prigozhin that he would be properly rewarded for his services.

Having initially denied everything, the Russian Foreign Ministry was obliged to amend its story, eventually acknowledging 'several dozen' Russian casualties, killed or wounded in the attack. The wounded had been 'provided with assistance to return to Russia, where they are now undergoing medical treatment at a number of hospitals'. The Kremlin's deniability was strained to breaking point. 'Russian servicemen did not take part in any capacity whatsoever [in the operation],' maintained the spokesperson, 'and no Russian military equipment was used.' The troops were merely 'Russian citizens who went to Syria of their own free will for various reasons ... and the Ministry does not have the authority to comment on the validity or legality of their individual decisions.'

As with all the other conflicts he provokes around the world, Putin views Syria as a means to blackmail the West. The tension surrounding the confrontation and the threat it poses to global stability put the Americans on the defensive; they find themselves obliged to sit down at the negotiating table with Putin, on terms that are advantageous to him. What does Putin want from these negotiations? Ideally, he wants a return to the old days, when the world was divided into recognised spheres of influence, allowing Moscow and Washington to maintain autonomy of action in their sector of the globe, with a guarantee of non-interference in the other's affairs. Most importantly, such an outcome would ensure the impunity of Putin and his inner circle to travel and spend their money anywhere in the world without constraints.

When Western countries dutifully came to the table after Russian interventions in Georgia, Syria and the Donbas, they assumed that Putin shared their desire to find solutions, to end wars that were – and still are – causing human misery and taking human lives. But the Kremlin's overriding motive in talks with the US and the EU was to secure a better strategic position for itself, which frequently meant simply freezing the conflict. The confrontation in the Donbas, for instance, was carefully prolonged by Moscow as a means of undermining Ukraine's independence. Putin pretended to the West that he wanted a diplomatic accord to satisfy all parties and persuaded the EU to include him in negotiations as a peacemaker, whereas, in reality, he was an instigator and a warmonger. The evidence of what all this was leading to is now plain for the world to see – and we are far from reaching the end of it.

The same is true in Syria. Putin has no interest in ending the fighting, because it is to his advantage to deepen the conflict and thereby secure for himself a role of global influence. By keeping Bashar al-Assad in power and tying down US troops on the ground, Putin has created the illusion that he holds the key to peace in the Middle East. But peace is not on his agenda. What he really wants is to boost his domestic approval ratings by publicly humiliating Washington and its allies in scenes that can be shown nightly on Russian television. At a time when the Russian people are suffering poverty, recession and isolation from the rest of the world, a foreign war in which Moscow is seen to be sticking it to the Western 'enemy' is a dog whistle call to the Great Russian sense of pride, which precludes criticism of the man who claims to be fighting for the honour of the Motherland.

A common thread in nearly all of Putin's foreign ventures has been a determination to support authoritarian rulers – those who maintain their grip on power through the use of force against a dissatisfied population. In 2014, he tried with all his might to prevent the overthrow of the dictatorial, pro-Moscow Ukrainian leader Viktor Yanukovych when a groundswell of popular discontent made his position untenable. In that case, Putin failed; but he did much better in Syria, where his resolute intervention rescued the murderous Bashar al-Assad from the vengeance of a population revolted by his record of oppression. In Belarus, too, Putin's unwavering support has become the crutch on which the unpopular president, Alexander Lukashenko, has come to rely. In 2021, Lukashenko violated all international norms to detain a Western airliner overflying Belarus in order to arrest one of his many vocal critics. The Kremlin was alone in the international community in coming to his rescue, emboldening the Belarusian leadership to continue its crackdown on domestic dissent.

It is not hard to understand why Putin is doing this. He supports endangered dictators because he knows that he himself is in the same category, haunted by fears that he too might be overthrown by the Russian people. Putin was concerned by the so-called 'colour revolutions' in Ukraine and Georgia, where popular uprisings ousted repressive regimes and replaced them with democratically elected governments. His alarm deepened in 2011, when the Middle East was rocked by the events of the Arab Spring, in which the leaders of Tunisia, Egypt, Yemen and Libya were all toppled. While the West greeted the uprisings as a victory for democracy, Putin viewed them as ominous harbingers of chaos and destabilisation, which he believed were covertly stoked by the CIA. Later the same year, the threat came closer to home as hundreds of thousands of demonstrators took to the streets of Moscow and St Petersburg, protesting about the rigging of parliamentary elections. The aforementioned demonstrations were briefly dubbed the 'snow revolution', a worrying augury that Russia was not immune to the bacillus of revolt. Putin's response was to blame Washington. He accused Hillary Clinton, the US secretary of state, of fomenting unrest in Russia as a prelude to a Western-sponsored coup, aimed at bringing about a regime change similar to those in Georgia and Ukraine.

Putin's stock reply to criticism of his aggressive foreign ventures is to protest that the West is doing worse. He is quick to highlight alleged Western transgressions, including interference in the internal affairs of sovereign states, the attempted 'imposition of democracy' and military intervention. But at the same time, the Kremlin claims for itself the right to a 'sphere of privileged interests' in the former Soviet territories and a 'right to defend our compatriots wherever they live'. A 2017 report for the Foreign Relations Committee of the US Senate, titled 'Putin's Asymmetrical Assault on Democracy', pointed out the inherent contradiction between the two positions:

> If Putin can demonstrate to the Russian people that liberal democracy is a dysfunctional and dying form of government, then their own system of 'sovereign democracy' – authoritarianism secured by corruption, apathy, and an iron fist – does not look so bad after all. As the National Intelligence Council put it, Putin's 'amalgam of authoritarianism, corruption, and nationalism represents an alternative to Western liberalism … [which] is synonymous with disorder and moral decay,

and pro-democracy movements are "Western plots" to weaken traditional bulwarks of order and the Russian state.'

If the West had paid more attention to Putin's public pronouncements in recent years, the February 2022 invasion of Ukraine might not have come as such a surprise. In July 2021, he published a long treatise, setting out Russia's claims on the country. The essay's title, 'On the Historical Unity of Russians and Ukrainians', was an indication that he has little time for an independent Ukrainian state.

> Russians and Ukrainians are one people and the wall that has emerged in recent years between Russia and Ukraine, between the parts of what is essentially the same historical and spiritual space, is a great misfortune and tragedy. These are … the result of deliberate efforts by those forces that have always sought to undermine our unity. The formula they apply is – divide and rule. Hence the attempts to sow discord among people, to pit the parts of a single people against one another.

In his essay, Putin names the malevolent 'forces' who he claims are bent on sowing division between Moscow and Kiev. Historically, he says, they have included Ukrainian nationalists who sought alliances with Poland or Germany in order to sabotage the 'brotherly' bonds with Russia. In the Second World War, some Ukrainian leaders were willing to collaborate with the Nazis in the struggle against Soviet domination, and Putin draws a direct – and defamatory – comparison between them and the modern Ukrainian independence movement:

> The Nazis, abetted by collaborators from the Organisation of Ukrainian Nationalists, did not need Ukraine, except as a living space and slaves for Aryan overlords. Nor were

the interests of the Ukrainian people thought of in February 2014. Public discontent was cynically exploited by Western countries who directly interfered in Ukraine's internal affairs and supported a coup. Radical nationalist groups served as its battering ram. Their slogans, ideology, and blatant aggressive Russophobia have become defining elements of state policy in Ukraine.

Putin equates the democratically elected government of today's Ukraine with the Nazi collaborators of 80 years ago, casting the Western democracies in the role of Hitlerite aggressors:

> The leaders of modern Ukraine and their external 'patrons' prefer to overlook these facts. And we know why: if they bring about the weakening of Russia, our ill-wishers are happy with that. Ukraine is being turned into a springboard against Russia … comparable in its consequences to the use of weapons of mass destruction against us … under the protection and control of the Western powers. We are witnessing direct external control and the deployment of NATO infrastructure.

He then hints that he is ready to re-take the lands he believes should belong to Russia, advancing a number of spurious claims to prove that Moscow would be justified in doing so.

> In 1954, the Crimean Region of the RSFSR was given to the Ukrainian SSR, in gross violation of legal norms that were in force at the time … The right for republics to freely secede from the Soviet Union was the most dangerous time bomb planted in the foundation of our statehood and it

exploded … in 1991, when all those territories and people found themselves abroad overnight, taken away from their historical motherland … It is crystal clear that Russia was blatantly robbed.

Having established the narrative of historical injustices and interfering foreign enemies 'robbing' Russia of her rightful territory, Putin lays out the pretexts on which he might take it back. Just as Hitler alleged mistreatment of ethnic Germans in the Sudetenland as a reason for its annexation, Putin cites tales of oppressed Russians in eastern Ukraine, bullied, abused and demanding the Motherland come to their rescue.

[They] have peacefully made their case. Yet, all of them, including children, have been labelled as separatists and terrorists. They have been threatened with ethnic cleansing and the use of military force … after the riots that swept through Ukrainian cities, after the horror and tragedy of Ukrainian neo-Nazis burning people alive. Russia has done everything to stop the fratricide … but Ukraine's representatives, assisted by Western partners, depict themselves as 'victims of external aggression' and peddle Russophobia. They arrange bloody provocations in Donbas, pandering to their external patrons and masters.

The Ukrainian government, says Putin, is no more than 'a tool in foreign hands', being used to wage war on Russia. In the face of such injustice, Russia will not stand idly by.

The machinations of the anti-Russia project and its Western authors are no secret to us. We will never allow our historical territories and people close to us living there to be used against

Russia. And to those who would undertake such an attempt, I would like to say that this will result in the destruction of their own country.

It is worth pausing to consider what psychological impulses lie behind Putin's decision to write his July 2021 article, which appeared like a bolt from the blue. If you read it carefully, its language is very much in the tradition of the pseudoscience that Stalin and Brezhnev used to come up with. On closer analysis, though, we can see it as a natural result of the evolution of Putin's views on Ukraine and a conscious political provocation that betrays his very concrete, real-world intentions.

At first, Putin had no strong opinions about Ukraine – like most Soviet and Russian people, he simply didn't think about it because it didn't impinge directly on the daily life of their country. Ukrainian independence was no great tragedy; he probably regretted the loss of Crimea, but it wasn't something worth fighting for. As the Putin regime evolved, however, he began to realise that 'post-imperial nostalgia' could be a useful tool to deploy at times of economic decline. He based his imperial idea on a couple of ideological tropes: the concept of a Slavic brotherhood of the three nations – Russia, Ukraine and Belarus – which Putin borrowed from Solzhenitsyn; and the old Slavophile movement, which venerated the Russian empire and believed that owning Ukraine was vital to keeping the empire going. These were the deep-seated historical stereotypes that got him into thinking that Ukraine is an inseparable part of Russia – and now, as a result of Putin's rhetoric, there's a good part of Russian society that believes it, too. Putin's thesis represents a deep historical prejudice that is unlikely to disappear anytime soon.

Putin's discovery of these post-imperial possibilities might have remained a matter between him and his conscience if history hadn't intervened. When the Ukrainians ousted Yanukovych, Putin saw it as an attack on Russia's sovereignty, a personal slight that kick-started the transformation of his personal beliefs into a national policy. And the essence of this policy is that Russia must control Ukraine at all costs. So, annexing Crimea clearly wasn't the end of things: it was just an intermediate step on the path to the full-scale invasion of 2022.

Putin has little or no hesitation about the use of military force. Spurred on by the military General Staff, he has long accepted that everything that is happening is now the first phase of the Third World War. When he massed Russian military forces on Ukraine's borders in the spring of 2021, it may have begun as a bluff; he may have intended to use the show of intimidation as a means to extract concessions from NATO and the West. But if he had genuinely wanted to negotiate with the Americans, it was unlikely that his public proposals would have been so blatantly unacceptable. Putin was demanding a block on NATO expansion into Ukraine and Georgia, and a ban on NATO forces in the countries of the former Warsaw Pact, both of which the West had always made clear it was not prepared to accept.

The reality of the situation was very different. The fact is that Putin and part of his entourage genuinely believe that all the problems inside Russia and in the countries surrounding it are the result of hostile American special operations. Putin genuinely believes – and genuinely fears – that if the Americans have missiles in Russia's neighbouring states against which even the bunker in which he now hides will provide no protection, it means they intend to use them. He has a deep-seated conviction that everyone wants to tear Russia apart and gobble up its natural resources.

Such a distorted view of the world convinced Putin that the only solution is the creation of a belt of buffer states around Russia. And for this to work, the Americans must be made to recognise Moscow's right to dominate this 'zone of influence' and to hold sway over the sovereignty of countries located in it. The problem for Putin and his associates was that they did not know how to get Washington to sit down at the negotiating table and agree to Russia's demands. Economic levers, the type of 'energy blackmail' that can be used against Western Europe, have very little impact on the United States. Putin tried to cause trouble in the US elections as a mechanism to influence its politicians there, by creating havoc and chaos among the electorate, playing on their fears for their personal security or political corruption. Those methods might work in some countries of Western Europe, but in the United States threats and provocations result not in fear, but in reciprocal antagonism.

For all those reasons, Putin concluded that apart from the never-ending threat of the nuclear arms race, his most effective bargaining mechanism was the instigation of international conflicts. The Kremlin fomented political and humanitarian crises in Syria, in Libya and in Venezuela, followed by the 2022 invasion of Ukraine. There were, though, significant downsides. The Russian public may have approved of the bloodless annexation of Crimea by the Kremlin's 'polite little men', but having their sons called up to serve in a foreign conflict against a fellow Slav nation is considerably less attractive. And then, there are the practical questions that arise from it. The Kremlin can occupy Ukraine, but what does it do next? How does it feed the population? And, God forbid, what happens when local partisans start to fight back? When sabotage begins? Ukraine is not Chechnya: there are 30 million people in mixed Russian-Ukrainian families currently living in Russia and neither they nor anyone else has any appetite for war.

What do ordinary Russians think? Regardless of the truth or otherwise of such claims, the Russian people have been endlessly told that NATO is a danger; but for the Russian in the street, it hardly matters whether the flight time of a US missile is 20 minutes, as it is now, or 5 minutes, as perhaps it might be if it were launched from

Ukraine or Eastern Europe – in either case, the end result is the same because, unlike Vladimir Putin, they don't have a bunker to run to.

Putin is weaker than he makes out, and his solution for domestic weakness is almost always aggression abroad. He knew the adverse consequences that military intervention in Ukraine would have on East–West relations, and while he says he is prepared to weather that storm, he has begun work on an insurance policy. Throughout its history, when Russia has encountered difficulties in its relationship with the West, it has threatened to make common cause with China. Stalin used the triumph of Mao Zedong's communists in 1949 to put pressure on the newly founded NATO alliance. Brezhnev, Chernenko and Andropov all flirted with Beijing when relations worsened with Washington. And Putin is making the same move today.

There is, however, a difference: in former times, Russia held the whip hand, while China was the weaker party, economically, politically and militarily. Moscow could therefore manipulate the relationship to its own advantage. But that has changed. China has outstripped Russia in all respects, making Putin's gambit decidedly risky. His hope is that Russia could find a strategic and civilisational solution to its struggle with the West by offering to become China's junior partner. It has been done before – Putin's role model is the great Russian prince, Alexander Nevsky, who agreed to kowtow humiliatingly to the rulers of the Horde in return for their support against the West. But Putin is in a weak position if he thinks he can use economic talks with the Chinese as a counterbalance to deteriorating relations with the USA and Western Europe. My own experience of working with Chinese companies taught me that the Chinese are tough negotiators. We supplied them with several million tons of oil per year, helping to construct rail border crossings to transport it, and we reached agreement on a pipeline to China from Angarsk in Siberia. In all our negotiations, the Chinese were quick to exploit every advantage they held over us. The only way we could get a fair price for our oil was by demonstrating to them that we had the capacity to sell it on the European market where rates were higher, so the Chinese could not demand a cut-price deal from us. Putin does not have that luxury. If he wants to sell to China to spite the West, Beijing is not going to be generous in the terms it offers. The Chinese offers so far have been remarkably bad. According to the leading Russian oil and gas analyst, Mikhail Krutikhin, Gazprom's sales in 2021 went for an average of $170 per thousand cubic metres of gas, compared with the European gas price of $270 per thousand cubic metres. Rosneft's sales of oil were similarly uneconomic. Putin has failed to learn the lesson that China and Chinese companies will never fail to take advantage of the geopolitical follies of a would-be trading partner. Not only has Putin agreed to unprofitable commercial contracts, he has also made concessions in the historic border disputes on Russia's eastern frontier, ceding territory to China on the Amur and Ussuri rivers.

The geopolitical benefit to Russia from all these concessions is very doubtful. But Putin's real aim in signalling that the Kremlin is willing to take on the role of junior partner to Beijing is to cause alarm in Washington. It has raised the stakes in East–West negotiations, forcing the West to turn a blind eye to some of the domestic and foreign policy misdemeanours of the temporary occupant of the Kremlin. There is real alarm in some European capitals that Beijing will henceforth have a hidden role in determining Moscow's future policy direction. In my opinion, the alarm has been raised too late – this is now the reality with which we have to live. Indeed, the main problem for Putin is not the reaction of the West, but the potential discontent of the Russian people. Russians are much more wary of Beijing gaining influence over their domestic affairs than they are of Paris or Berlin. Putin's spin machine has helped to dampen domestic discontent, but it won't be able to do so forever.

Putin is the victim of a disastrous geopolitical miscalculation. Strategically, China doesn't need a junior partner, and it will never quarrel with the West in order to side with Russia. Quite the opposite. China's long-term interest is possibly to see Russia fall apart so it can snap up our Siberian territories. It doesn't want Russia clinging on to its coattails; and it has no interest in helping to prolong the lifespan of Russia's unviable centralised state, if that were to become necessary. China will not go to war over this, but neither will they offer to help us.

CHAPTER 19
A BLUNT INSTRUMENT

Despite their nations' long and recent history of antagonism towards each other, the world was somewhat surprised by the friendship on show between Vladimir Putin and Donald Trump. There were theories about the Kremlin using compromising material to blackmail Trump into acquiescing in Putin's international scheming, and other suggestions that Trump felt indebted to Putin in helping him win the presidential election. But the real reason for their mutual affinity was that both men are cut from the same cloth.

Donald Trump looked enviously at Putin's model of autocracy, his regal style, his contempt for civic institutions and his crude populism. It seems to me that he would have liked to enjoy such powers himself, overriding the democratic checks and balances that maintain democratic continuity in the US. But this was not a model on which future East–West stability could be built.

The noxiousness of such a recasting of the US democratic model and its toxicity for world peace was evident from the January 2021 events in Washington, DC. The storming of the US Capitol and the need for thousands of National Guardsmen to 'protect law-makers from the American people' played into Putin's hands. It allowed Russian state media to decry the US political system as riddled with double standards. 'The problem is that America's views of its own democracy ... are quite different from when they are applied to other countries,' reported Russian state television. The theme of US hypocrisy trended on Russian social media, includ-ing jokes about alleged American involvement in fomenting politi-cal revolts in former Soviet states. 'Because of international travel restrictions,' one post read, 'it has been announced that this year the United States of America will be staging a coup at home.' 'Why did the Washington coup fail?' asked another. 'Because there wasn't a US embassy on hand to provide tactical support ...'

The departure of Donald Trump in 2021 opened the way for change, and a recognition of the benefits that can flow from a reset in East–West relations. But the undermining of Western liberal democ-racy seemed to have emboldened Putin. Far from engaging with the new administration, he stepped up his campaign of aggression with a series of damaging cyberattacks on key infrastructure targets in North America and Western Europe. In May 2021, ransomware operations carried out by criminals reportedly linked to the Russian Foreign Intelligence Service disrupted the largest fuel pipeline in the United States, leading to shortages across the east coast, the shut-down of fuel stations, panic buying and the cancellation of American Airlines flights. The White House was still debating how to respond to the SolarWinds hack, which stole data from multiple branches of the US federal government, as well as from NATO, Microsoft and the European Parliament, when further cyberattacks in June shut

US Capitol under siege on 6 January 2021

down everything from the Republican National Committee to kinder-gartens in New Zealand and supermarkets in Sweden.

The scale of the onslaught forced the issue to the top of President Joe Biden's agenda. When he met Putin in Geneva a week later, he gave him a list of 16 areas of critical infrastructure that should be exempt from cyberattacks. Putin nodded, smiled and did nothing. Biden pledged that the Russian attacks would 'not go unanswered', but his national security adviser, Jake Sullivan, conceded that options were limited. He hoped a mix of public measures and private cyber-retaliation might force 'a broad strategic discussion with the Russians', but acknowledged that stiffer penalties were problematic. Economic sanctions had shown little evidence of success and there were few potentially effective sanctions left to impose. 'I actually believe that measures that are understood by the Russians, but may not be visible to the broader world, are likely to be the most effective in clarifying what the United States believes is in bounds and out of bounds, and what we are prepared to do in response.'

Sanctions have been the West's go-to response when the Kremlin transgresses yet another norm of international behaviour, but they are not a perfect solution – and the Kremlin has made a point of thumb-ing its nose at Western efforts. In the summer of 2015, as a riposte to Western sanctions, Russian state television showed pictures of moun-tains of French cheese being bulldozed into the ground in Belgorod, near the border with Ukraine. In the village of Gusino, entire legs of smuggled Spanish jamon were burned to a crisp before being thrown into a pit alongside flattened foreign tomatoes, while local officials looked on with satisfied grins usually reserved for the disposal of Class A drugs. That such wanton destruction of high-quality food failed to draw any widespread criticism in a country where pensioners struggle to make ends meet was indicative of the two-edged nature of sanc-tions as a tool of political pressure. The Kremlin has conditioned domestic public opinion to view Western measures as an affront to Russia's dignity and a vindictive attack on ordinary Russians; rather than leading to outcries against their president, they tend to strengthen feelings against the West. Putin's cheese and ham roast was his response to the Western sanctions imposed in the wake of the 2014 Ukraine and Crimea crises. The Russian agriculture minister, Alexander Tkachev, was filmed in a patriotic plea for the nation to 'do everything in its power to ensure that consignments of [Western] food are … destroyed on the spot'. Mobile incinerators were wheeled into border towns, deployed like Katyusha rocket batteries to protect Russia from this latest foreign menace. The spectacle was intended to appeal to Russian pride, to evoke memories of past conflicts and command a spirit of national unity in the struggle against foreign foes.

The success of the Kremlin's campaign was a warning to the West not to play into such a damaging narrative. The sanctions imposed in response to Putin's 2022 invasion of Ukraine are necessary, but after the end of the war and the restoration of Ukraine's sovereignty, they too have to be carefully calibrated. In the longer term, it is not readily apparent that by making the daily life of ordinary Russians harder, we will make them more quickly realise what rogues they have for leaders. When Russians hear Western politicians speaking in the media about sanctions directed against Russia, they feel humiliated, as though they are being targeted and attacked, and this opens the door for the Kremlin's propaganda. I want to stress how important it is to be very accurate in your language when talking about Russia. We often hear the words 'sanctions against Russia'. This is an erroneous approach, because if we talk about the Russia of 144 million people, such broad sanctions against the country as a whole cannot change anything.

The perception of being bullied and humiliated by the West plays into the hands of those nationalists who want Russia to isolate herself from the global community. It allows the Kremlin to frame Western sanctions as punishing the Russian people, rather than the regime, a manifestation of continuing foreign attempts to undermine and contain Russian power. Unrefined sanctions simply make the Russian population look more favourably at their own government and less favourably at the West.

Putin called the wave of sanctions triggered by the invasion of Ukraine 'a declaration of war', while Dmitri Medvedev attempted to frame them as an attack on 'all Russian people'. In his first ever post on Telegram, one of the few social networks still freely accessible in Russia, Medvedev called the sanctions yet more evidence of the 'West's frenzied Russophobia'. The West must avoid providing the Kremlin with fuel for this propaganda by making it clear that its sanctions are directed at Putin and his government cronies who launched the Ukraine war. The state machine is run by a relatively small group of people who are responsible for the bad things that are done. Behind them there are more or less two organisations: the presidential administration and the FSB. It is this system that is turning the state into what we know it as today, and it is the men and women who keep this system afloat who need to be the targets of sanctions.

It is well known that sanctions are an imperfect tool. Their impact can be hard to assess and often takes many years to become apparent; but that does not mean they should be discarded entirely. Correctly targeted sanctions are crucial for applying pressure on regimes that flout international law and treat their citizens like slaves. Sanctions can punish unacceptable behaviour and discourage further breaches. But they must be used carefully to be effective. This is because the first people to suffer from unfocused sanctions are the population generally, while the powerful people – the people who run the regime – can find ways of getting around them. Branko Milanović, an international economist at the City University of New York, warned that the first effect of indiscriminate sanctions is to worsen social inequality, because their primary impact is on the people who have the least power and are the most economically vulnerable. 'Blanket sanctions ... are fundamentally wrong. Their objective is ostensibly to change the behaviour of a certain government. But ... they punish people who actually don't have any influence or very small influence on what the government does.'

In his annual telethon in June 2021, Vladimir Putin put a brave face on the 'sanctions battle', minimising the suffering of the Russian people and suggesting that the Russian economy had actually benefited. 'We have not just adapted to the sanctions pressure. In some ways, they even did us good: replacing imported technologies with our own gave us an impetus to production ... The world is changing and changing rapidly. No matter what sanctions are applied to Russia, no matter what they frighten us with, Russia is still developing, economic sovereignty is increasing, defence capability has reached a very high level and, in many important parameters, has surpassed many countries of the world, and in some of them, even surpassed the United States.'

It is true that the Kremlin's embargo on the importation of Western foodstuffs prompted improvements in domestic agricultural production, in particular a broadening of the cheese and dairy sector. But 'import substitution' has fallen short of its targets and poor quality knock-offs of European favourites have failed to meet consumer demands. Overall agricultural production has increased, but not sufficiently to counter negative impacts. A 2019 study by researchers from the Russian Presidential Academy of National Economy and Public Administration (RANEPA) and the Centre for Economic and Financial Research (CEFIR) calculated that the Kremlin's food embargo costs Russians $70 per person per year in higher priced fish, meat, cheese and vegetables, a significant sum in a country where many pensioners survive on little more than $200 a month. 'Five years after the introduction of counter-sanctions,' the study noted, 'Russian consumers continue to pay for them from their own pockets. Although a few industries have experienced a positive impact from the import substitution policy, most of them are not effective enough to change general price dynamics.' In short, the Kremlin's ban on food imports has had little impact on the West, but continues to penalise ordinary Russians.

When people suffer, however, it is human nature to look for someone to blame, and this can be a less than rational process. The Kremlin has had success in manipulating people's emotions, deflecting blame away from itself and pointing the finger instead at the ubiquitous 'common enemy.' Putin has created the narrative of a West motivated by irrational hatred of Russia and of the Russian people, and has applied it not only to sanctions, but to any criticism of his regime. Even the most factual critiques are dismissed as 'Russophobia'. When Kremlin power brokers are targeted for personal sanctions as a result of their actions, they routinely attribute it to Western bigotry. 'I have not heard anything about any violation of human rights,' Yevgeny Prigozhin declared in a statement to the BBC when he was added to the sanctions list, 'and I am sure that this is an absolute lie. My advice to you is to operate with facts, not your Russophobic sentiments.'

The suspension of trade in Russia by Western companies such as Starbucks, popular clothing brands, hotels and restaurants that followed Putin's invasion of Ukraine, together with the exclusion of Russia from sporting events and Eurovision, had the potential to make ordinary Russians feel they were being victimised and to provide fuel for the Kremlin's claims of Western Russophobia. The lesson for the West is that, in the longer term, sanctions will need to be finely tuned and their purpose clearly explained; they must target those who profit from the corruption and lawlessness of the Putin regime, while making clear to the Russian people what the aim of the measures truly is.

The West can remove ammunition from the Kremlin spin doctors by differentiating between the crooks in the leadership and Russia as a whole. Be clear who the opponent is; do not use Russia as a scapegoat for the West's own problems, as has happened in American politics. Yes, the Kremlin sought to meddle in US elections, but its role shouldn't be exaggerated. Democracy in America is put at risk by the behaviour of its own politicians, by the rise of populism and developments in global social trends, not just by the malevolent force from the East. Superhuman powers should not be assigned to a president who Navalny and many others now refer to as 'the old man in his bunker', a leader who makes increasingly rare public appearances and fears the world beyond the Kremlin walls. It's a mistake to engage with the hysterical polemics promoted by Russian state media, or with the conspiracies propagated by the Russian Ministry of Foreign Affairs. Trying to refute spokesperson Maria Zakharova's contention that the British state poisoned the Skripals in order to frame Russia, or that Navalny poisoned himself, only plays into their hands. It is best to deal with the realities and the facts, and to avoid playing into the Kremlin blame game. As Professor Daniel Drezner, author of *The Sanctions Paradox*, points out, when sanctioned regimes fear they are failing to keep their population onside by using the 'common enemy' tactic, they will increasingly 'enact repressive measures'.

Recent events have demonstrated that a dictatorship has finally been established in Russia. Any hint of decorum has been cast aside. The electoral process has become a smokescreen. Putin's political opponents are not allowed to run in the elections, criminal cases are fabricated against them; and, finally, in some cases, they are poisoned. As Putin and his stooges become increasingly helpless and desperate, they openly resort to violence to quell dissent.

Since the original imposition of sanctions in 2014, the West has got better at tailoring and explaining its measures, but there is still more work to do. The Americans gradually pivoted to individually targeted sanctions. That was very painful for those named individuals. But here, too, not enough effort was put into explaining why these particular sanctions were being applied to these people. As a result, their effect was lessened, because the Russian authorities told their citizens their own version of the story, that the Americans were punishing Russia for daring to have an independent foreign policy.

Personal sanctions that target specific people for clearly specified reasons have the potential to curb the influence of Putin, his friends and the regime's sponsors. Sanctions should target the perpetrators of illegal orders and political repression, individuals who distort the workings of a normal state. That includes judges, security officials, prosecutors, intelligence services, as well as the sponsors and asset holders of Putin's inner circle. The sanctions' targets should be people and businesses who directly violate, sponsor or facilitate the spread of corruption, disinformation and illegal influence in the West, or promote human rights abuses in Russia.

Who are these people and how are they affected? Oleg Deripaska, the founder of Rusal, until recently the largest aluminium producer in the world, is an example of someone targeted by personal sanctions against members of Putin's entourage. To remain as rich as Deripaska has in Putin's Russia means total subservience to the Kremlin. Few of Putin's oligarchs are more influential and loyal than Deripaska, as the Mueller Report amply demonstrated. In 2018, the United States Treasury nominated Deripaska for sanctions as a result of his 'having acted or purported to act for or on behalf of, directly or indirectly, a senior official of the Government of the Russian Federation', as well as his 'claims to have represented the Russian government in other countries'. This had a staggering impact on Russia's main share index, which slumped by 11 per cent when the sanctions came into effect.

Deripaska's public pronouncements suggest quite strongly that targeted sanctions can work. In late 2020, he complained that the measures against him were part of a 'war' against Russia, 'no better than a bombing raid on our cities or direct attacks on our borders'. Deripaska's words reflect the extent of the disconnect between the ruling elite and the people of Russia. 'Those who directly or indirectly provoke sanctions against [us],' he added, 'should logically be considered to have betrayed the country and suffer the corresponding judicial consequences.' I responded to Deripaska at the time: 'So, [the West] preventing people from spending millions abroad while they are nominally employed as civil servants in Russia, or refusing to allow into their countries those people who go unpunished for torture and murder in Russia, amounts to a hybrid war? To me this is actually just basic morality.'

Alongside Deripaska, the US Treasury Department in 2018 targeted a number of people close to Putin: oil, gas and mineral tycoons Vladimir Bogdanov, Suleiman Kerimov, Viktor Vekselberg and Igor Rotenberg; Putin's former son-in-law Kirill Shamalov; former prime minister Mikhail Fradkov; head of the Security Council Nikolai Patrushev; Gazprom CEO Alexey Miller; and Viktor Zolotov, head of Putin's Praetorian Guard, the Rosgvardiya. It was a warning to the corrupt officials of the Kremlin and a signal to the Russian business community that has for so long propped up this authoritarian junta that they are not safe, and Putin cannot protect them forever.

Paradoxically, the Kremlin criminals who accuse their critics of being 'Russophobes' and 'foreign agents' have nearly all stashed their cash in Western countries, via shell companies or under the names of family and friends who live abroad. They do so because they know that keeping their money in Russia exposes it to the ravages of a predatory state, renowned for its arbitrary confiscation of private property. The existential paradox of any kleptocratic system is that those who have stolen money do not trust the regime that has let them steal it. They seek to hide this dirty money where it cannot be taken from them. It is estimated that well over $1 trillion of private Russian money is in foreign banks, and, while some of it is perfectly legitimate, a very large amount of it is not. Capital outflows have increased markedly in recent times, much to Putin's displeasure.

These thieves must not be allowed to continue hiding their money in the West, using the financial centres of London and New York to launder cash stolen from the Russian people. If the West wishes to combat the criminals in the Kremlin, it must agree to be more transparent and more decisive in its actions. During the election campaign of 2020, then President-elect Biden pledged that he would 'issue a presidential policy directive that establishes combating corruption as a core national security interest and democratic responsibility'. He undertook to 'lead efforts internationally to bring transparency to the global financial system, go after illicit tax havens, seize stolen assets, and make it more difficult for leaders who steal from their people to hide behind anonymous front companies'. The strengthened sanctions announced by Washington, Brussels and London in March 2022 suggest that the West is finally getting serious about ending the old practices of financial secrecy for Putin and his criminal associates. While the war in Ukraine continues to rage, while the Putin regime is killing people en masse, no sanctions can be considered too harsh. Western governments might even be criticised for leaving obvious loopholes and opportunities for circumventing them. What I am talking about is the medium-term and the longer-term future.

The Magnitsky Act is another proven tool to push back against Russian human rights abusers, and it is right to extend its application to those people involved in persecuting, poisoning and arresting Alexei Navalny. It is not a question of new laws, but of enforcing existing legislation, as the United States did when it designated the GRU and two of its specific officers, the FSB, three research institutes and five Russian government officials linked to the use of a chemical weapon in contravention of international law for the nerve agent attacks on Navalny and the Skripals. These attacks have brought home to some Western leaders that they, too, are under threat. One German politician told me plainly, that 'it's only the door of my house that separates me from Putin's assassins. No one is protecting me.'

When respected Western politicians sat on the boards of Putin's companies, notorious for their corrupt schemes and for pilfering from the Russian budget, it made it harder to go after these organisations. Most prominent among them was the former German chancellor, Gerhard Schröder. At the end of his term in office in 2005, Schröder agreed to become head of the shareholders' committee of the Nord Stream consortium, the natural gas pipeline project linking Russia to Germany, which he had helped launch a matter of weeks earlier. Schröder later became chairman of the board of Nord Stream AG, as well as chairman of the board of Rosneft when the company was already under sanctions for its role in the conflict in Ukraine. The purpose of Nord Stream was to bypass traditional transit countries, such as Ukraine and Poland, to funnel Russian Arctic gas supplies under the Baltic Sea directly to Germany. The project was controversial from the outset, notably for the central role played by long-term Putin ally and former Stasi agent, Matthias Warnig. Critics warned that the pipeline would open the door for Putin to threaten the curtailment of gas supplies to Ukraine and Poland without endangering supplies in the West, a particularly vindictive means of coercion. So, the decision in the wake of the Ukraine invasion to block Nord Stream marked a substantial turning point.

I have long felt there is a dearth of strong Western leadership. But the recent decisions to freeze assets, not just of those Russians who take part in operations directly against the United States, but also those who fight the free press, who violate human rights and take part in corruption, will have a real impact. Enforcing sanctions is crucial, but it is vital to apply them alongside developmental goals, supporting the people within Russia who are seeking to make a positive difference. The Kremlin's attempt to insulate the Russian people from the truth about the war in Ukraine risks turning Russia into another North Korea, with a population hermetically sealed from the outside world. This must not be allowed to happen. Cultural and scientific exchanges, assistance in education and the raising of the new generation must be maintained where possible, as only this will help to build the civil society of the future. No matter how well intentioned those who suggested imposing sanctions in the fields of culture, education and science might have been, this is not sensible in the longer term; once the war is over and Ukrainian sovereignty has been guaranteed, it will be vital to restore cultural ties between Russia, Europe and the broader West in the future. If this does not happen, the West will struggle to show itself to be an ally of the Russian people, rather than simply a force determined to topple its government.

CHAPTER 20
YOU ARE NOT SAFE

At the beginning of July 2018, along with many people in the United Kingdom, I opened my newspaper to discover headlines about a middle-aged couple in the southern English city of Salisbury who had fallen mysteriously ill. Four months earlier, Salisbury had been the scene of the attempted assassination by Kremlin agents of a former Russian military intelligence officer, Sergei Skripal, and the British media were already making a connection between the two events. As someone with first-hand experience of Vladimir Putin's methods, I knew this did not make sense. In the minds of Putin's regime, Skripal was a legitimate target – a person who had expressed his disgust at the men running his homeland by cooperating with the British; but the couple in the latest story had no involvement with Russia or indeed with politics of any sort. Dawn Sturgess and Charlie Rowley were in their mid-40s, unemployed and existing on the fringes of British society. Dawn, who was a mother of three children, had a history of drug abuse and she and Charlie were living in hostels for the home-less. The couple were known to scavenge in litter bins and recycling containers. Why on earth would Vladimir Putin select them as targets for his hit squads?

In the weeks that followed, the terrible truth emerged. On the morning of Sunday, 30 June, Dawn Sturgess had unexpectedly collapsed. An ambulance was called and Dawn was taken to hospital. Later that day, Charlie Rowley fell ill and he too was rushed to hospi-tal. Dawn's condition worsened and she fell into a coma. The doctors decided she could not be saved and, on 8 July, her life support system was switched off. When Wiltshire Police concluded that foul play was involved, the story became national news. Two days later, Charlie regained consciousness. The hospital reported that he was no longer in a critical condition, but his health had been severely impaired; an unknown substance had inflicted serious damage on the functioning of his central nervous system.

Charlie told the police officers who came to see him that he had discovered a bottle of Nina Ricci perfume in a charity shop bin. After they opened it and Dawn sprayed herself with the contents, they had begun to experience symptoms of dizziness and nausea. When blood samples from Dawn and Charlie were sent for analysis to the British government's Defence Science and Technology Laboratory at Porton Down, it became clear that they – like Sergei Skripal and his daughter before them – had been poisoned by the Novichok nerve agent. The BBC reported that police were working on the hypothesis that the fake Nina Ricci bottle had been left over from the attack on the Skripals and had been disposed of 'in a haphazard way'.

It all made sense. The agents sent by Vladimir Putin to murder a former Russian intelligence operative had assumed their job was done and had simply thrown away a vial of deadly poison, with no regard for the harm it could do to the person who might stumble across it.

As it happened, that person was Dawn Sturgess, an innocent woman completely unconnected to the Machiavellian world of the Kremlin, a mother, a friend, a partner, a precious human soul. When Charlie gave her the Nina Ricci perfume, it is easy to imagine how happy it would have made her, how delighted Dawn would have been with such a show of affection. But it would be the cause of their terrible fate.

The unmitigated cynicism of Putin's regime was demonstrated by its response to the global outrage at its actions. By early September, the Organisation for the Prohibition of Chemical Weapons – the body that polices compliance with the International Chemical Weapons Convention – had concluded that the Novichok that killed Dawn Sturgess was from the same batch used against the Skripals, and the British police revealed that the two suspects in both cases were serving members of the Russian special services. The Kremlin, as was to be expected, denied any involvement in the attacks – it could hardly do otherwise – but at the same time, it gave Russian state media the go-ahead to glory in its murderous deeds.

The state television station, Channel One, sneered that the accusations against the Russian special services were 'the usual British Russophobia', but simultaneously boasted that the Kremlin would always hunt down 'traitors' such as Sergei Skripal. 'Being a traitor to the Motherland ... is one of the most hazardous professions,' gloated the presenter of the evening news, Kirill Kleimenov. 'Whether you are a professional traitor or you just burn with hatred for your mother country, I would warn you very strongly not to flee to England. There's obviously something wrong over there – there have been lots of examples ... so many strange incidents when people get hanged or poisoned, or they die in helicopter crashes and fall mysteriously out of windows.'

The cynical charade of pleading innocence but confirming with a nod and a wink that 'we did it' is characteristic of Putin's macho posturing. When the two suspects were identified as GRU operatives 'Alexander Petrov' and 'Ruslan Boshirov', Putin gleefully put them up for an interview with the Russian propaganda channel, RT. The ostensible purpose was for the men to deny they had carried out the deed, but the prepared script they were given to memorise was so ludicrously implausible that it was clear Putin was ridiculing the British authorities and all those involved.

Speaking in a learned-by-rote monotone, Petrov and Boshirov claimed that they had been innocent tourists. 'Our friends had been suggesting for a long time that we visit this wonderful town [Salisbury]. There is a famous cathedral there. It is famous for its 123-metre-high spire ... and for its famous clock, the first clock to be invented in the world.'

When the interviewer seemed mildly surprised that the men had flown all the way from Moscow to visit a clock, Petrov explained, 'Well, our plan was actually to spend some time in London and then travel to Salisbury. It wasn't a business trip. We went to the railway station to see the timetable ... But when we arrived in Salisbury on 3 March, it was blocked up with snow, so we could only spend half-an-hour there ... The town was covered with muddy slush. We went back to the station and took the train back to London.'

Having examined CCTV recordings of Petrov and Boshirov walking in Salisbury, Scotland Yard had concluded that this first visit was a reconnaissance trip to locate and survey the house where their targets – Sergei Skripal and his daughter, Yulia – were living. When they returned the following day and spent much longer in the city, the GRU-men's presence coincided with the moment the Skripals were poisoned.

'Maybe we did approach the Skripals' house that day [4 March],' Boshirov shrugged, before correcting himself. 'But we don't know where it is, so I can't say for certain ... At lunchtime, it started snowing

Ruslan Boshirov and Alexander Petrov snapped on their mission to kill Sergei Skripal

again so we left Salisbury earlier than we had planned.' Asked if they had been carrying Novichok in a Nina Ricci perfume bottle, the men expressed incredulity. 'We're normal blokes,' laughed Boshirov. 'It'd be silly for normal blokes to be carrying women's perfume. The British customs always check all your luggage, so they'd have had questions about normal blokes carrying women's perfume in their luggage, wouldn't they …'

Even the RT interviewer, Margarita Simonyan, herself an active participant in the propaganda charade, couldn't hide her surprise at the crudity of the men's denials. At one point in the interview, she is seen looking witheringly at them and saying, 'You seem to be sweating … Maybe you'd like some air conditioning?'

In another clumsy PR exercise, Charlie Rowley was invited to the Russian embassy in London, where Ambassador Alexander Yakovenko was photographed welcoming the man who had nearly been killed by the emissaries of Yakovenko's boss and whose partner had died an agonising death at their hands. In a cynical concoction of 'alternate facts', Yakovenko told Rowley that it was probably the Americans or the Czechs who had poisoned him and Dawn, and invited him to come to Moscow, where he would 'get better medical treatment than he was receiving in the UK' and might even be able to meet Vladimir Putin.

The events of 2018 and the Kremlin's public response to them bear the unmistakable hallmarks of countless similar operations in the past. I am aware that the Kremlin special services have continued to manufacture chemical weapons, which are banned by international treaties. They did so in Soviet times and they are doing so now. Secret laboratories produce poisons that have resulted in a number of unsolved deaths, in addition to the attack on Alexei Navalny. Since Putin came to power, the capacity of the poison labs has seemingly been developed and updated in line with new developments in the biochemical sciences, keeping pace with the Kremlin's demands for specific poisons for specific operations. The main requirement, it appears, is that the symptoms they produce must deter the medics and investigators of foreign countries from identifying the hand of the Kremlin.

The use of polonium in the 2006 murder of Alexander Litvinenko, for example, was a deliberate calculation. Polonium is dispersed in water and has no taste, so a person is unlikely even to know he has been attacked; and unlike most other poisons, there is no antidote for it. The FSB was well aware that cases of polonium irradiation are so rare that doctors do not test for it, meaning that the cause of death is unlikely to be discovered.

In Litvinenko's case, the FSB was unlucky. They had counted on the fact that most victims of polonium poisoning die within a few days; but Litvinenko's strong physical condition allowed him to survive for three weeks, which gave the medics at London's University College Hospital time to investigate all the possible causes of his sickness. It was only on the day before his death that they finally checked for polonium; had Litvinenko died a day earlier, the killers would have got away undetected. And if the doctors hadn't have figured out that it was polonium, the British police would never have traced its distinctive trail of alpha radiation across London and back to Moscow.

Under Vladimir Putin, there has been a dramatic rise in the number of political poisonings. Anna Politkovskaya, the investigative journalist who wrote critically of Putin's activities in Chechnya, was unsuccessfully poisoned before she was eventually shot in 2006. The anti-Kremlin Ukrainian President Viktor Yushchenko was fed deadly dioxin at a dinner in 2004 with security officials loyal to Moscow, but survived with disfiguring injuries. In 2003, Yuri Shchekochikhin, a vocal opposition member of the Russian Duma, died from the effects of unexplained radiation exposure. In 2004, Roman Tsepov, a former bodyguard to the St Petersburg mayor Anatoly Sobchak and, briefly, to Vladimir Putin, was poisoned with an unidentified substance. An official investigation declared the cause of death unproven, but sources within the investigative team suggested symptoms compatible with radiation poisoning. And in August 2020, the Russian opposition activist, Alexei Navalny, spent two and a half weeks in a coma after being poisoned with a new type of Novichok while returning from Siberia to Moscow. Investigations uncovered the identities of the FSB agents who had smeared the deadly nerve agent on Navalny's clothes, but the Russian authorities refused to bring criminal proceedings against them, declaring that there was no evidence of a crime having been committed.

A common factor in all of these cases has been the immense suffering the poison inflicts on its victims. Polonium, for instance, rots and destroys the human body from within, eating up the internal organs with no way to alleviate its terrible, inexorable torture. The evidence suggests that the Kremlin's aim is not just to kill, but to kill with such inhuman cruelty that it will intimidate and terrify its enemies and potential future enemies worldwide – an exemplary killing that will not allow anyone to forget it and will not allow anyone to feel safe, wherever they are.

The Litvinenko operation was aimed not just at Litvinenko himself, but also at his boss, the exiled anti-Putin oligarch, Boris Berezovsky. The FSB's assassin, Andrei Lugovoy, spent the evening before the murder sitting in Berezovsky's office, spreading polonium on to his furniture, making a show of Berezovsky's vulnerability, only to spare him and kill his lieutenant. Putin was saying, 'We could have killed you, but we didn't; you are at our mercy ...'

State-run Russian television offered the usual tongue-in-cheek denial – 'It wasn't the Kremlin who did this, because it had nothing to gain from killing Litvinenko' – before identifying the real target of the exercise. 'If the Kremlin wanted to exterminate its opponents, think about it …,' said the smiling presenter. 'Stalin had Trotsky knocked off, not Trotsky's chauffeur. Not Trotsky's dog … Litvinenko isn't Trotsky. I'm sorry, but Litvinenko is Trotsky's dog!' If the FSB had murdered 'Trotsky's dog', they had murdered him at his master's heel. The message was clear: we know this is a Western country, we know you think you are protected; but we have the power and you are not safe.

In Stalinist times, the communist leadership despatched teams of assassins around the globe to hunt down 'traitors to the Motherland'. During the brief window of East–West rapprochement under Boris Yeltsin, that sort of thinking was abandoned, but Vladimir Putin has brought it back. A law passed in July 2006 gave the security forces the explicit right to kill enemies of the state at home or abroad. 'Special operations divisions of the Federal Security Service [FSB],' states article 9.1 of Federal Law No. 153-FZ, 'may be deployed, by decision of the President of the Russian Federation, against terrorists … located outside the territory of the Russian Federation in order to eliminate a threat to the security of the Russian Federation.' Specifically mentioned as legitimate targets are people, such as Boris Berezovsky, who call for political change in Russia, described in legal jargon as 'individuals … aiming to forcibly change the constitutional system of the Russian Federation'. It's a formula that allows the FSB wide discretion, and it has been widely deployed. FSB commanders no longer need to request permission to kill; the law is in place and no one is going to punish them.

Speaking about the poisoning of Alexei Navalny, Putin laughed at calls for an investigation. 'Who needs him [Navalny]?' he sneered. 'If somebody had wanted to poison him, they would finish him off.'

When he was asked in March 2021 if he thought Putin was a killer, Joe Biden had no hesitation in answering in the affirmative. Decisions on the legitimate use of force are made by the leaders of many states and this in itself does not make them murderers. Force may be justified if it is used in the public interest, following a proper legal process and when no other means is possible. The key phrases are 'due process' and 'in the public interest'. The arbitrary and unjustified decisions taken by Putin, or by his entourage with Putin's consent, meet none of these criteria. They are common criminal acts of violence and murder carried out in the venal interests of corrupt individuals.

CHAPTER 21
MAKING MARTYRS

When Alexei Navalny flew back to Russia on 17 January 2021, I'm sure he knew he would be arrested and sent to jail. He had been poisoned five months earlier by the Russian secret police, the FSB, on the orders of Vladimir Putin. His crime was to reveal the corruption and self-enrichment of the president at the expense of the Russian nation.

I had myself travelled exactly the same path 18 years earlier, so I understood better than most why Navalny took the deliberate step of being imprisoned, possibly for a long time. As I explained earlier, I knew that when I confronted Putin in 2003, I was likely to be arrested.

I had pointed out the corruption in Vladimir Putin's Kremlin and Alexei Navalny had done the same. After he was poisoned, he had been flown for treatment to Germany and could easily have stayed in relative safety abroad. He chose to return because he had wanted to make a difference to the future of Russia, but he was arrested at the gates of Moscow airport. Like me, he was tried on nonsensical charges of embezzlement. A court in February 2021 sentenced him to three-and-a-half years in a labour camp; and in February 2022 he was put on trial again, facing charges that carried a maximum penalty of 15 years.

Will Navalny's sacrifice change things? I hope so. I can say with certainty that my denunciation of corruption in the Kremlin, followed by my ten years as a political prisoner, made many more Russians aware of the big questions facing our country today. It gave me the opportunity to continue promoting the values of freedom and democracy. Putting Alexei Navalny in jail and keeping him there may seem like a solution for Putin, but it creates a very public martyr that the world will find hard to ignore.

For the Russian people, even those who dislike figures such as Navalny, there is a recognition that the willingness to suffer persecution and imprisonment is a token of integrity in the pursuit of a moral cause. Memories remain strong of Soviet-era dissidents such as Sergei Kovalev, Anatoly Shcharansky, Lyudmila Alekseeva and Nobel Peace Prize winner Andrei Sakharov. Navalny in jail is a rallying point. For much of the Russian intelligentsia it makes the situation black and white – you can either support Putin and the continuation of the status quo in Russia, or you can support the fight for democracy, through Navalny.

There have been calls for me to take a more central role in opposition politics, which is something I have considered doing in the past. But I do not wish to repeat the example of Boris Berezovsky, who came to London and railed against Putin without achieving much, before ultimately asking the Kremlin to allow him to return to Russia and dying before he could do so. Instead, I am committed to working with all the representatives of the progressive opposition, including Navalny, Garry Kasparov, Andrei Pivovarov, Dmitry Gudkov and others. I want to contribute something constructive,

Alexei Navalny at a court hearing in Moscow, February 2021

taking an objective view of East–West relations, to propose solutions that will benefit the people of Russia, America and the world. Now, with history hastening its march, I am convinced more than ever that the future lies with us. There is ample and growing evidence that the Putin regime is becoming desperate, resorting to ever greater violence and repression to thwart the aspirations of the Russian people. The decision to invade Ukraine was an irresponsible gamble with genuine potential to rebound on Putin and his cronies. This is the moment to find hope and to take action.

In the spring and summer of 2021, there was a very public display of the Kremlin's despairing struggle to hold back the tide of change. The wall of an electrical substation in St Petersburg's Pushkarsky Park became the setting for an exploration of memory, truth and freedom that summed up the dynamic of a regime gripped by panic. Overnight on 14 July, a banner appeared on the substation wall. In the style of the Beatles' *Revolver* album, it depicted a series of faces that most Russians would recognise, including the murdered investigative journalists, Anna Politkovskaya and Anastasia Baburova, the murdered opposition politician, Boris Nemtsov, the slain human rights activist, Natalya Estemirova, and other victims of the struggle for freedom of expression.

The inscription on the banner, 'Heroes of recent times', was a homage to those who had been brave enough to ask questions of Vladimir Putin's regime and have lost their lives as a consequence. It was also a reference to a mural that previously, briefly, had adorned the substation wall, a smiling image of Alexei Navalny, titled 'A hero of the new era'.

The people in the banners and the murals are the folk the Kremlin fears most, men and women that Putin's government would like society to forget. The Navalny image was discovered at 6am on 28 April and had been painted over by 10.30am. The banner, too, was

The short-lived banner honouring 'Heroes of Recent Times' in St Petersburg's
Pushkarsky Park

An official removes Alexei Navalny's likeness from the same St Petersburg wall

swiftly removed by the authorities and its creators were tracked down and fined.

But almost immediately, a new image appeared in the park; this time not a victim, but an enforcer. The anonymous serviceman, dressed in camouflage gear, equipped for battle, with his face hidden behind a balaclava, could have come from any one of the Kremlin's tools of repression: the OMON riot police who bludgeon and arrest those who dare to voice their opinions on the streets, the masked FSB agents who raid the apartments of journalists and businessmen, or the 'little green men' sent undercover to invade foreign countries. The inscription now read, 'A hero of our time', the title of Mikhail Lermontov's famous novel of 1840 whose main character, Pechorin, is recognised by Russians as the symbol of the superfluous man who can find no place in a stagnating, backward-looking society.

In the weeks that followed Navalny's return to Russia, the state's masked and camouflaged enforcers had been deployed in cities throughout the country, making over 13,000 arrests in response to the nationwide protests against the corruption and theft that Navalny had exposed. The hulking riot police in their thick body armour and visored helmets, universally known as 'cosmonauts', remain anonymous, unworried by personal responsibility, dispensing violence with impunity. But for Putin, there is a dilemma. His modus operandi has been to allow his cronies to pilfer from public funds as a reward for keeping him in power. If they go too far and their greed is embarrassingly publicised, he would normally dispense discreet punishments to curb their appetites. To do so now, however, would be to admit that Navalny and his fellow corruption-busters were in the right, to risk appearing weak in the face of the opposition. With his back against the wall, Putin chose instead to abandon restraint. He sent Navalny to jail on trumped up charges, then set about destroying his movement and his followers. Using the pretext of the COVID crisis to outlaw demonstrations, the Kremlin ruled that any public gathering would henceforth require an official permit and then routinely refused to grant these permits for opposition protests, allowing the cosmonauts a free hand to intimidate, beat and arrest.

Navalny's Anti-Corruption Foundation, the FBK, was singled out for denunciation. 'Under the guise of liberal slogans,' declared the Moscow Prosecutor's Office, '[it] is engaged in creating conditions for destabilising the social and the socio-political situation … with the intent to overthrow the foundations of the constitutional order.' Driven by the fear of a 'colour revolution' like the ones that so terrified Putin when they occurred in Georgia and Ukraine, the Kremlin declared Navalny's Anti-Corruption Foundation an 'extremist group', a designation previously reserved for terrorist organisations such as al-Qaeda. Anyone deemed to have been associated with FBK or its leaders in the 12 months leading up to the designation was subject to retrospective prosecution and a ban on standing for public office. 'Association' was defined as anything from attending a then-legal demonstration, to posting a supportive message online or merely 'liking' a message by someone else. Sharing FBK's investigative reports was now considered 'disseminating extremist material'.

The catch-all nature of the legislation gave the Kremlin an alarmingly free rein to extend its crackdown. Two of my own media organisations, MBK Media and Open Media, were promptly targeted. These were independent news sources, providing uncensored information to a Russian public that is otherwise deprived of non-state-sponsored reporting. When their online presence was again blocked in August 2021, there was no official announcement and no explanation, other than an indication that it was part of a wider move to target websites which 'incite unrest, extremist activities, or participation in unauthorised rallies'. Vitaly Borodin, whose Kremlin-backed organisation's denunciations provided the pretext for the crackdown, declared

A very different 'Hero of Our Time' is revealed

publicly that investigative journalists are worse than terrorists. Under such circumstances, Russia under Putin has become a killing field. According to the Committee to Protect Journalists, an international NGO that tracks attacks on the press across the globe, at least 58 reporters have been murdered in connection with their work in Russia since 1992. Against a background of such violence, I decided it was no longer possible to continue operating; to do so would put the editorial staff of MBK Media and Open Media at too great a risk. In my statement at the time, I warned that 'these political repressions, including the silencing of journalists and human-rights defenders, demonstrate the regression of Putin's regime and of Putin personally towards the archaic Soviet model, with the added factor of his own personal greed and that of his ruling circle.'

Even before the Navalny ruling, the Russian Prosecutor's Office had declared my political movement Open Russia and my philanthropic organisations – the Future of Russia Foundation, the Khodorkovsky Foundation, the Oxford Russia Fund and European Choice – to be 'undesirable organisations'. The Khodorkovsky Foundation has for over 20 years helped thousands of children from disadvantaged families to get a good education in Russia and in top European universities. The Oxford Russia Fund, which provides scholarships for Russian students to study at Oxford University, has helped hundreds of young Russian men and women by covering their fees, accommodation and travel costs. Closing down these schemes only increased Russia's isolation, depriving her citizens of engagement and dialogue with Europe. They have forced many hopeful and active young people to leave their own country. Unfortunately, the trend of intimidation and political repression is growing ever greater.

After the initial onslaught on Navalny, myself and my associates, an increasing number of independent media platforms has been targeted. Meduza and the Dossier Center had their websites blocked. The investigative media outlet, Proekt, was banned in retaliation for its embarrassing revelations about Putin and other officials. Proekt had carried exposés of Putin's brutal placeman in Chechnya, Ramzan Kadyrov, of Yevgeny Prigozhin and the interior minister, Vladimir Kolokoltsev; it had reported on the Kremlin's bungled response to the COVID crisis and had run a carefully sourced story in 2020 revealing that Putin has an unacknowledged daughter by a secret mistress. Eight Proekt journalists, including its editor, Roman Badanin, were added to a register of 'foreign agents', along with the staff of the US-funded Radio Free Europe/Radio Liberty. The ruling made it illegal for other news organisations to link to or quote from their reports, on pain of criminal charges.

As long ago as 2001, the threat to free speech in Russia had prompted me to set up a training scheme for young journalists, in which promising reporters from regional newspapers, television and radio could learn from prominent figures in the industry. Guest lecturers from independent journals such as *Novaya Gazeta*, *Kommersant* and the online gazeta.ru tried to develop a spirit of questioning curiosity in our young journalists, but found the task harder than they had expected. One lecturer said he struggled to convince the trainees that they should always distrust the official version of stories promulgated by the central or local authorities. He said they had lost the journalist's natural reflex to question the motives of politicians and PR men, so he had to make them promise always to ask themselves, 'Who benefits from this story?'

In the years since then, independent-minded TV channels and newspapers have been targeted, threatened or taken over by Putin-friendly billionaires. Their editors are now made to attend regular 'discussions' with the Kremlin's media-oversight team, at which their editorial lines are dictated to them. The editors are instructed to avoid reporting issues of economic and social shortcomings and are pointed instead towards puff pieces about the government. They are instructed to adopt a critical approach to the West, promoting the perception that the Western democracies are in social and moral decline, while Russians should be thankful to Putin that they live in a stable, morally upright nation. Konstantin Ernst, the chief executive of the main state TV channel, Perviy Kanal, and the man who orchestrated the grandiose patriotism of the opening ceremony of the Sochi Olympics, explained the media's role in terms redolent of Bolshevik ideology. 'The main task of television today,' Ernst declared, 'is to mobilise the country',' adding that 'informing the country' is merely 'task number two'.

The result of the Kremlin's new media-propaganda nexus is a caricatural representation of an America riven by racial injustice, where rampant Russophobia is surpassed only by identity politics so out of control they risk triggering a full-blown ethnic war. As for Western Europe, the picture painted by the Russian media is of societies dominated by LGBTQ+ activists, which they depict as a degenerate 'Gayropa'. The influential, pro-Kremlin TV presenter Dmitry Kiselev, known as 'Putin's mouthpiece', announced on air that gays 'should be prohibited from donating blood and sperm, and in the case of a road accident, their hearts should be either buried or cremated as unsuitable for the prolongation of life'. During the Tokyo Olympics, Olga Skabeyeva, the main presenter of Rossiya 1's primetime talk show, *Sixty Minutes*, delivered a startlingly homophobic commentary over images of Tom Daley, Britain's gay, gold-medal winning diver, while Alexei Zhuravlyov, a member of the Russian parliament, explained that the Russian competitor came only third because he was 'constantly forced to puke at the sight of those queers'.

Putin's increasing reliance on stoking chauvinistic Russian nationalism to maintain his support base in difficult economic times has led him to depend on ever-more extreme expressions of xenophobia.

America and Europe are now depicted as spoiling for a fight with Russia, inciting anti-Russian unrest in former Soviet republics considered part of Russia's 'near-abroad'. In recent years, Putin has sought to propagate a simplistic narrative of jealous foreign rivals, desperate to hurt Russia. 'It has always been thus,' he wrote in 2021:

> from times of ancient folklore through to our modern history. Our opponents or potential opponents have always used very ambitious, power-hungry people to attack Russia. People, including Russians, are growing tired. In all countries of the world, people's irritation has grown, and there is displeasure, including about living conditions and income levels. When a person's living standards decline, he starts blaming the authorities … And, of course, people in Europe, in the US and in other countries are trying to take advantage of that.

As always, truth is the first casualty of war. Nuanced and balanced reporting has no place in the new polarised media landscape. Investigative journalism in Russia, seeking to correct the Kremlin's narratives and hold the powerful to account, is a dangerous business; but a small group of courageous men and women continue to do so, upholding the honourable tradition of Politkovskaya, Baburova, Estemirova and others. When the leading business newspaper, *Vedomosti*, was taken over by a Putin crony in 2020, many of the editorial staff resigned in protest to found their own journal, *VTimes*. Articles on corruption and economic mismanagement by the Kremlin brought swift retaliation. In 2021, the Kremlin placed *VTimes* on its list of 'foreign agents', with a consequent, disastrous withdrawal of advertisers. Announcing that the journal could no longer continue to function, the editors acknowledged defeat in the unequal struggle against state control.

When we launched *VTimes* last year, we announced that we were creating not a propaganda tool, but a high-quality independent media outlet and a platform for the free exchange of constructive opinions. We are proud to say that we achieved that aim. But we have now seen for ourselves that the authorities have no time for professional, non-government-controlled media … The 'foreign agent' label has destroyed our business model. Advertisers are unwilling to cooperate with a 'foreign agent' and we cannot blame them for that.

The 'foreign agent' law, which I mentioned earlier, allows the authorities to penalise any media outlet, NGO or independent organisation that receives funds, including even nominal grants and advertising, from non-Russian sources. It requires them to label anything they publish – from lengthy articles and reports to one-line tweets – with a lengthy, sinister-sounding description of their 'foreign agent' status, making their material virtually untouchable. Distributing or quoting from it without appending the 22-word 'foreign agent' label in typeface twice as big as normal could entail serious legal consequences, with heavy penalties, including prison sentences for repeat offenders.

Ministers and senior Kremlin officials reinforced the hysteria surrounding independent journalism by alleging that Russian non-state media sites are tools of the West. The director of the Foreign Intelligence Service, Sergey Naryshkin, accused Proekt, Insider and iStories of working for Western spy agencies, claiming that the Navalny poisoning was the work of Western agents, carried out so that troublemaking journalists could make Russia look bad, and warning of further such 'attacks' in the future. 'We expect new provocations ahead of the [2021] parliamentary elections. We have information about which points will be hit, but we will not say anything publicly yet. The United States is looking for an external enemy, so they point the finger at us.'

Naryshkin alleged that the source of much independent journalism, the Netherlands-based investigative and fact-checking organisation, Bellingcat, was a front for Western intelligence. 'Bellingcat is needed to exert pressure,' Naryshkin wrote. 'They use dishonest methods. The information they use in their investigations is false and unverified. This group includes a number of former intelligence agents. They're prepared to carry out any task for money. Bellingcat, Navalny's organisations, Proekt, iStories, the Insider — they're all interconnected. It's a complex [intelligence] operation that involves great skill and effort.'

When journalists and activists have tried to defend themselves against the Kremlin's legal intimidation, they have found their advisers subjected to threats and violence, further darkening the outlook for civil society in Russia. The human rights lawyers, Team 29, which represented defendants in several politically motivated cases, including that of Navalny's Anti-Corruption Foundation, were forced into liquidation following harassment by the authorities. Team 29's website was blocked by the Russian censor, Roskomnadzor, allegedly for linking to material from the Prague-based NGO 'Freedom of Information Society', a designated 'undesirable organisation'. In an interview with the Meduza website, Team 29 lawyer Yevgeny Smirnov spoke of the Kremlin campaign against them. '[We] received threats. They said we were a bone in the throat not only of investigators, but also of other people, people in government agencies. Therefore, the decision was made to bomb us with all their might.' Meduza itself has remained operational only by having its headquarters in Latvia, reducing staff salaries and appealing for readers' donations.

Foreign journalists in Russia have also been targeted. Radio Free Europe/Radio Liberty was hit with a $2.4 million fine, which it challenged in the European Court of Human Rights; but before the court could consider the case, the Kremlin had frozen RFE/RL's bank account and sent bailiffs to seize property from its Moscow bureau. In August 2021, the BBC's Sarah Rainsford was expelled with no explanation after more than two decades covering the country. Rainsford believes that her detailed knowledge of Russia, her fluent Russian and her ability to speak directly to ordinary Russians were perceived as unwelcome by the Kremlin:

> The reality is that they don't want people like that here. It's much easier to have fewer people here who understand and who can talk directly to people and hear their stories … to have people who don't speak the language, don't know the country so deeply. [I]t is indicative of an increasingly difficult and repressive environment. [They're] coming for the press, [for] Russian journalists, the few who are left that have been trying to report independently, freely, in extremely difficult circumstances, about Russia to their own people.'

OVD-Info, a Russian non-profit organisation that keeps track of legal data, reported that the 'scale of detentions, administrative and criminal prosecution in connection with the protests of January–February 2021 is by far the largest in the entire history of modern Russia; it demonstrates the complete lack of readiness on the part of the authorities to respect the rights of citizens to freedom of peaceful assembly and, conversely, their readiness to resist protests by any means, including illegal ones.' According to Andrei Kolesnikov of the Carnegie Moscow Center, Putin has 'decided to lock in the results of his first 20 years in power by rolling back liberalism in domestic and foreign policy. The state is now very sincere in its brutality and is not prepared for any more efforts of normalisation.'

The Kremlin's dependence on force to maintain its grip on society doesn't come cheap. The state's need for a loyal and ruthless security apparatus to enforce the application of arbitrary, unpopular laws is reflected in the greatly increased budgets for the security services. A 2020 investigation by Proekt revealed the exponentially growing numbers of Russian citizens employed to control their fellow citizens' behaviour and being paid higher than average wages to do so. The FSB has seen its budget increase year on year, increasing by 70 per cent since 2012, as more and more heavily equipped riot police are despatched on to the streets. The men in the balaclavas may currently have the upper hand in Russia, but the fact that they are needed reveals the weakness at the heart of the Kremlin. Bereft of ideas and ideals, with an open-minded and determined young generation rising up against them, Putin and his cronies will continue to live in fear.

The reason for the crackdown on free speech and the media is not hard to discern. Independent journalists pose no threat to the Russian people; quite the contrary – by creating a culture of accountability they work in society's interest. They do, however, scare those in high places who have secrets to hide. Vitaly Borodin, the Kremlin 'expert' who likened reporters to terrorists, has done his utmost to discredit the journalists at Open Media by accusing them of being a vehicle for my political revenge. '[They] are financed by Khodorkovsky, a fugitive oligarch, who's currently trying to pull off some kind of political coup with Navalny's help. How come Khodorkovsky suddenly decided to become a journalist? He's certainly not a journalist by trade – he's a crook and a villain.'

Putin uses people like me and Navalny to scare those Russian citizens who have swallowed the Kremlin's indoctrination. But there is a new generation emerging, young Russians who were born after the end of the Soviet Union, who have known only the rule of Putin and his cronies. Opinion polls show that these young people have low levels of trust in the current regime; for them, it is not enough for Putin to boast that he is the man who 'ended the chaos of the 1990s'. The new generation came of age after that; they grew up during the oil boom of the early 2000s and have suffered the subsequent collapse in living standards, the degradation in civil freedoms, and the increasing reliance on base nationalism and international aggression. Such posturing may work with older Russians, but not with the young generation. The award of the 2021 Nobel Prize to the independent Russian journalist Dmitry Muratov, editor of the courageous investigative newspaper, *Novaya Gazeta*, was a boost from the international community to the cause of freedom of expression in Russia.

Putin has become trapped by the extremist element of his support base, people he had previously been able to play off against more moderate voices. The extremists are now dictating policy and the Kremlin is terrified that it has lost touch with young Russians who have no truck with scare stories about the West or warnings about the supposed moral degradation of society. A July 2021 poll by the Russian Public Opinion Research Centre, VTsIOM, showed clearly that the under-30s reject the Kremlin's demonisation of personal freedoms, including the right to same-sex marriage.

The Kremlin's panicked response has been to try to prevent people accessing 'undesirable' news from outside Russia. The vaunted 'sovereign internet' project is a Russian version of China's 'Great Firewall', isolating the country from the outside world, scouring social networks for unwelcome material. But it is an unwinnable battle. Putin has neutralised the print media and terrestrial broadcasters, but he is struggling to control information online. He has restricted Facebook and Twitter; he has closed down news websites operating in Russia; but he has not been able completely to block overseas sources and independent Russian sites have continued to operate by moving their operations to Latvia and Lithuania. For those Russians willing to seek out alternatives to the Kremlin's lies – mostly the young, educated, urban generation – there is information available. They can see for themselves the atrocities that Putin has committed in Ukraine, and the intermingling of Russian and Ukrainian families – tens of millions have relatives over the border – has resulted in an unstoppable wave of damning mobile-phone images flowing into the country.

The result has been the emergence of two populations in Russia – the 'TV population', the compliant majority who consume and believe Putin's propaganda; and the 'internet population', a growing minority, who want to make their own minds up. These are the people who staged the public demonstrations against the war in Ukraine, risking arrest and a record that will restrict their future access to employment. Families have been split by arguments between older, pro-Putin parents and independent-minded children. It has caused acrimony, but the subject is at least being discussed and, as more information emerges about the crimes and failures of Putin's war, the debate will widen.

The experience of Chechnya, where Putin spent years struggling to subdue a defiant nation, demonstrated the impact on public opinion of growing Russian casualties. Mothers of soldiers who perished in the fighting formed pressure groups that the Kremlin found hard to silence, and something similar is happening again now. The Russian constitution states that only professional soldiers will be sent into war zones – conscripts are specifically exempted. But on social media, there are numbers of mothers testifying that their sons have been sent into battle, having been falsely told they were taking part in an exercise. Unlike the geographically and ethnically remote Chechnya, Ukraine is a next-door country populated by fellow Slavs, so the emotional impact will be even more powerful.

CHAPTER 22
A BRIGHTER FUTURE

I firmly believe that Russia is not doomed to remain in thrall to the repressive personalised model of autocracy that has been imposed on her by Vladimir Putin. I am convinced that my homeland can become a normal country, blessed by the benefits of market-oriented liberal democracy. There are some who claim such a transformation is impossible, that it is precluded by history, geography and the mentality of the Russian people. When I was in New York many years ago, I met with a prominent correspondent from the *New York Times*, whose ancestors had emigrated from Russia at the start of the twentieth century. He told me that Russians are 'genetically unfit for democracy', that Russians need a father figure in the form of a strong, autocratic ruler who will both punish them and protect them. But it is not only Americans who have sacrificed themselves in defence of the universal rights proclaimed by the US Declaration of Independence; Russians, too, have fought and died for 'Life, Liberty and the pursuit of Happiness'. And sooner or later, the Russian people will build a true democracy for themselves and for their children.

It has been traditional in Russian historiography to equate democracy with the European 'West' and autocratic despotism with the Asiatic 'East'. It is not that we believe these stereotypes to be accurate descriptions of today's geopolitical reality, simply that they have become shorthand in our history for the two models of governance we feel we have been torn between. Russia sits geographically at the intersection of East and West but, for 500 years, the West has been the more important influence on her. There is every likelihood, even in today's difficult times, that Russia will cement her enduring cultural and ideological union with the Euro-Atlantic civilisation she belongs to.

Shortly before my arrest in October 2003, I reflected on the weight of Russia's history that makes our challenge so much greater than that of Western nations. 'Our country has a history of serfdom and slavery. A very brief exception to this ended recently,' I wrote, referring to the democratic experiment of the 1990s. 'And, unfortunately, the psychology of society is the psychology of serfdom. In this situation, the responsibility of a successful businessman is to support the democratic process, regardless of its potential problems. This is the moral duty of people – a duty to our own children to take part in this process.' Despite my optimism for the future, I did not disguise or play down the damaging impact of centuries of autocratic rule in Russia, both on the political and judicial structures of the state and on the minds of the Russian people.

Regrettably, we still do not have the institutions of civil society, which would allow us to hand this function over to political parties and public organizations. For a society like ours, with a history like Russia's, this is normal. We have to understand this, but we also have to struggle to change it. First of all, through education – preparing the future generation. We must say that we have a choice … a real choice: between people in military uniforms and a civil society. Our strength is pretty much equal. And the problem is not that one side has military uniforms and weapons while the other side has nothing. The problem is the mentality.

I set up Open Russia, to help create the missing institutions of a strong civil society and – even more importantly – to change the 'mentality of slavery' that I identified as holding back the nation's progress. This is what the *New York Times* correspondent was referring to when he told me that Russia could never be a democracy. He was expressing a point of view known as historical determinism, or path determinism, which states that Russia's destiny is fixed and can never be changed – that Russia's history and the Russian mentality mean it must forever remain a despotic, centralised autocracy.

Let's look at the historical evidence for this. It is a fact that up until the middle of the thirteenth century, the city states of Novgorod, Kiev, Pskov and elsewhere had been developing a participatory form of governance in which citizens were allowed to have their say, laws were respected and the princes who ruled them could be removed from power by the people. It wasn't democracy as we know it today, but it was similar to what was happening in the rest of Europe. Then, in 1237, disaster struck. The Mongol hordes, highly militarised warriors from East Asia, stormed into Russian lands, capturing and enslaving the population. The Mongol Yoke would last for 240 years, disrupting Russia's economy and setting back her development as a European state.

It is a long-accepted shibboleth of our thinking that Russia needs to be governed by the iron fist; that her vast size and ethnic, linguistic and national diversity make her unsuitable to freedom and democracy. For these reasons, even Catherine the Great, who began her reign as a champion of liberal ideas, ended up endorsing the old system of autocracy.

> The possessions of the Russian Empire extend upon the globe to 32 degrees of latitude, and to 165 of longitude. The Sovereign is absolute, for no authority but the power centred in his single person can act with the vigour proportionate to the extent of such a vast dominion. The extent of the dominion requires that absolute power be vested in the one person who rules over it ... All other forms of government whatsoever would not only be prejudicial to Russia, but would provoke its entire ruin.

What could be clearer? Russia, Catherine asserted, is too big and too unruly ever to be suited to democracy; only the strong hand of centralised autocracy can keep such a disparate, centripetal empire together and maintain order among her people.

For their part, the Bolsheviks were little different. They, too, imposed a despotic centralised rule that enslaved the very workers and peasants they had claimed to liberate. Writing in the 1960s, the great Soviet writer Vasily Grossman compared Russia to a 'slave girl' held captive by Lenin's tyrannical zealots:

> Lenin's intolerance, his contempt for freedom, the fanaticism of his faith, his cruelty towards his enemies, were the qualities that brought victory to his cause ... and Russia followed him – willingly at first, trustfully – along a merry intoxicating path lit by the burning estates of the landowners. Then she began to stumble, to look back, ever more terrified of the path

stretching before her. But the grip of his iron hand leading her onwards grew tighter and tighter … While the West was fertilised with freedom, Russia's evolution was fertilised by the growth of slavery.

Vladimir Putin has inherited and exploited the form of governance established by his tsarist and socialist predecessors. Like the Mongols, like Catherine and like Lenin, he too wields autocratic power, arguing that the Yeltsin years of botched democracy are proof that Russia needs strong rule from above. But our nation's centuries of autocracy have been paralleled by another current of thought. Russia's so-called Westernisers have argued for the rejection of despotism and a decisive turn towards Western values – European-style constitutionalism and social justice. It was a view that has found plenty of support among the Russian intelligentsia and is a tradition to which I count myself an adherent today.

It is true that the model of governance in Russia for almost a millennium has been autocracy, albeit with fairly powerful local self-government that was not destroyed until the time of Stalin. But this does not mean Russia cannot change; she is not condemned to remain forever outside the community of free, democratic nations.

Putin is the latest in the line of Russian autocrats and there are indications that he will be the last. The world is changing; no country – not even North Korea – can hide its archaic practices from the eyes of the world. Where Soviet leaders once retreated behind a wall of secrecy, keeping their abuses hidden and their people in ignorance, Russia today has been swept by the winds of transparency. The outside world can see in, and the Russian people have more chance to see out. Putin's response has been to increase internal repression, crack down on opposition, and crush individuals and businesses that don't toe the line. It is the behaviour of a leader who knows he is surrounded by inimical forces, retreating deeper into his bunker, ordering his timorous generals to go out and beat back the unstoppable enemy advance.

Putin uses the myth that the Yeltsin years are proof that a liberal economic order and democracy are not feasible for Russia and that only he and his hardline model of centralised autocracy can keep Russia safe. But justice is the basic moral imperative for successful government and independent polls have shown that most Russians believe the Kremlin leadership is corrupt, motivated not by love for Russia but by self-enrichment. On a moral level, the regime is disowned even by its usual supporters, a significant indicator that real political change is imminent. It is no longer 'stability and continuity at all costs' that the Russian people crave; our country yearns for reform.

According to human rights experts, as many as one in six of Russia's entrepreneurs have been put on trial; prisons hold thousands of them, many of them victims of fabricated legal suits, facilitated by a corrupt criminal justice system. The Levada Center think tank calculates that, in any given year, more than 15 per cent of Russians are forced to bribe bureaucrats and other agents of the state. The country is ruled by Putin's personal clique, elected by no one and devoid of any legal authority; parliament is run by one party, the United Russia Party of Vladimir Putin, which anyone who wants to be properly assured of their business's future has to support in some way or other. Such constraints have discouraged the most enterprising members of society, depressed economic activity and filled a vital cohort of the population with resentment for the regime.

The Russian Federation needs new areas of development; it needs modern infrastructure, cheap and fast transport links, and modern industry. None of this is possible unless Russia emerges from the isolation it has been pushed into by the current regime. The resources to achieve all this exist; they simply need to be utilised in a rational manner, rather than bartered for the loyalty of the crooks and cronies of the Kremlin.

• • •

In March 2021, I was in London, exiled from my country and waiting by the telephone. It had been a couple of hours since I had last heard from Moscow and I was getting anxious. When the fate of your homeland is at stake, living in exile is an ordeal.

The news I was hoping to hear was from the Open Russia movement, which was taking part in a conference of municipal representatives called to discuss the activities of independent council deputies and their plans for the next round of elections. It was a run-of-the-mill event that in normal countries would attract little attention, a fleeting mention in the media – think, a Lib Dem discussion forum in the UK, or a Democratic strategy group in the US. But Russia in 2021 was not a normal country; things are different there. At 10am Moscow time, the conference began its proceedings and a few minutes later, armed police burst in, yelling, 'Don't move! You are all detained!'

Two hundred men and women, young and old, delegates and journalists, were dragged away and bundled into police buses. They were respectable folk – people like Ilya Yashin, Council Leader of Moscow's Krasnoselsky District; the ex-mayor of Yekaterinburg, Yevgeny Roizman; the executive director of Open Russia, Andrei Pivovarov; the publicist, Vladimir Kara-Murza; and municipal deputy, Yulia Galyamina – but that didn't save them. No one was given the chance to object. Yulia tried to ask the police what she had done wrong – 'I didn't break any law; I'm a municipal deputy, an elected representative' – but she got no answer. Only after they had been booked and cautioned in a Moscow police station were the arrestees told that their crime was 'associating with an undesirable organisation'.

Russian police arrested 200 opposition politicians and municipal deputies for taking part in a forum with an 'undesirable' organisation, Open Russia

The concept of 'undesirable' is a complicated issue that Vladimir Putin has made simple: in Putin's Russia, the Kremlin decides who is desirable and who is not. Independent political parties, institutes and think tanks fall unsurprisingly into the latter category. My own affiliated organisations, the Open Russia Civic Movement and the Institute of Modern Russia, are allowed to work freely abroad, but in Russia they are proscribed. Cooperating with either of them makes you liable to detention under Article 20.33 of the Administrative Code of the Russian Federation; you get a 15,000-rouble fine for your first 'offence' followed by escalating penalties if you don't learn the error of your ways.

In the days that followed the attack on the municipal forum, the police forcibly entered the apartment of Open Russia's Moscow coordinator, Maria Kuznetsova. On the pretext of looking for 'materials relating to undesirable organisations', they took away her laptop and memory sticks. They raided the offices of my news organisation, MBK Media, seizing documents and computers. On 17 March, the Kremlin wrote to Twitter, demanding they ban MBK Media from using their services. When Twitter declined to comply with this and other similar demands, the communications censor, Roskomnadzor, used jamming technology to 'throttle' the speed of its tweets in the territory of the Russian Federation.

Vladimir Putin has come to believe he can tell the Russian people whatever he wants. He can tell us that black is white and he expects us to believe it – or, at least, to pretend that we believe it. During the COVID-19 pandemic, the Kremlin did what all other European countries were doing – it released regular updates on the number of deaths caused by the virus. But even the most cursory analysis revealed that deaths in Russia were being grossly underreported. On 13 March 2021, for example – the day of the police raid on Open Russia – Putin's state media told the Russian people that a total of 91,695 of their fellow citizens had perished so far. But at the same time, a simple glance at the record of excess deaths – that is, the number by which the current year's deaths exceed those of previous years – showed that the real figure was more than 400,000. When Alexei Raksha, the (now former) senior statistician at the state statistics agency, Rosstat, pointed out the discrepancy, he was removed from his job.

What's most worrying is that the vast majority of people thought that this was normal – that this was just how governments behave. Russians are not stupid; people knew Putin was lying, but there was no protest, no outrage. People in Russia have been conditioned to believe *there is nothing we can do about it*. Years of oppression by an uncaring, authoritarian state have instilled the belief that the individual is impotent in the face of the machine. Two centuries ago, Alexander Pushkin created an enduring image of the little man – the *malenky chelovek* – who is nightmarishly pursued by a bronze statue of the tsar on horseback and pounded into exhaustion, submission and, eventually, death. Russian society has come to accept that the authorities will abuse and bully and deceive us, and that nothing can be done to change it. The reaction to the lies about COVID deaths, to the collapse of efforts to build a modern economy, to the crushing of civil liberties, the persecution of journalists and opposition politicians, the ingrained corruption and the trampling of free speech, is the same as it always has been – a shrug, a sigh and maybe a few jaundiced jokes about the system we live under.

This is no longer acceptable. It is time to end the mentality of acceptance. It is time for Russians to know that the individual is not powerless, that the state can be challenged. And all this needs to be done quickly. Because without it, things will never get better. If we fail to create a new cohort of confident, educated citizens, aware of their rights and responsibilities, willing to stand up for the ideal of an open, free civil society, Russia will continue to founder under the weight of oppression. A 2021 report by the Chatham House research institute explains why these changes are so urgent. 'Any chances for a post-Putin Russia to build a viable democratic political system are lower now than they were in the 1990s,' the report says. 'Although nearly two generations of Russians have grown up since the collapse of the Soviet Union, they have done so largely under Putin ... any remaining chances for meaningful democracy are rapidly evaporating.' And the reason for this?

> Apart from a limited number of institutions either accepted or tolerated by the Kremlin, Russia's civil society is non-existent and therefore has no experience or track record. This begs the question of how realistic it is to expect the emergence of advanced democratic institutions after Putin leaves office, when there are currently no foundations to speak of. In the early 1990s, a hunger for democracy compensated for the absence of institutions and expertise, and there was a clarity among the general public about which democratic models were to be adopted and a willingness to see the process through. Today, that hunger has been replaced by disappointment

It is imperative, therefore, that we work to nurture the courageous, independent-minded citizens who will be capable of leading a future democracy in Russia:

> the country will need a new professional cadre of elite bureaucrats and policymakers, along with the resources for their rapid mobilization. The conditions needed to achieve this are not present in today's Russia, and it will therefore take a long time to develop and establish new elites from scratch.

The Chatham House report is sobering, albeit perhaps too pessimistic. Of course it will not be easy to build the new civil society Russia needs, but we are already hard at work doing so. Organisations such as the Open Russia Foundation are busy helping to educate our young generation in the values of free-market democracy, to create the new class of civic activists that Chatham House is calling for, willing to question and probe, ready to shape the society that many want to see.

The task is challenging. Current conditions in Putin's Russia are very different from the reality of Western democracies. There has, for instance, been much talk in the United States about a so-called 'deep state' made up of covert, ill-intentioned people who wield power and influence over the running of the country while never showing their faces or revealing their identity. Speculation reached ludicrous proportions with the QAnon conspiracy theory claiming that a secret cabal of Satan-worshipping paedophiles, led – improbably – by Bill and Hillary Clinton, were pulling the nation's strings and that only Donald Trump could be trusted to defeat them. In Russia, the 'internal state' is not a joke, but a reality. As I have shown, it is a network of informal power that stands above and outside the law, living off privilege and permeating the institutions of the official state. Putin and his cronies control justice and the law, dictating verdicts in key court cases, granting each other the right to control state industries, creaming off billions of dollars.

Only by ditching the unaccountable autocracy of the few – the 'inner state' clique in the Kremlin – in favour of democratic institutions reflecting the will of the many can Russia hope to realise its full potential. Our previous attempts at democracy – the short period between the February and Bolshevik revolutions, the 1990s – were built on shaky foundations and were not a success. To succeed, a future Russia must build a firm democratic base, of the kind that has long been established in the West, with proper weight given to the voices of all electors and an effective separation of powers to bind the leadership into a system of checks and balances.

. . .

When I reflect on the years I have spent in the West since December 2013, when the Kremlin loaded me on to a German plane and sent me off into the unknown, I am struck by how much has changed in Russia. Back then, there was a move to restore relations with the West in advance of the Sochi Olympics. My release along with my friend and business partner, Platon Lebedev, as well as the women from Pussy Riot, was a gesture in this direction. When I first arrived in London, I felt there was a chance for gradual democratisation in my homeland; at that time, I didn't see any pressing need for me to get involved in international politics.

But things started to change. First there was Ukraine's Maidan revolution in February 2014, followed by the annexation of Crimea, the Kremlin's intervention in Donbas, backing for Assad in Syria and finally the invasion of Ukraine in 2022. Putin doesn't understand that people everywhere are motivated by a desire for liberty. That's why he continues to parrot the old refrains, fulminating about 'the machinations of the West', 'Russia surrounded by foreign enemies' and 'whoever is not with us is against us'.

I could no longer stand aside. In March 2014 I flew to Kiev and addressed the crowds on Maidan Square. I told them there is a different Russia from Putin's Russia, a Russia that wishes you well, a Russia that sees its future together with yours, a common, European path of democracy. I took a plane to Donbas three days before the war broke out to bring the same message of hope. And I took the decision to intensify the work of my socio-political organisation, Open Russia.

Back then, it was still possible to engage openly in political activity, so I supported young candidates for the State Duma and municipal

Addressing the crowd on the Maidan in Kyiv, March 2014

councils; I established several popular online publications; and I organised the 'Enough!' campaign against Putin's cynical manoeuvring to extend his time in the presidency. We knew Putin wasn't going to just throw in the towel, but there was still hope of managed change. This hope took a major blow in 2020, when Putin's shameless rewriting of the constitution to perpetuate his own grip on power proved beyond doubt that Soviet totalitarianism was back. Now people started to be arbitrarily imprisoned simply for expressing their opinions, with the clear message to everyone else that they should think twice whether it was worth the risk. Those who didn't get the message started to be labelled 'foreign agents', which means a de facto ban on working in many professions, or 'members of undesirable organisations', which means prison sentences, or – worst of all – 'extremists', for which the prison sentences are numbered in many years. As I mentioned, our own journalists and almost all our publications were declared 'foreign agents' and all our funds labelled 'undesirable'.

The closure of our organisations and publications in Russia under the threat of Kremlin repression does not mean the end of the fight. We have found new ways of working, with editorial boards based abroad, journalists in Russia writing under pseudonyms, young political activists learning their trade via the internet and even some in-person training. We get much valuable help and information from democratically minded supporters who work in government jobs; human rights lawyers provide assistance to activists, journalists and bloggers seeking to defend themselves against state-sponsored persecution. Such methods alone will not lead to a change of power in Russia, but we have another much more ambitious target: when the current regime reaches its final, inevitable collapse – inevitable because of the weight of its own mistakes and the vulnerability of its ageing leader – we must ensure that Russia is not allowed to stumble into yet another era of authoritarian rule.

To do this, we are redoubling our work on educating the young generation, providing support for civil rights, training hundreds of independent journalists and grassroots activists. We are increasing our output of opposition publications and seeking alliances with other political forces that are committed to a law-based future for the new Russia. In the current global climate, it isn't easy: the world has seen a rising tide of authoritarianism; people have become wary of changes associated with globalisation; political leaders have lost the trust of society, and society itself has failed to respond to the new challenges in constructive ways. Populist politicians promising simple, easy solutions have found unwarranted support: in some countries, especially the young democracies of Eastern Europe, social institutions have crumbled and autocracy has returned.

Our overriding concern is that when change comes in Russia, the country does not follow the same path. Despite all the problems, I have faith in my nation. I would be delighted if Vladimir Putin were gradually to share the autocratic presidential power he now wields with an honestly elected parliament, an independent judiciary and a coalition government. I would rejoice if a new president were to be a man or woman of compromise, a conciliator, a guarantor of citizens' rights, eschewing the authoritarianism that has done so much damage to my country in the past 20 years, ready to work with a coalition of opposition forces and other branches of political power. The likelihood that events will develop that way is, sadly, not high. Rejecting the template of 'strongman' rule is not easy and Russians have become increasingly seduced by the nostrums of simplistic populism. Unlimited presidential powers, the cult of personality and authoritarianism all militate against change, but the system is under strain. The repression of political opposition, the curtailing of social mobility, the ageing of Putin and his entourage, Putin's extrajudicial arbitration of constant conflicts between competing factions of his inner circle, and the refusal to engage in dialogue with society have created fertile ground for politicians from outside the current structures. After Putin leaves, there is likely to be a brief period of rule by his appointed 'heir', followed by an inevitable political crisis and a relaunch of how the country is run, perhaps involving a shift away from presidential autocracy via a constituent assembly towards a parliamentary, genuinely federal republic. We, the democratic opposition and our friends in the West, must encourage and be ready for this future.

A future democratic Russia will arise because her people now recognise that freedom is better than unfreedom, and that a society of free people is best equipped to deal with the challenges that humanity faces. But we recognise that before we can demand changes from others, we too must be willing to change ourselves. Each of us has flaws. While denouncing and condemning the current regime – a necessary process for reforming the state and healing society – we must remember that forgiveness is dearer than punishment. A new society cannot be built through anger and revenge. The true, lasting solution is not the settling of scores, but the introduction of genuine institutional reforms to the benefit of all.

My task, the task of the democratic opposition and the task of our friends in the West, involves the preservation of a viable alternative to the current reality in Russia; it involves helping people who are prepared to become the personnel of this alternative to gain experience of political struggle. We have created, and will continue to create, platforms for free discussion of the country's future. We have told, and shall continue to tell, the truth in writing and in film. We are fighting, and shall continue to fight, for the rights of political prisoners, and against repressive, anti-constitutional laws. I envisage Russia as a law-governed state with an independent judiciary and an independent parliament exerting broad budgetary and executive powers. If these conditions are met, there is no reason that a future Russia cannot be welcomed into the global community of nations, to her deep and lasting benefit and to the equal benefit of the West.

ABOUT THE AUTHORS

MIKHAIL KHODORKOVSKY

In the early 2000s, Mikhail Khodorkovsky was the wealthiest man in Russia, the head of the giant Yukos oil company, and ranked 16th on the *Forbes* list of world billionaires. But his pro-democracy, anti-corruption views led to a clash with President Vladimir Putin, who had him arrested in 2003. Convicted on politically motivated fraud charges, Khodorkovsky spent ten years in Putin's prison camps, recognised by Amnesty International as a prisoner of conscience. Since his release in December 2013, Khodorkovsky has lived in Switzerland and the UK. He now leads the philanthropic Open Russia organisation, promoting political reform in Russia, including free and fair elections, the protection of journalists and activists, the rule of law and media independence. He has been described by the *Economist* as 'the Kremlin's leading critic-in-exile'.

MARTIN SIXSMITH

Martin Sixsmith studied Russian at Oxford, Leningrad and the Sorbonne. He was a Slavics Tutor at Harvard and wrote his postgraduate thesis about Russian poetry. From 1980 to 1997 he was the BBC's correspondent in Moscow, Washington, Brussels and Warsaw. From 1997 to 2002 he worked for the British government as director of communications and press secretary to several cabinet ministers. He is now a writer, presenter and journalist. He is the author of non-fiction titles including *Russia – The Wild East*, *Putin's Oil* and *The Litvinenko File*. His bestselling 2009 book, *The Lost Child of Philomena Lee*, was adapted for film and became the multiple Oscar-nominated *Philomena*, starring Steve Coogan and Judi Dench.

ACKNOWLEDGEMENTS

The authors wish to acknowledge the invaluable help of Maria Logan, Elena Cook, Albert DePetrillo and Hana Teraie-Wood in the production of this book.

PICTURE CREDITS

p.ii Khodorkosvky behind bars – © TATYANA MAKEYEVA/AFP via Getty Images

p.5 Khodorkosvky and Putin – © Sovfoto/Universal Images Group/Shutterstock

p.6 Khodorkosvky and Putin 2 – © Sovfoto/Universal Images Group/Shutterstock

p.9 Police at a Navalny protest – © Sergey Ponomarev/New York Times/Redux/eyevine

p.14 Khodorkovsky at school, Kino Lorber – © Mikhail Khodorkovsky

p.19 Young Mikhail Khodorkovsky – © Thierry Esch/Paris Match via Getty Images

p.20 Annie Lennox in Red Square, Moscow 1989 – © Adrian Boot / Urbanimage

p.24 Interview with Khodorkovsky – © Ivan Sekretarev/AP/Shutterstock

p.27 Inna Khodorkovskaya – © Sovfoto/Universal Images Group/Shutterstock

p.31 Margaret Thatcher in Moscow, 1987 – © Steve Bent/Mail On Sunday/Shutterstock

p.37 (top) Margaret Thatcher hugs a little girl, Moscow – © Peter Turnley/Corbis/VCG via Getty Images; (bottom) Margaret Thatcher greets Moscovites during official visit, 1987 – © DANIEL JANIN/AFP via Getty Images

p.43 People stand on a barricade in front the Russian White House in Moscow on August 21, 1991 – © ALEXANDER NEMENOV/AFP via Getty Images

p.46 Boris Yeltsin meets leading industrialists and bankers in the Kremlin, 1997 – © Sovfoto/Universal Images Group/Shutterstock

p.65 (top) Protesters with statue of Felix Dzerzhinsky, 23 August 1991 – © Alexander Zemlianichenko/AP/Shutterstock; (bottom) The Lubyanka, 1963 – © Popperfoto via Getty Images/Getty Images p.115 Screengrab of Viktor Zolotov speech – © Uncredited/AP/Shutterstock

p.126 Khodorkovsky arriving at his trial in Moscow surrounded by prison guards, 2009 – © Sergei Ilnitsky/EPA/Shutterstock

p.129 Mikhail Khodorkovsky arrives at the courthouse in Moscow – © MIKHAIL SMIRNOV/AFP via Getty Images

p.140 Khodorkovsky behind bars in the courtroom, surrounded by press – © TATYANA MAKEYEVA/AFP via Getty Images

p.177 Khodorkovsky in YaG-14/10 prison camp, Siberia – © Thierry Esch/Paris Match via Getty Images

p.178 Vasily Aleksanyan sits in court – © ZUMA Press, Inc. / Alamy Stock Photo

p.181 Khodorkovsky reunited with parents Marina and Boris, and son Pavel, December 2013 – © REUTERS / Alamy Stock Photo

p.182 A woman shows support for Khodorkovsky during a rally, Moscow, 14 April 2007 – © UPI / Alamy Stock Photo

p.199 Vladimir Putin in Tuva, 2007 – © DMITRY ASTAKHOV/RIA NOVOSTI/AFP via Getty Images

p.203 Pussy Riot perform at the Cathedral of Christ the Saviour, Moscow – © Sergey Ponomarev/Shutterstock

p.207 Olympics Pussy Riot protest, Sochi, 2014 – © Morry Gash/AP/Shutterstock

p.211 Yevgeny Prigozhin serves Vladimir Putin at a banquet near Moscow, November 2011 – © REUTERS / Alamy Stock Photo

p.225 FBI Wanted poster for Yevgeny Prigozhin – © Pictorial Press Ltd / Alamy Stock Photo

p.235 A woman at Joseph Stalin's memorial ceremony, Moscow, 5 March 2016 – © YURI KADOBNOV/AFP via Getty Images p.267 US Capitol under siege on 6 January 2021 – © Evelyn Hockstein/The Washington Post via Getty Images

p.283 Ruslan Boshirov and Alexander Petrov, Fisherton Road, Salisbury, 4 March 2018 – © Metropolitan Police/AP/Shutterstock

p.291 Alexei Navalny in a cage, Babuskinsky District Court, Moscow – © Alexander Zemlianichenko/AP/Shutterstock

p.293 'Heroes of recent times' banner in St Petersburg's Pushkarsky Park – © Petrov Ivan Sergeevich

p.294 A worker paints over graffiti depicting Alexei Navalny, St Petersburg – © REUTERS / Alamy Stock Photo

p.297 Mural of masked, helmeted figure, St Petersburg – © Darya Borisova

p.316 Police officers detain a woman in Moscow, March 2021 – © Victor Berezkin/AP/Shutterstock

p.322 Khodorkovsky speaks during a rally in Independence Square in Kiev, 9 March 2014 – © UPI / Alamy Stock Photo

INDEX

Page numbers in *italics* refer to illustrations.